GUI-BASED DESIGN AND DEVELOPMENT
FOR CLIENT/SERVER APPLICATIONS

GUI-BASED DESIGN AND DEVELOPMENT FOR CLIENT/SERVER APPLICATIONS

USING POWERBUILDER, SQLWINDOWS, VISUAL BASIC, PARTS WORKBENCH

Jonathan S. Sayles
Peter Molchan
Steve Karlen
Gary Bilodeau

John Wiley & Sons, Inc.
New York • Chichester • Brisbane • Toronto • Singapore

Designations used by companies to distinguish their products are often claimed as trademarks. In all instances where John Wiley & Sons, Inc. is aware of a claim, the product names appear in Initial Capital or ALL CAPITAL LETTERS. Readers, however, should contact the appropriate companies for more complete information regarding trademarks and registration.

This text is printed on acid-free paper.

Copyright © 1994 by John Wiley & Sons, Inc.

Library of Congress Cataloging-in-Publication Data:

GUI-based design and development for client/server applications : using
   PowerBuilder, SQLWindows, Visual Basic, PARTS Workbench / Jonathan
   S. Sayles . . . [et al.].
      p.   cm.
   Includes bibliographical references.
   ISBN 0-471-30304-6 (paper)
   1. Client/server computing.   2. Graphical user interfaces
(Computer systems) I. Sayles, Jonathan.
   QA76.9.C55G85   1994
   005.2—dc20   94-3148
                                                                  CIP

Printed in the United States of America
10 9 8 7 6 5 4 3 2 1

Dedication

The authors would like to thank the following persons (without whose help this book would have wound up like so many well-intentioned but ultimately destined-for-vaporware projects); First and foremost, thanks to Diane Cerra—our ever-so-patient and just-as-persistent editor-in-chief ("Don't call me chief!") at John Wiley & Sons. We would like to the following companies: Sybase, Microsoft, Powersoft, Gupta, and Digitalk for providing software, service, and support. We would like to thank specific individuals of the companies: from Powersoft Corporation, Rachel Stockton, Chuck Barbaro, and Peter Treadway; and from Digitalk, Barbara Noparstak.

Other individuals who were of invaluable help to us in our endeavors include Drew Hannah of Connecticut Mutual Life; Chuck Adams of Infinity Systems; Paul Ruhlo; Olga Matyczyk, Walter Matyczyk, and Walter Matyczyk Jr.; MaryEllen, Christopher, and Jamison Sayles.

We would like to thank The Systems Group, Inc., for permitting us the time off from our normal obligations to complete the book.

Finally, all the authors would like to thank their families for their patience and long suffering without their respective husbands and dads. We're finally finished, and we can't wait to start our next book. ("What?" "Stop hitting me dear, it's embarassing in front of the readers! Okay, I promise I won't do anymore books . . . this year!")

To be continued . . .

Sincerely, the authors

JONATHAN SAYLES
PETER MOLCHAN
STEVE KARLEN
GARY BILODEAU

Gary Bilodeau:
I dedicate this to my daughter, Renee who was born during the writing of this book, and to my wife, Jennifer, for all her support.

Steve Karlen:
There is only one thing harder than being an author . . . being an author's wife. We both work as computer consultants for ten to twelve hours a day and come home exhausted. While I slave away behind my faithful word processor, she faithfully supports my endeavors, serves as my sounding board and editor, and, in her spare time, keeps our household running like a clock. She knows I appreciate her, but she has no idea how much. This book is as much hers as it is mine.

I'd also like to thank Jon Sayles. He gave me my start in this business, has always insisted on receiving my best effort, and continues to provide new avenues for me to express myself. Lastly, I'd like to thank Bob Hoffman and Ahmed Sako, two of the most intelligent technicians I have ever met. Much of what I know about client/server technology I have learned from them. I am very thankful for the time they have invested in me.

Preface

"When I see my first advertisement for Object-Oriented JCL, I'll know that the data-processing apocalypse is upon us!"—an anonymous speaker, DB-Expo, 1992.

In the movie *Indiana Jones and the Last Crusade,* Harrison Ford must make a leap of faith in order to obtain the Holy Grail. He stands before an abyss, an enormous chasm between two cliffs, and after a spell of (understandable) reluctance, strides forward . . . and onto a translucent (special effects) bridge, upon which he walks safely across the chasm, and into the next act.

The artificial drama produced in this scene represents Hollywood at its celluloid best. We can only wish that reality were so carefully scripted, and that it came complete with safety nets, stuntmen and stuntwomen ready and able to take the risk out of our own personal adventures.

Today, mainframe data-processing professionals feel the same anxiety we are meant to believe that Harrison Ford experienced, when they look out into the swirling tempest of information surrounding the new technology apocalypse, which consists of C/S (client/server), OO (object orientation), and GUI (heretofore to be known as C/S-OO-GUI).

Fearing the lack of job security and their own professional future (no special effects and stunt doubles here), mainframe professionals who have begun reading the tea leaves of their trade know they must retrain and learn the new technologies in order to survive and flourish into the next decade. A question, however, that looms large in their minds is—"Exactly how?"

There is a lot to learn in the new technologies, a lot of ground to cover. And noticeably absent in the books and articles in print on the subjects is any attempt to translate mainframe concepts, procedures, and skills into their C/S-OO-GUI counterparts. Because the vast preponderance of literature on these topics has been written "of the C programmers, by the C programmers, and for the C programmers" garden-variety mainframe professionals feel left out in the cold—a situation we hope this book alleviates.

In *Developing GUI/Client Server Applications,* we will be presenting an introduction to GUI, client/server, and object orientation, as standalone technologies (the theory), and through real-life application design and development (the implementation). We have taken many measures to ensure that mainframe programmers can translate their current professional skill set into the new world order—trading in their current skills and knowledge base for new skills, and a new knowledge base. This has meant developing analogies, and describing what mainframe technology can be directly transferred into client/server-OO-GUI technology, what mainframe technology is not transferrable, and what positively brand-new concepts and techniques exist in the new technologies that have no counterpart on the mainframe. Mainframe programmers who don't wish to start all over, beginning at page one of the technology primer will appreciate the efforts taken. These efforts will allow them to leverage their hard-earned professional skills.

However, this book is not solely for mainframe professionals. College students and data-processing readers with Pascal, C language, dBASE/Clipper and other PC/LAN backgrounds are not going to be left baffled by a profusion of arcane TSO/ISPF* analogies, mnemonics, and examples. In fact, they will probably pick up the new culture of C/S-OO-GUI faster and more easily than the mainframe programmer who has spent the last five to twenty years using mainframe tools and languages to develop 3270 applications with JCL,† COBOL, and so on. This is not because they are any more intelligent than mainframe developers, but because both the hardware and software components of C/S-OO-GUI are, for the most part PC- and LAN-based, written in C by C developers, and designed and optimized for the C programming-language culture—a culture about as far from the mainframe COBOL development culture as you can get without falling into Academia.

Following introductory chapters on GUI, client/server, and object orientation, we present chapters on four of the most commercially successful, powerful, and exciting client/server, object-oriented application development toolkits (PowerBuilder, Visual Basic, SQLWindows, and PARTS Workbench). The chapters on the four products walk you through the process of building a model client/server application using each of these four products. You will see how to define

---

*TSO/ISPF—Time Sharing Option, Interactive Systems Programming Facility, an IBM mainframe development environment/workbench.
†JCL—Job Control Language, IBM's control language for executing programs in batch mode on the mainframe.

application objects, windows objects, and code database access and business logic using the same application with each of the tools.

Suggested Approaches to This Book

Given the variance of backgrounds in these new technologies within the MIS community, we have structured the book so that there are several ways you can make the most of it:

Introduction to C/S-OO-GUI

Unless you have a strong technical and/or theoretical background in C/S-OO-GUI technologies, read "Introduction to CC/S-OO-GUI Technology," "Introduction to Client/Server," "Introduction to GUI," and "Introduction to Object Orientation." These chapters contain terms, concepts, definitions, vocabulary, and features and facility information. They lay the necessary foundation for an understanding of C/S-OO-GUI technology. This background will prepare you for the terms, acronyms, and mnemonics that you will encounter throughout the rest of the book.

A Note to Windows and OS/2 Users

C/S-OO-GUI technology represents both a base-development platform and a target for application design, development, and delivery by the four products discussed in later chapters. Even if you have a strong background in the use of OS/2 or Microsoft Windows products such as Microsoft Excel, Word for Windows, Microsoft Access, DB2/2, and so on, we feel that you should read these chapters. This is because the intuitive style of use, and simplified operations that are so much a part of the working environment of C/S-OO-GUI products masks an incredibly complex infrastructure. This infrastructure is the domain of C/S-OO-GUI application development. Thus, you must acquaint yourself with the technology that lies behind the pretty visuals and slick interfaces. You have to know the theory and application of C/S-OO-GUI, along with the operations of end-user computing.

The Sample Business Application

Following the introductory chapters, we present a short description of a sample GUI-client/server application. This chapter is important, in that it describes the business purpose and client/server-GUI components of the sample business application used in subsequent chapters developed with the 4GLs.

The Four Product Chapters

Following the Sample Business Application chapter, we present four chapters, each of which focus on separate software products (Power-

Builder, Visual Basic, SQLWindows, and PARTS Workbench), and more specifically, how to construct the sample application using these products. These chapters show the actual step-by-step processes taken in building the application: the procedures, scripts, and toolsets used. These chapters represent the "rubber meets the road" portion of this book, as theory (the C/S-OO-GUI intro chapters) and reality (the sample business application) meet on the battlefield of real-life application development.

It is important to note here that the intent of the product chapters is to relate the theory of C/S-OO-GUI to the reality and experience of C/S-OO-GUI development in some depth, and with actual business requirements, through the development of an executable GUI-client/server application. These chapters, we hope, will clarify the usually vague theoretical concepts of C/S-OO-GUI, and that you will gain a deeper understanding as you see the implementation of GUI, object-oriented and client/server techniques and facilities at work—process by process and screen snapshot by screen snapshot.

It is important to understand that these chapters are not meant to be a comparison of the products, and under no circumstances should they be used as part of a buy/no-buy decision* regarding the products.

And Behind Door Number Three . . .

If your shop has not yet chosen its C/S-OO-GUI tool, it is probably (as you read this sentence) looking at two or more of the products in the remaining chapters. We therefore recommend that you read all four chapters, with an eye towards strengthening your understanding of the central C/S-OO-GUI technology, terms, approaches, and concepts. Each chapter is written by a different author. Each delivers a slightly different message, or point of view on the subjects. Note that we recommend reading all four chapters, even if all four products are not currently under consideration at your shop. Software contenders change quickly in the C/S-OO-GUI arena. Today your company may not be looking at PARTS Workbench, tomorrow it may! Studying technology for the moment (learning only about what you will use next week, next month, and next quarter) is like living for the moment used to be in the 1960s, a luxury you find out only too late that you cannot afford.

If your shop has chosen a strategic† C/S-OO-GUI product, read just that chapter in depth. This will prepare you for further training to be delivered by your company or outside specialty training firms in the

---

*Such strategic decisions, with far-reaching consequences, should be made on the basis of a comprehensive product analysis, going far beyond the scope of the material presented in this book.
†In our experience, once a technology reaches strategic status in the minds of executives-who-make-the-buy-decisions, any technical and/or empirical discussion is deemed irrelevant.

subject. The implication here is that these chapters are not meant to replace qualified, professional stand-up instruction in PowerBuilder, Visual Basic, SQLWindows, and PARTS Workbench. Once again, the purpose of these chapters is to solidify the reader's understanding of C/S-OO-GUI technology. Training and tutorials are available from the vendors, their authorized training partners, and independent consulting firms.

Finally, we hope you enjoy the rest of this book. We are confident that you will get a great deal of information from it, and hope that you can use it to your advantage in your career.

Contents

Introduction to C/S-OO-GUI Technology and the C/S-OO-GUI Development Workbench

The Way We Were

For the first three decades of MIS computing (the sixties, seventies, and eighties), application professionals were content to know two, three, or maybe four technologies. Generally, if you had a solid grasp of COBOL and JCL as well as either IMS or CICS, you were a valued asset to your company, with a decent (if not overly glamorous) career path—and you were secure in your job. If you knew ALC (Assembler Language Coding—in the sixties, seventies, and eighties it was referred to as BAL—Basic Assembler Language) you were known as a technical guru (or in the vernacular, a most valued nerd).

For decades this limited technology foundation of between two and four mainframe products was enough to qualify you for life membership in the data-processing community. But, oh, how things have changed over the past four years!

A description of the technical apocalypse that has become the nineties needs no introduction. If you glance at the current trade journals you'd think that if you are not working on object-oriented or downsized/rightsized-client/server-GUI* applications—all running on the "UNIX du jour"—you might as well move into the storage closet (right next to the card punch), or maybe become part of some exhibit on ancient computing in a technology museum ("Look over

---

*GUI—*Graphical user interface,* a popular icon/colored windows-based/mouse-driven presentation style of user interface, available in such products as Microsoft Windows, OS/2, and Motif.

Museum of ancient technologies.

there, son. That's a COBOL programmer. See how tense she looks? That's from tracing GO TO branches over five thousand lines of spaghetti code. What's a GO TO? Son, whatever they're paying those teachers of yours at the computing academy, it's not enough!").

"The Reports of My Death Have Been Greatly Exaggerated."—W. C. Fields

In fact, COBOL, JCL, IMS, and CICS are not ready for the life hereafter as of this writing. Mainframe systems are flourishing and there's plenty of work out there for people who still remember how to spell PERFORM THRU and trace register assignments in a dump (albeit, mostly maintenance work—remember, that's how the COBOL programmer in the museum got all her crow's feet and worry lines). All the good work (*good* being defined as: development, little or no on-call responsibilities, well paying—maybe this should be first—I'll leave that up to you, fun, and in demand—they're not laying off SQLServer and PowerBuilder developers) is being done in the object-oriented, client/server, and GUI technology. And guess what . . . the canyon that divides MIS-Nova from MIS-Antiqua is only going to get wider and more pronounced over the next five years.

Whether or not PCs and local area networks will ever replace mainframes (and actually save companies money) is no longer a debatable issue. The new technologies have enslaved the hearts and minds of prominent MIS individuals (you know, the ones who sign the purchase orders at your shop). Hence, it is no longer a question of "Will we be going client/server?" only a a question of "When will we be going client/server—this week or next?" According to trade journal surveys and independent research by companies such as Forrester, Inc. and the Gartner Group, if you work in a Fortune 1000 company, the answer to the that last question is probably "last year."

"All right," you say. "I won't try to buck the tide another minute. I've made up my mind, and starting today I'm going to learn C and become the world's best ex-COBOL programmer turned client/server developer. I'll take the MIS world by storm, and give myself job security well into the next century." Not so fast. While we would never try to stop you from learning C, that computer language alone will hardly give you the hottest resume in a headhunter's* collection. C programmers are coming out of every community college, technical college, and plain old Ivy League college faster than you can spell GO TO. You'll need more. Specifically, you will need the theoretical background—client/server concepts and facilities, object-oriented concepts and facilities, GUI concepts and facilities—and you will need to learn one or more GUI-client/server 4GLs such as PowerBuilder (Powersoft, Inc.), Visual Basic (Microsoft, Inc.), SQLWindows (Gupta, Inc.), or PARTS Workbench (Digitalk, Inc.).

To C or Not to C

3GLs are no longer in favor with an MIS world attempting to code, as one of our students presented the edict from management, "better, cheaper, faster."† And while COBOL is a 3GL (you can almost think of COBOL as "assembler language run through a thesaurus"), C is yet another 3GL, flexible and powerful, but unfriendly, non-Englishlike, and little better in the current opinion of corporate America at producing better, cheaper, faster (and particularly *maintainable* better, cheaper, faster) business applications than COBOL. What seems to be able to do better, cheaper, faster are client/server, object-oriented 4GL workbenches.

---

*The term *headhunter* refers to data-processing placement professionals—men and women who recruit technical developers for jobs in corporate MIS.
†Another student told us that the *real* meaning of the phrase "to develop systems better, cheaper, faster," was in fact "to develop systems cheaper, cheaper, cheaper!"

4GL Workbenches have been around for several decades. Traditional, character-based, 3270-mainframe 4GLs such as APS (Inter-Solv) and CA-Telon (Computer Associates) have survived the CASE onslaught of the eighties, and represent a proven means of developing systems better, cheaper, faster with their macro-style languages, integrated debugging tools, and database access painting capabilities. The traditional 4GL workbenches have spawned a group of "new wave 4GL workbenches," such as PowerBuilder, Visual Basic, SQLWindows, and PARTS Workbench.* These products are designed to allow developers—and in some cases, power end users—to build OS/2 or Microsoft Windows-based graphical-client/server applications.

These new wave (client/server, object-oriented) 4GL workbenches are not just nonprocedural programming languages. The new wave 4GL workbenches contain graphically oriented, intelligent, and fully integrated development toolsets that incorporate most of the advances made in hardware and software technology in the past ten years. They are PC- and LAN-based development products featuring flexible, powerful, Englishlike, nonprocedural languages, macros and function libraries, integrated toolsets, integrated debugging facilities, and so on. The new wave 4GL workbenches are designed and optimized for the rapid and simplified development and deployment (better, cheaper, faster) of GUI, client/server and object-oriented PC applications that run on a variety of operating systems and most of the standard PC/LAN hardware platforms. As a final note, it is important to understand that even with all the attention these products receive in the press, the new wave 4GL Workbenches are at the bottom end of the technological S curve.

The S curve is a metaphor that represents a contemporary financial theory about trends and directions in new technologies. At the bottom of the S curve technology advances come quickly and cheaply. At the top end of the S curve the same measure of advances come slowly and expensively, if they come at all. Mainframes and virtually all associated mainframe technology—with the possible exception of DB2—is at the top end of the S curve. The technology is being invested in parsimoniously, or sometimes not at all, by the vendors.

PCs, LANs, and all associated PC technology (i.e., C/S-OO-GUI) are at the bottom end of the S curve. Technological functionality and price/value for PC technology is going up the S curve as explosively as it is inexpensively. Hardware prices (as measured in processing capacity) are dropping like the mercury in a thermometer in Anchor-

---

*You should note that the vendors (Powersoft, Microsoft, Gupta, and Digitalk), have dropped any and all references to the term 4GL from their marketing literature. They describe their products solely in terms of being "object-oriented, client/server application development toolsets."

age—in January. And while IBM still wants to be your "beast of burden," with mainframe servers for galactic-scale legacy applications, don't bet that by the time you read this, even previously untouchable large-scale production applications in your shop won't be under consideration for a client/server rewrite.

The inexorable march down the C/S-OO-GUI path is a data processing inevitable. We don't think it's too much to predict that the use of a new wave 4GL workbench such as PowerBuilder, Visual Basic, SQLWindows, PARTS Workbench, or some similar product, is a C/S-OO-GUI application development fait accompli. In other words, these products, in our opinion, represent the future of a client/server-object-oriented-GUI application development and delivery into the next generation of computing technology.

So if you are a developer looking to update your skills in a marketable way, we highly recommend that you pick up a copy of one of the products discussed in this book. These products are currently dominating the C/S-OO-GUI market, and we feel that they will continue to dominate them over the next decade for the very good reason (as you will see) that these are superior tools.

Overview of C/S-OO-GUI

Not that the vendors have any trouble telling you this. In fact, to begin our introduction to the various technologies, we thought it would be appropriate (given the ubiquity of C/S-OO-GUI marketing in the trade journals, something we felt all our readers would be familiar with) to study contemporary C/S-OO-GUI jargon as an end in itself. Take a look at the following advertisement a reader might find in any data-processing database magazine:

> Looking for a client/server, GUI, object-oriented solution to your development problems? Welcome to the world of high tech. Welcome to the Acme GUI-client/server workbench. This product features Windows-based nonprocedural development tools, the means (through object orientation) to create reusable application components, tight integration with a number of PC/LAN-based relational DBMSs, and much more.

Did you wonder how many of the buzzwords in that paragraph would mean anything to the average reader? Or mean much past a vague notion? Can you imagine a less suitable profession for ambiguous and unintelligible definitions than MIS and software development? Perhaps the medical profession? Let's explore the buzzwords in this advertising jargon and see if we can get started on the road to clear, intelligible, and useful definitions.

Client/Server Computing

Client/server computing, by all accounts, represents the new DBMS Holy Grail for the nineties and beyond.* There is no hotter buzzword, no faster way to sell a product than to call it "client/server." Unfortunately, the sheer commercial success of client/server technology has made it simply irresistible as a buzzword for new technology. Products from every technological walk of life have sprung onto the market waving the client/server flag and watering down its meaning.

Unlike relational database technology (with Dr. Codd's 12 abstracts delivered to the ACM), object orientation (with Tom Atwood's object-oriented manifesto), and GUI technology (with Charles Petzold's treatise on GUI design from Microsoft) there is no single-source definition, or client/server Ten Commandments that MIS and client/server vendors have bought into as the absolute client/server definition. Given this lack of formality, let us begin our own definition with the most basic and broadest client/server characterization allowable, and work our way up from there to the more specific, closed, and contemporary definition of client/server:

- A client is any program that requests processing.
- A server is any program that delivers processing.
- Client/server computing is thus any application system where separate autonomous programs request and deliver processing to and from one another.

If you take this definition to its logical conclusion, you can call quite a good percentage of existing data-processing applications client/server computing. Take, for example, a traditional call using application interface:

- From within 'Program A "
  . . . procedural logic . . .
  Call "ProgramB" Using Field1, Field2, Field3;
- From within 'Program B "
  . . . procedural logic to populate Field1, Field2, Field3
  Return;

Most online mainframe application systems qualify as client/server under this definition (all except standalone batch COBOL modules). Other examples of valid client/server computing (by this most basic definition) include database query and reporting packages like QMF (IBM), Paradox (Borland), FoxBase (Microsoft), dbExpress (Computer Concepts Corporation, Inc.), as well as various types of server prod-

---

*Forrestor Research, Inc. has estimated that the total client/server application development tools market will exceed $4 billion worldwide by 1996.

ucts: (file, fax, and database servers such as Sybase/SQLServer, Oracle, Informix, XDB, SQLBase, DB2/2, etc.).

"That's all well and good," you might say. "But if I go around referring to my shop's 25-year-old COBOL/CICS mainframe applications as client/server systems, although I might be technically accurate by your definition, I will get taken off the list of potential attendees for future Sybase/PowerBuilder classes." Granted. Contemporary data processing/MIS culture (as represented by positions taken by Microsoft, IBM, and others), has formulated a loose—but widely accepted—pseudodefinition of client/server technology, which is a bit more specific and—not terribly surprisingly—is associated with certain commercially successful software offerings rather than on a published theory or mathematical model.

In other words, there is still no formal definition of the term *client/server* agreed upon by all parties participating in client/server tools-based development and product delivery. However, there are certain common traits and characteristics shared among the commercial software conventionally known as client/server products.

A good definition of client/server computing that accounts for these common traits can be found in *Client/Server Computing,* written by Alex Berson, and published by McGraw Hill:

> Distributed computing, where at least one portion of the application system resides on a PC or Intelligent Workstation . . .

While Mr. Berson's definition seems to be only slightly more specific than our first general definition, it actually does a good job at covering the range of what is accepted as client/sever, without being so general as not to be of any use in discussing the technology. The key term to understand in Mr. Berson's definition is *distributed.*

What Can You Distribute?

An application system can be divided into three separate functional components: the user interface—representing screens, panels, reports, and so on, all parts of an application which the business user gets their hands on, or sees; the business logic—representing the formal policies and procedures automated in the software as logic or code; and database access—the storage and retrieval of information from one or more electronic filing systems. Client/server technology provides the means by which to distribute these three application system components across various hardware/software platforms, such as PCs, workstations, local area networks, and even mainframes. This distribution allows application designers and developers to optimize the system for better access to data, system responsiveness and

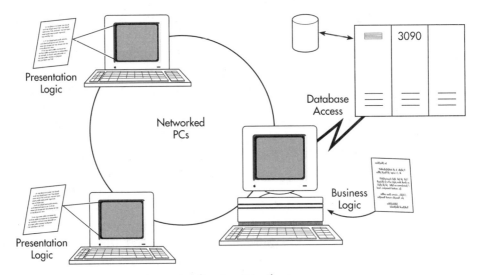

Application Distribution.

performance, and integration with other applications or commercial software.

Toward an Enterprise Client/Server Architecture

An architecture (in most MIS discussions) refers to the framework or hardware/software infrastructure that supports application development and delivery. Currently, most large shops have rather sophisticated architectures consisting of mainframes, servers (by conventional definition local area networks), and PCs or standalone workstations.

In an attempt to describe the most useful methods of distributing the user interface (UI), business logic (APPL), and database access (DBMS), throughout an enterprise composed of mainframes, servers, and PCs, the Gartner Group produced a classification of various types of Client/Server architectures currently being deployed by the Fortune 1000 (Table 1.1).

As you can see, there are six different combinations of application system component distribution. In Chapter 2 on graphical user interface in a client/server environment, we will be discussing these (and much more about client/server) in greater depth.

Is That All There Is to Client/Server?

For the purposes of this chapter, yes. However, the major client/server vendors (Microsoft, Powersoft, Sybase, Gupta, etc.) are motivated both technically and commercially to improve their products, and are feverishly incorporating other advanced, contemporary technologies under the umbrella of client/server. This advanced technology includes graphical user interfaces (GUI), object orientation, and relational DBMSs.

Client/Server-Architecture	MAINFRAME	SERVER	PC
Monolithic	UI APPL DBMS		
Intelligent Presentation	DBMS APPL		UI
Distributed Data Access	DBMS	DBMS	APPL UI
Distributed Application Logic	DBMS APPL		APPL UI
Distributed Data Access APPL & Application Logic	DBMS APPL	DBMS	APPL UI
Distributed Database	DBMS	DBMS	DBMS APPL UI

Source: The Gartner Group, *Client/Server Computing* abstracts

Table 1.1 Method of application component distribution.

GUI, or graphical user interface software, is the contemporary standard for end-user presentation delivery. Unlike client/server, there is a formal definition for GUI. It was set forth in the late 1980s by IBM in their CUA (common user access) announcements and documentation. The CUA approach to application system interfaces, part of IBM's SAA (systems application architecture), involves presenting information in a standardized format, using graphical icons, windows, dropdown menus, and pointing devices (mouse) technology, in place of PF-key (program-function key), character-based, nonstandard interfaces, traditionally the method of delivering mainframe-3270-based applications.

The primary impetus for CUA was (unfortunately, this has been lost in the furor over this new and exciting technology), to standardize and simplify applications for the casual end user. We emphasize the term *casual user,* to set those people apart from power end users, or those working constantly with computers, such as data-entry clerks and PC professionals. While it has been proven beyond a doubt that GUI technology is the superior approach for software destined for casual (occasional) use, GUI-based software for power users or heavily used screen-driven applications such as data collections applications has been accepted at a slower pace.

None of which is about to halt the GUI juggernaut. In the minds of contemporary MIS professionals, GUI technology has succeeded in delivering systems that are far more visually appealing, systems that require shorter learning curves for end users, systems with more advanced functionality, and systems that have proven to cut down on costly data-entry errors. Quite simply, GUI applications are accepted as providing a better user interface. But a better user interface (like a GUI) comes with a price tag.

GUI: A Swan of a Technology

If you've ever seen a swan swimming gracefully about in a pond, you might think that their efforts were simple and expedient. Upon closer inspection, however, you would find that the swan's legs are moving like little automobile pistons, in considerable and frenetic efforts to manage the swan's apparent effortlessness, grace, and appearance.

This same concept of on the surface ease of effort and simplicity belying—and to a large degree masking—substantial work and complexity under the surface describes both GUI technology delivery and development. While the end product of a quality GUI application is indeed, ease of use and a simple, attractive, and efficient human interface (Figure 1.1), the design and programming efforts required to build GUIs has heretofore been anything but.

In fact, Gartner Group, in a July 1992 report on client/server, makes a statement to the effect that in many cases the only verifiable savings obtained by client/server technology are due mainly to reduced data entry errors because of the inclusion of GUI front ends to applications.

Windows and OS/2 APIs

Until the advent of 4GL Windows development tools such as SQL-Windows, PowerBuilder, and Visual Basic, programming for Microsoft Windows GUIs and OS/2 Presentation Manager software was done using 3GL and object-oriented programming languages such as C, C++, and Smalltalk making calls to Windows and OS/2 API (application programming interface) functions and macros.

The code required to produce even simple Windows applications using native C/Windows API programming is event-driven,* generally complex, and can be difficult for mainframe developers—or for that matter, any developers except experienced C programmers—to write (C/Windows API programming includes a particularly steep

---

Event-driven refers to a style of procedural programming and application design, whereby any and all external events (mouse clicks, mouse movement, tabbing, and so forth) cause events to occur within the application system, which are either queued or handled immediately by pockets of code written specifically for those events.

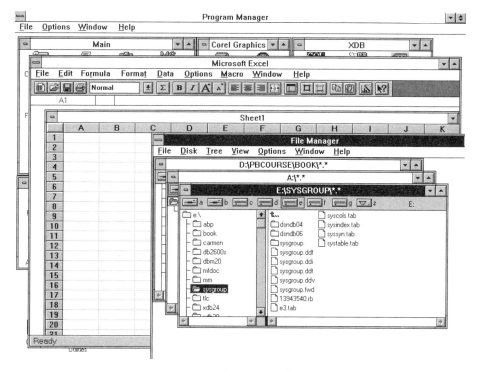

Figure 1.1 A sample GUI application screen.

learning curve for mainframe COBOL personnel). However, with the advent of the new wave 4GL workbenches such as Powerbuilder, Visual Basic, SQLWindows, and PARTS Workbench, this is no longer an issue, as these products generate the C/Windows API code and allow mere mortal developers to build sophisticated GUI applications with relatively the same effort (past the initial learning curve) that it would take to build character-based applications.

New Wave 4GLs to the Rescue

The synergy between GUI technology and our new wave 4GLs is no accident. Because of the difficulty in developing custom applications in Windows/API-C programming without a simplified means to produce custom GUI applications quickly and cheaply, GUI technology (for a while) ran the risk of becoming a niche platform, accessible only to software developers with heavy C/systems programming backgrounds. But with the advent and acceptance of the new wave 4GLs, GUI technology has been given an enormous boost in momentum and prominence, and has become a legitimate contender for the huge store of corporate applications currently operating in character-based mode. The new wave 4GLs are the key to the continued success of GUI in MIS, as is object orientation.

Object Orientation

One of the major software design and development advances of the past decade is object technology. *Object technology** is a group of advanced programming languages and database systems that share a common set of guiding principles—object orientation. Object-oriented programming languages (OOPL), object-oriented analysis and design (OOAD), and object-oriented database systems (OODBMS) share a minimally defined set of rules and regulations. These rules have been documented in various object-oriented "manifestos" by authors such as Rumbaugh, Martyn, Grady/Booch, and Yourdoun. And while there is no single precise textbook definition of object orientation approximating Dr. Codd's relational database theorems, there is a general consensus that, for a technology to call itself object-oriented, its technology must support or enforce a group of software design and programming practices such as: *inheritance*—the ability of a software object such as a program, window, window control, or database to physically and logically *inherit* (receive) all aspects of an ancestor software object, *encapsulation*—the ability to create software objects that contain all elements of logic and all elements of data in a single, defined structure, and *messaging*—the method of invoking objects.[+]

GUI and OO: More Synergy

As software trends and directions occur, little seems to happen in a vacuum in the DP world. Over the past decade object orientation and GUI have become the trend in the software development universe, and (wouldn't you know it), they wind up sharing important features.

As it turns out, windows (GUI) application development is best addressed using languages that refer to graphical objects rather than mere fields and records in a control block. Windows macros and controls exist in class libraries (another OO construct) and use messaging to communicate with one another and with the end user. Many of the terms and concepts of GUI programming have their roots in OO technology. Thus, a natural synergy exists between OO and GUI. As you will see in the later chapters of this book, most of the major C/S-OO-GUI vendors have built in the capability to include a small-to-large degree of object orientation into the application development environments of their respective products.

---

*Object technology is more than a single product or feature. It is a formal method, a way of thinking about and approaching software design and development. As such, *object orientation* (as a term) is similar to *CASE* or *information engineering* as terms. There are many object-oriented products, just as there are many CASE tools.

[+]See Chapter 4, Introduction to Object Orientation, for more detail on object orientation.

Overview of the Four Products

Now it is time to discuss the 4GL Workbench products that we will use to build our sample business application. This chapter presents only an introduction to each product (the "what") and a bit of background on each company. Subsequent chapters will describe the use of the product (the "how to") in an actual development procedure.

PowerBuilder 3.0

PowerBuilder is an object-oriented, graphic, client/server development toolset, used to build and deliver commercial Microsoft Windows applications. PowerBuilder 1.0 began shipping in June 1991, and quickly gained widespread recognition from developers as a high-performance graphical development platform. PowerBuilder 2.0, which began shipping July 1992, offered greatly expanded object-oriented features, as well as improved SQL-development options. PowerBuilder 3.0, which began shipping in September 1993, has extended the object orientation even further and provided more advanced SQL functionality, including extensions to the point-and-click development interface to the DBMS, and more sophisticated graphics options.

PowerBuilder's stated targets are large-scale Fortune 1000 companies and government agencies that are looking to leverage the gains and strategic business opportunities associated with client/server-based information systems. Powersoft, a publicly held and traded company, states that as of June 1993 more than 2,600 organizations were using PowerBuilder, and that over 13,400 licensed copies had been sold. In order to manage this extremely rapid growth, Powersoft has been proactive in establishing several support options.

Education partners. Taking their model from the Novell, Inc., certification process, Powersoft has established an in-depth Education Partners program that provides course instruction, stand-up training, and consulting certification in PowerBuilder. Courses are offered at the company headquarters in Burlington, Mass., and in many other cities throughout the United States, by the (as of this writing) more than 30 Powersoft Education Partners. The program is also offered internationally through Powersoft's European headquarters and distributors who are authorized and certified in PowerBuilder training.

Support, consulting, and other services. Powersoft also provides customers with an extensive variety of support plans, including consulting services, an electronic bulletin-board system, a FAXBACK system (offering technical tips and techniques), and a Compuserve forum. Powersoft maintains ten field offices throughout the United

States and Canada to sell and support its products. Powersoft also distributes and sells PowerBuilder and supplementary services through relationships with over 70 authorized resellers (VARs, value added resellers). European operation headquarters are located in Maidenhead, England. Powersoft offers product support, education, certification, and consulting throughout Europe, the Pacific Rim, and Latin America.

Supported platforms and DBMSs. The list of supported development platforms, execution platforms (where PowerBuilder generated applications may run), and DBMSs is shown in Table 1.2. You should note that this list increases quarterly, and should a technology you need supported not appear on this list, please contact the company to get a current update.

Digitalk

Founded in 1983 by Jim Anderson, George Bosworth, and Barbara Noparstak, in 1985 Digitalk became the first company to provide commercially available object technology on the PC with a product called Methods, followed by Smalltalk/V in 1986. Digitalk has since delivered versions of Smalltalk/V on DOS, Macintosh, Windows, OS/2, and in 1993 for AIX on the IBM RS/6000 platform.

The maturity of Digitalk and its object-oriented Smalltalk/V is a significant advantage to developers. Because Smalltalk/V has been used in the field longer than any other PC object technology product, it has a richer set of class libraries—about twice as many as the most

Development Platforms	Execution Platforms	DBMS
Microsoft Windows 3.1	Microsoft Windows 3.1	ALLBASE/SQL
OS/2 2.1	OS/2 2.1	Database Manager and DB2/2
		Informix
		Micro Decisionware Database Gateway to DB2
		ODBC
		Oracle
		SQL Server
		GUPTA SQLBase
		Sybase
		Watcom SQL
		XDB

Table 1.2   PowerBuilder platform and product support.

popular C++ compiler. The breadth and depth of these classes make application development faster and easier. Repeated building and testing of components over time has ensured that Smalltalk/V object classes are reliable. Today, over 100,000 people around the world are using Smalltalk/V. This installed base also forms the basis for the acceptance of new technologies from Digitalk.

In October 1990, Digitalk and IBM announced a major alliance: a development and license agreement for Digitalk's Smalltalk/V for Windows and OS/2 and its new PARTS product line, as well as for future products. The agreement was dramatically amplified in September 1991, when IBM named Digitalk to its International Alliance for AD/Cycle, the select group of eight companies whose products IBM endorses for its corporate customers.

In October of 1992, Digitalk delivered PARTS Workbench, the first in a line of products based on a parts assembly and reuse tool set technology that enables very rapid, visual application construction from prefabricated software components. This enables software developers to leverage the creation of components by reusing them again and again. PARTS technology is based on the Smalltalk/V object technology. In January 1993, Digitalk shipped version 2.0 of PARTS Workbench for OS/2 with a new 32-bit architecture making it smaller and faster than version 1.0. That year also marked the release of the PARTS COBOL Wrapper, a companion product for PARTS Workbench that allows easy integration with COBOL code and supports Micro Focus COBOL. The PARTS Relational Database Interface, another companion product for PARTS Workbench, allows integration with relational databases. This release, the first in a series of database interface parts, supports IBM OS/2 Extended Services Database Manager. Characteristics of PARTS Workbench are outlined in Table 1.3.

Digitalk Professional Services. Digitalk Professional Services is a source for information on Smalltalk/V design methodologies, object-oriented technical and managerial topics, technology assessment and

Development Platform	Execution Platforms	DBMS
OS/2 2.0, 2.1 Microsoft Windows	OS/2 2.0, 2.1 Microsoft Windows (soon to be released)	SQL Server Oracle IBM Extended Services Database Manager DB2 and others

Table 1.3   PARTS Workbench, platform and product support.

transfer, and project definition. Both consulting and education services are offered.

Direct Connect. Direct Connect is Digitalk's online support and information service. Direct Connect is a direct link to Digitalk technical support, available via a local phone number in more than 750 cities in 30 countries. The Direct Connect service provides the latest information about Digitalk development environment, access to Digitalk technical support personnel, a communication channel with other Digitalk product users and extensive databases of technical information including code, commonly asked questions, and problem reports.

Microsoft Visual Basic 3.0

Visual Basic is one of hundreds of products brought to you by Microsoft. If you don't know who they are, let me be the first to welcome you to planet Earth. Founded in 1975, Microsoft has been a household world since the introduction of the IBM PC in 1980. Microsoft developed the operating system used in that personal computer (MS-DOS), which rocketed the company to its current status as the largest software vendor in the world. In fact, the original IBM PC came with MS-DOS 1.0 and the Microsoft BASIC interpreter.

Although BASIC had been around for years, Microsoft brought the language into the limelight by making it available to the general public. The language was used primarily as an educational tool for learning the basics of programming—it seemed that BASIC would never be a mainstream programming language.

Microsoft apparently felt differently. Microsoft made BASIC a viable language for PC application development by marketing several generations of BASIC compilers. BASIC began to catch on as a powerful, easy-to-learn, and easy-to-use PC programming language. In 1986, Microsoft released Windows. As Windows began to mature, the developer community was calling for a development environment and 4GL language for creating Windows applications. Visual BASIC for Windows was Microsoft's response.

Today, Microsoft Visual BASIC Version 3.0 is one of the leading client/server application development tools for Windows. Its success has been a result of several factors: the product, the organization, and support.

A superior package in its own right, VB owes a great deal of its success to the add-on products developed by other vendors. These include everything from additional controls to database API middleware, which gives Visual Basic the benefit of tremendous vendor support. Microsoft's ODBC database connectivity has given VB access to some of the most popular database formats, allowing for significant enterprise connectivity.

Microsoft as an organization has also contributed to the product's success. Sales, product support, Microsoft University classes, Microsoft Consultant Relations Program, Microsoft Developer Network, and the forums they maintain on Compuserve are all important services software developers can rely on.

SQLWindows

SQLWindows is a client/server development tool developed by the Gupta Corporation and has been one of the leading client/server development products on the market for several years. The company was started in 1984 by Umang Gupta, vice president of Oracle's microcomputer division, and Bruce Scott, coauthor of the original Oracle database engine. In 1986, Gupta released the first SQL database engine designed for PC networks, called SQLBase Server. In 1988 Gupta released SQLWindows 1.0, one of the first client/server application development systems for Windows. Today Gupta is a leader in the client/server development arena, and their products are used by many Fortune 500 companies and major companies throughout the world.

SQLWindows 4.0 contains several powerful tools used for developing client/server applications. The Corporate Edition comes with TeamWindows, used for managing client/server projects; SQLWindows software to develop the GUI for client/server application, Quest, a graphical interface to SQL based database engines; ReportWindows, used for developing reports; and SQLBase, a powerful SQL based database engine scalable from laptops to LAN servers. SQLBase is available for use in DOS, Windows, OS/2, NetWare (NLM), and Sun. SQLWindows can connect to a multitude of other SQL based database engine with the use of Gupta's SQLNetwork. SQLNetwork provides connectivity to such database engines as IBM's DB2, OS/2 Database Manager, and AS/400; Microsoft and Sybase's SQLServer; HP ALLBASE/SQL; and Informix.

Support, consulting, and other services. Gupta offers several types of technical support services, from a baseline service to premium corporate support. Gupta offers consulting and training through specialists at Gupta and many certified training partners.

2

Overview of Client/Server Technology

Client/Server

If you've never heard of client/server before reading this book, you're probably much better off than you realize. Some of the top technicians in the field have struggled for a succinct definition of client/server and what it really means. Most experts define client/server as a broad set of ideals that have so many different implementations, a single one-line definition is either so broad that it says nothing, or too deep while still leaving things out.

To clearly explain what client/server is, where it came from, what it means, and where it's going, we have to talk about a variety of different hardware platforms, operating systems, software choices, and communications terminology. My advice is sit back, relax, be patient, and enjoy the ride.

Choose Your Weapons

Before we can jump into a discussion of the different things that make up client/server technology, we need to carve out some common ground and make sure we are starting from the same place. Depending on your background (PC coder, mainframe programmer, or DP manager), some of these terms and concepts may be familiar and comfortable while others remain dark holes in your understanding. Browse the next few pages and confirm or supplement your knowledge.

The Corporate Mainframe: Centralized Data Processing

For the last 30 years, the mainframe computer has been the center of data processing as we know it (Figure 2.1). Referred to by most as the *host,* the mainframe represents a large, central platform with virtually

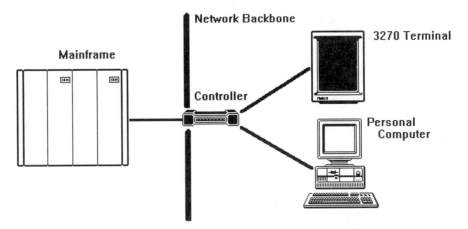

Figure 2.1   A typical mainframe topography.

unlimited resources. From a programmer's view, the mainframe appears as a central CPU (central processing unit) with vast quantities of memory, disk space, and assorted peripheral devices (printers, optical readers, and so on) accessible and shared by hundreds or thousands of programmers and users via a video terminal.

This one device can support all the tasks a shop requires. At any given moment, the mainframe can support programmer activities (editing, compiling, linking, testing, etc.), user applications (data entry and online applications), and batch activities. Various pieces of software and hardware work together to give all these people with different jobs access to the resources they need.

The key to the mainframe is centralization. All operations are performed and all data is stored at the same logical location. In reality, what a programmer sees as a single device may in fact be multiple physical devices operating in tandem. A mainframe can simultaneously support a user in Los Angeles just as efficiently as a user in Boston. The Los Angeles user has access to the same data, same programs, same databases, and same printers as the Boston user. All hardware maintenance occurs at a central location. If disk space runs out, a new drive is installed. If the CPU resources need upgrading, the mainframe can be expanded.

In most medium and large shops, you will find a mainframe. In 70 percent of those shops, that mainframe will be IBM. "Big Blue" has had a stronghold on the mainframe market since its inception, and despite their recent organizational upheaval will likely continue to be the standard in the future. This domination of the market is part of what contributed to IBM's success. IBM developed and instituted what most shops have now adopted as a standard. In general, if your hardware is IBM and your operating systems are IBM, you had a much greater chance of integrating your applications than you did if your hardware was from different vendors. This standardization also made it easier to find computer support personnel. It was easier to find an IBM programmer than a DEC programmer, as they were more common and, as a result, less expensive to hire.

IBM mainframes are based on the mature 370 architecture. Established business operating systems, TP monitors, software, databases, and utilities make the mainframe a permanent data-processing establishment. However, despite the vast capacities available, corporate America is approaching capacity thresholds. Furthermore, the costs associated with purchasing, maintaining, and upgrading mainframe systems to keep up with rapidly escalating needs has become prohibitive.

The mainframe provides centralized access to programming resources, data resources, and application environments. Its capacity, size, and speed make it the logical choice for the execution of complex, CPU-intensive tasks, and the storage of large files or databases.

Multiple Parallel Processor Machines—The Next Generation

Multiple parallel processor machines (MPP) are the future of data processing (Figure 2.2). These machines are not made of just one expensive microprocessor but rather many inexpensive processors working in tandem. Today's MPP machines can be made of as many as 64,000 processors working together. The MIPS (millions of instructions per second) these machines can produce leave IBM's most powerful mainframe looking like a tinker toy.

While just coming into their own, MPP machines are currently too unstable to use as production machines. They are continuing to progress and are showing up more and more in advanced prototype

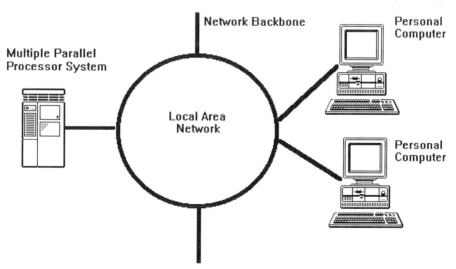

Figure 2.2 Multiple parallel processor machines.

environments. Their operating systems are primarily UNIX derivatives and their applications will be endless. One of the most interesting examples of the MPP's future use is as a video server for the next generation of home cable networks, which allow someone to interactively request a movie to watch on TV. These machines are powerful enough to retrieve the video and sound of a movie from disk and present it to the customer via a cable network. These machines have the storage and MIPS to support over 150 users simultaneously. Although their cost is still high (yet not even close to the cost of a mainframe) and their reliability is still questionable, they represent the future of client/server.

Minicomputers—Midrange Platforms

The minicomputer arrived as an alternative to the mainframe for shops that did not require the strength and capacity or could not support the cost of purchasing and maintaining a mainframe (Figure 2.3). The minicomputer is a scaled-down version of the mainframe. Still a centralized environment, the minicomputer is a central CPU that supports hundreds of users offering the services of the memory, disk drives, and peripherals it has available. Although capacities are not as great, processing speed and power is not that far off.

Initially, minicomputers were a decentralized solution. The Boston office would have their own minicomputer while the Los Angeles branch supported a computer of its own. If data needed to be shared between the Los Angeles and Boston branches, the exchange was often unreliable at best. Data was shipped via tape or transmitted nightly over telephone lines. When application programs changed, software installation had to be done at two different sites. In exchange

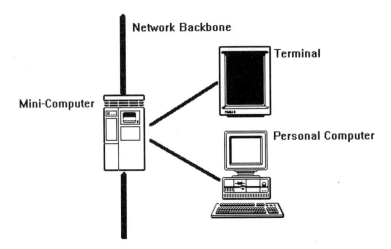

Figure 2.3   A typical minicomputer topography.

for these inconveniences, maintenance costs fell and performance improved. Different corporate areas felt they had more control over the cost and use of the DP resources they needed.

The major problem minicomputer users experienced was the lack of standardization. For years, the minicomputer market has been crowded with players like Digital Equipment Corporation, IBM, Hewlett Packard and Unisys, to name a few. Each manufacturer has its own operating system, standards, languages, and communication techniques. This reality forced a shop to standardize on a particular manufacturer or dabble in all the problems associated with system incompatibilities.

The minicomputer provides a centralized resource to many programmers and users while being decentralized in a larger organization view. Certain efficiencies are gained by this decentralization while others are lost. Standardization has always been a problem.

Workstations—Not Just for Lab Use Anymore

The term *workstations* (commonly but incorrectly equated to PCs) was coined in the UNIX world (Figure 2.4). A workstation is similar to a minicomputer in that it provides access to one or many users sharing its available resources. Workstations differ in their architecture and capacity. Built around CPUs with radically different instruction sets (RISC, or reduced instruction set CPU), running different variants of the UNIX operating system, workstations provide a more decentralized resource. A shop typically needs more workstations to support an operation than it would minicomputers. In the past, a workstation was found primarily in scientific environments. Over the past few years, the workstation has been making considerable inroads

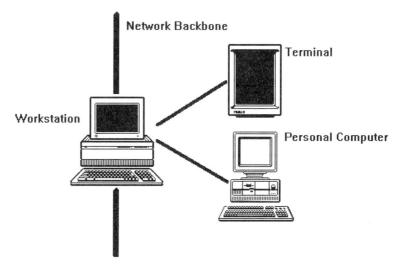

Figure 2.4   Workstations and their connections.

into the business environment, primarily due to the advances made in client/server technology.

Personal Computers—The Key to Client/Server

The term *personal computer* or PC was apropos when PCs were first introduced (Figure 2.5). A PC is a truly decentralized platform providing dedicated CPU, memory, and disk resources to one user. Costs have fallen, maintenance is insignificant, and productivity enhancements have been significant. The PC's success has been primarily due to its independence. A user running an application on a PC has access to features previously unavailable anywhere else. Graphical user interface (GUI) and dedicated CPU resources are the primary ones. The introduction of the PC into business computing environments has led to a whole new generation of applications. However, sharing data from this solitary outpost is even more of a problem. With all its power, the PC has been limited by the isolation inherent in its use.

Operating Systems—The Brains of the Operation

If a CPU and associated hardware are a computer's body, the operating system is its brain (Figure 2.6). Responsible for base input/output functions, disk management, task-management functions, and base communications, the strengths and weaknesses of an operating system translate into the strengths and weaknesses of a platform. The vast array of operating systems available across platforms can easily make anyone's head spin. Most mainframes run MVS but some run DOS/VSE. The two operating systems can communicate with one another but the interface is not always terribly efficient.

Digital's VMS, HP's HP/UX, and IBM's OS/400 are just a few of the more popular minicomputer operating systems. Each operating

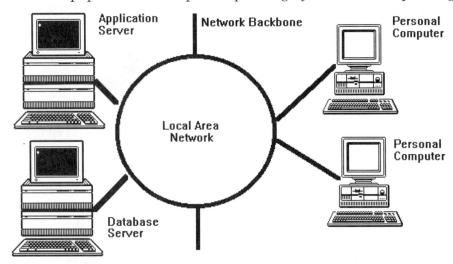

Figure 2.5   A PC local area network.

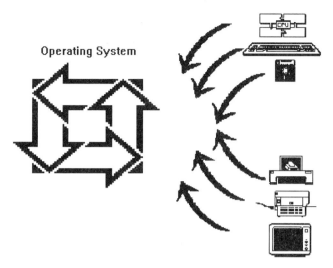

Figure 2.6 Operating systems and their functions.

system performs the same basic function, but not always in the same way. Furthermore, design and maturity play a major role in the success or failure of an OS. The number of UNIX variants available on the workstation market are astounding: UNIX, Sun OS/Solaris, IBM's AIX, and SCO's Xenix are but a few.

Other operating systems, such as NEXT, bear notice. NEXT is a new concept in operating systems. The operating system itself is made up of object-oriented building blocks. These blocks can be easily shaped into efficient, operating-system level applications. Furthermore, in the tradition of object-oriented programming, existing application code can be reused to produce new applications. Born to run on proprietary architecture, NEXT was recently ported to the Intel chip platform. The strengths of object-oriented development are undeniable and, if NEXT can provide object-oriented application development at an operating system level, they may just have a winner.

Apple computer's hardware and software offerings have always filled niche markets like education and graphic arts. Over the years, Apple has stopped boycotting IBM technology and begun to embrace or at least tolerate it. The current generation of Apple technology can not only communicate with Intel processor machines, but can run their software and read from/write to their disk formats.

A joint operating system venture between Apple and IBM called PINK holds the promise of integrating IBM advances and Apple ingenuity. Similar to NEXT, PINK is expected to be object-oriented and is another operating system to watch.

The real battle in operating systems is occurring on the PC front. The well established single-user operating system, DOS, has outlived its usefulness. Currently, DOS's successor, Microsoft's Windows and

IBM's next generation OS/2 are slugging it out. Windows' slick graphical user interface, cooperative multitasking, and preservation of DOS programs revolutionized PC computing. However, Windows, built on DOS, does not yet provide the kind of stability a truly robust 32-bit operating system should.

Although trailing in time and acceptance, IBM's OS/2 provides a more robust 32-bit operating system with preemptive multitasking and extended services, such as database manager and communications manager. OS/2 is technically superior and the logical corporate, large-application choice.

Microsoft has responded by diversifying the base Windows operating system into more specific operating systems, each with the same basic characteristics. Windows NT is a full-blown 32-bit operating system. Because of its size and requirements, NT is currently in use primarily as a server operating system. Window's next generation of desktop operating systems, code-named *Chicago,* is due out in mid-1994. Microsoft is also developing an object-oriented Windows based operating system, code-named *Cairo.*

At the same time, IBM has stepped to the plate with their base product and diversified. The latest release of OS/2 (2.1) supports the execution of DOS, Windows 3.1, and OS/2 applications under the same kernel. In order to accomplish this, IBM has had to pay royalties to Microsoft for the use of their Windows 3.1 microcode. As a result, IBM recently released a version of OS/2 for Windows. This product allows Microsoft Windows' users to execute DOS and OS/2 applications with a more efficient memory manager and preemptive multitasking, while not paying for Windows twice. This has further lowered the price of OS/2 and makes the competition for PC operating system dominance even more fierce.

Databases—The Storage and Retrieval of Information

Database technology is one of the driving forces behind the client/server movement. Specifically, the relational database has changed the face of data processing (Figure 2.7). Corporate America has a large portion of its available data stored in sequential file formats. Large tape datasets and flat files account for a considerable amount of current data. VSAM files and DL/I databases have supported the need for indexed data. The ever-increasing need for more information from that data has led to a move toward relational databases. The ability to access data from any angle across multiple independent tables has given programmers the ability to produce information previously unavailable because of the expense of processing large flat files. The stability and efficiency afforded today's relational databases has made multimillion-row tables a reality. More important, the general standardization of structured query language

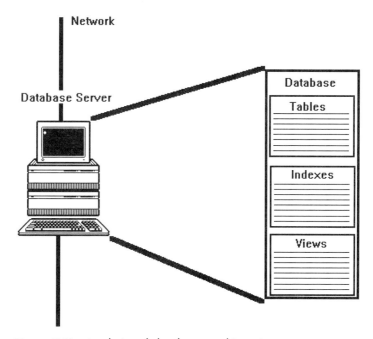

Figure 2.7   A relational database and its primary components.

(SQL) has made vendor choice a secondary consideration. Vendors such as IBM (Mainframe DB2 and OS/2's DB2/2), Sybase/Microsoft SQLServer, and Oracle are competing fiercely for domination. Other vendors such as Progress, Informix, Ingress, IBI (FOCUS), Gupta (SQLBase), and XDB (XDB) are not far behind. These databases have provided the cornerstone of client/server computing.

Communications—The Glue That Holds It All Together

Without overemphasizing the point, it must be made clear that communications is by far the most important concept to grasp when discussing client/server (Figure 2.8). Scores of books have been written on the developments in communications technology by itself—most of them hardly readable. Communications is a highly technical subject full of terms and concepts barely comprehensible by even the most seasoned professional. Despite its complexity, a rudimentary understanding of communications technology is critical to understanding client/server. Without entering into a deep philosophical discussion of communications, it should be said that communications technology is what allows us to tie different machines running different operating systems and different software to communicate with one another. Communications are accomplished by subscribing to a specific protocol or set of rules. TCP/IP is by far the most common protocol found on UNIX platforms. Net BIOS protocols on token ring networks tie most Intel-based systems together on local area networks

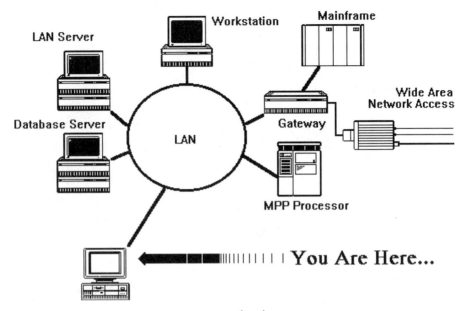

Figure 2.8   Networks: the BIG picture.

(LANs). SNA is used on most IBM-based mainframe systems to allow external access. Other emerging protocols such as IBM's APPC, SNMP, and CMIP are bound to become more prevalent in the future. Other advances in client/server communications technology such as DCE, DME, and Datahub will also become important.

On a local area network network operating system (NOS) front, Novell, Microsoft (LAN manager), and IBM (LAN Server) control a large piece of the market.

While physical communications are usually hidden from the average programmer, the client/server programmer will have to be aware of communications protocols and the functions they perform. In many cases, programmers will have to interact with communications layers to accomplish their tasks.

Client/Server—What Is It?

The era of corporate data processing began when the mainframe came into its own. As the mainframe became more powerful and more standardized, data-processing skill sets became more predictable. In most business-oriented firms, IBM was the standard. Skills such as JCL (job control language), SPF (system productivity facility), and COBOL (common business-oriented language) were tickets to success. A visible line was drawn between programmers and users. Each had specific knowledge and expertise the other generally did not possess and each was at the mercy of the ability and skill of the other.

Requirements and technology progressed together to produce new standards. The user community needed to move away from systems that accepted information from keypunchers and processed data in batch mode to systems that accepted input and processed queries in real time. Two environments emerged as online teleprocessing monitor standards—IMS and CICS. These environments allowed for the development of applications that collected data and process queries in real time. Data storage was moving away from the traditional flat file or tape format to indexed formats like VSAM, hierarchical database formats like IMS's DL/I, and relational formats like DB2.

Believe it or not, client/server principles first emerged in this environment (Figure 2.9). Systems analysts began to develop ways to combine online and batch processing to better serve the needs of the user. Data was collected all day online and, at night, files were deallocated from the online regions and used in batch systems. Batch systems ran against these files and updated other system files across the corporation. This was the first example of using radically different environments together to produce optimal use of both.

In a nutshell, that's what client/server is all about. Client/server is a new way of developing applications in order to use the resources available to the best of their ability. In the example above, online environments provided the user with instantaneous access to real-time data. However, in order to maintain adequate response time, the corresponding updates to other systems were left to batch systems which ran during off hours. In this fashion, programmers were developing systems that used the resources available to them, exploiting different environments for their strengths. As user need increased, so did the scope of client/server thought. As you might expect, there were some situations which required one online application to collect information previously collected by another online application. Analysts began devising ways for one application to communicate in real time with other applications to process these requests. One CICS application could feed data to another within the same CICS region. Then, programmers began to devise methods by which one CICS

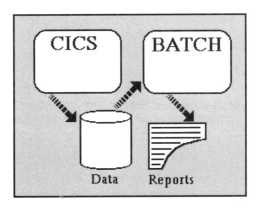

Figure 2.9   Client/Server processing in its infancy.

application could communicate with another CICS application processing in a different region. Eventually, applications were communicating with applications across regions routinely. Programmers began to view a request for information as a *unit of work*. One unit of work might require information from several systems across many regions.

Synchronous versus asynchronous processing became a critical design consideration. Critical transactions were processed *synchronously*—data was collected or processed while the user waited for a response. Less critical and CPU intensive units of work were processed *asynchronously*. Asynchronous processing involved the use of store and forward mechanisms. The user would collect data or make a request for information. The data or request was then formatted for transmission and shipped off to the appropriate region for processing. While the data was being processed, the user's application was freed up for further requests. Once back-end processing was complete, a response data stream was formatted, sent back to the user's region, and stored. A message was sent to the user telling him the results of his previous request were available for retrieval at his convenience. Using this model of processing, data-processing resources were being used together, in real time, to more efficiently process user requests. This is called *cooperative processing*—using CPU resources across platforms to process data together.

Client/server technology involves expanding this design theory to consider all of the resources a shop has available—mainframes, minis, workstations, and PCs—for their particular strengths and weaknesses, and to exploit their strengths to provide greater productivity and lower data-processing costs. While many terms have been emerging for this concept, the most appropriate is *enterprise computing*. Programmers are no longer mainframe oriented or language oriented. Programmers must develop systems that run across platforms in an enterprise and use all resources available for their best purpose.

How It All Ties Together

The first step toward considering client/server computing is to remove yourself from what you know and reconsider what you have. Most data-processing professionals have grown up with a particular specialty. A mainframe programmer, a PC jock, a UNIX expert—all have their own sphere of knowledge in which they feel comfortable. More often than not, each has a distinct lack of understanding of what goes on in other platforms available. Enterprise computing requires the programmer and analyst to understand all the computing resources they have available, what the strengths and weakness of each are, and how each platform can communicate with the others.

Fortune 1000 companies are investing in personal-computer technology at a staggering rate. Most of these PCs are interconnected with local area networks. These local LANs are often interconnected on a backbone network, which usually includes gateway communications to the corporate mainframe. Specific departments and different areas often require their own specialized resources. DEC VAX clusters, UNIX file and database servers, and IBM minis are often in evidence. These units are often available off the corporate backbone as well. Once you consider the resources available across your enterprise, you come to the realization that the CPU, memory, and disk space available for information processing is vast. The question you have to ask yourself is, how to make the best use of those resources as a group.

What Do You Look For?

The term *client/server* refers to the relationship between enterprise resources. On one end of a transaction is the client or service requester. On the other, the server or provider of resources. In its simplest form, client/server can reside in a simple local area network topology. Programs and data are often stored on a LAN file server. LAN-connected personal computers have their own CPU and memory resources. When a PC executes an application program that resides on the server, the program instructions are loaded into the PC's memory and use the PC's CPU resources for processing. By executing the server-resident application, the PC or client has made a request. The server will respond to the request by providing the program instructions for loading and execution. In essence, a client/server transaction has just taken place. We used the CPU and central-storage resources of the server to store a program and retrieve it for us and the resources of our PC to execute the program.

Client/server application design is a new way of thinking when designing and building an application. Personal computers and UNIX workstations have the corner on the market when it comes to user-interface technology. The advent of the graphical user interface has changed the face of computing. Ease of use, standardized look and feel, and the extensive online contact-sensitive help have made the GUI the new standard. GUI application development has also blurred the traditional lines between programmer and user. The user is now able to provide considerably more input concerning what the application looks like and how it reacts. More often than not, users can prototype the application themselves, leaving only the detail code and database access to the programmer. Many PC-GUI development packages allow for rapid prototype development, and approach a state of greater sophistication.

There are three distinct ways to consider a client/server application. The first is to enhance an existing mainframe system by adding a graphical user interface. Commonly called *3270 masking* or *screen scraping,* this technique involves using a PC-based software package to build a GUI interface to collect data. Once collected, the PC package will, in the background, populate existing host screens and simulate pressing the enter key. By utilizing this methodology, existing legacy systems can be left intact while giving the user community the benefits derived from a graphical application. Furthermore, a single PC application can maintain connections to multiple host systems and use these connections to update data across these systems at the same time. For example, an application can be developed to collect the name and address of a customer. That information may be required by several existing legacy systems. Once this information is collected, the PC application can update each of these systems in the background while the user moves on to collect more information. The same is true for information retrieval. If the information required exists on multiple systems, the GUI can retrieve the information and compile a more complete response.

If you choose to abandon legacy systems and start from scratch, or develop a new application using a client/server design, the issues become more complex. Any computer application requires the storage and retrieval of data. To make the best use of available technology, the natural choice is a relational database. The location of the data and the programs responsible for accessing and processing data is a complicated issue.

Data location depends on need, use, and size. Large data storage often requires a mainframe where DASD and processing cycles are the most significant. Also, any data that requires online access by other mainframe systems or is required by wide-area users may belong on a mainframe. The mainframe is the best choice for truly centralized access. If the data does not require the kind of access or scope described above, the choices become more diverse. Again, the key here is to make the best use of the resources you have available.

Most shops have the corporate mainframe, minicomputer or workstation servers, and LAN file servers at their disposal. All these platforms should be used for their specific strengths. The most productive platform is the local area network database server. Any data that can be kept local should be. Local database servers provide the best response to user requests since they are local and dedicated. Along the same lines, minicomputer and workstation resources also provide very efficient, cost-effective service. If accessed locally, these devices can provide the same types of service as a local area network server but with far greater resources in terms of disk space and CPU.

The complexity involved in designing an efficient client/server system lies in the theory that a database does not have to reside solely on a single platform. Data can be distributed across multiple platforms as required. Some examples follow.

When designing an application to collect data, the data may be stored locally on a LAN-connected server. During off hours or at specified intervals, the data may be uploaded to the mainframe or minicomputer to provide other applications access. If required, it is also possible to apply data to other platforms at the time a transaction is made. Special care must be taken under these circumstances to make sure the update is properly committed to both databases. These same principles hold true on an inquiry application. Sections of a centrally located database are often downloaded to local servers for faster access. Sometimes, updates to these local servers are made at periodic intervals from the central database.

These are only some of the ways in which data can be distributed across enterprise platforms to make the best use of available resources. As you can see, the permutations here are considerable. Furthermore, just when you thought you had enough to consider—here's more.

The programs which process data can be distributed across enterprise resources the same way data can. On a simple level, Sybase/ Microsoft SQLServer allows for distributed processing through the use of stored procedures. Executing a stored procedure in SQLServer causes the transaction to be executed on the server instead of local CPU resources.

Programs which must process complicated queries or updates may need to reside on a mini- or mainframe where the MIPS exist to handle the request efficiently. Other routines may reside on the client workstation where the GUI resides, and still others may reside on intermediate resources.

Where does it all end? Well, it doesn't—that's the point. Client/server application design involves a fundamental shift in "the big picture." As application designers, we are all used to embracing a large task and breaking it down into processes. We are also used to compiling a list of all required data items and arranging that list into logically related packages. To take advantage of enterprise computing, you need to add a few more variables to your design criteria.

What Are the Enterprise Resources Available in My Shop?

The first step toward enterprise computing is to compile a larger view of your organization's resources. Take inventory of the hardware platforms your shop maintains and begin to understand what is available to you. You need to know what kind of hardware your shop has and how that hardware is configured. For each platform you need to understand what operating systems are installed, what applications are currently running there, and whether the platform is currently over- or underutilized. Specifically, you need to know CPU size and speed, memory available, disk space available, and video display characteristics. While you're asking, find out if there are any planned enhancements or money in the budget for potential upgrades. For example, you may find the PCs in your shop do not have the kind of resources you need, but that your department is either planning upgrades or would consider doing so to further your project.

In general, if you're considering a client/server application over a more traditional design approach it's usually for one of two reasons: that your shop is attempting to bring their mainframe costs under control by downsizing or right-sizing applications using C/S or that this project depends upon utilizing the most current technology available to make it a success. In other words, users are screaming for better response time or a graphical user interface or both. In either case, the key platform in your enterprise system will be your front-end processor—usually a PC or workstation.

If this platform is a PC, a decision needs to be made concerning what operating system you require. It is the operating system which will drive the hardware requirements. Most shops have invested a great deal of money stocking up on PCs but often purchased them in stages. As a result, most shops do not have a standard PC configuration but rather a wide variety of configurations based on the most reasonable and current configuration at the time of purchase. You must either take the lowest possible configuration and use it as your guideline or secure funds for upgrades.

How Are Those Resources Interconnected?

With the front-end resource a given, compiling information on back-end resources first depends on the extent of platform communication available. Remember, communications is the heart of client/server, and is often the most difficult piece to find out about and understand. Where to start? Start at the front end and work out.

If your shop has PCs, more often than not it has a local area network. *LANs,* by definition, are groups of PCs interconnected with at least one server. Typically, a LAN will have many different kinds of servers, each providing a specific service. For example, the *standard file server* is used simply to store user-data files and work-storage space. The *application server* is configured to support the different application programs users are sharing. *Database servers* are machines configured especially to handle the rigors of shared relational databases. There are others. Each server on your LAN should be examined to determine configuration and resources available. Basic communication on the LAN is most often handled by a network operating system (NOS) and is usually transparent to the user. The type of LAN you are running and the NOS are very important in determining how you can programmatically communicate over your LAN to other platforms.

From your LAN, you need to determine how to communicate with the rest of your enterprise. Two scenarios are common. First, each PC may have an emulation card installed directly, which allows that PC to be direct wired to a mainframe. This scenario is a holdover from the initial installation of PCs when LANs were an unproven technology. The more common scenario today is external access through a gateway server hanging off the LAN. This gateway server is a machine specially configured with hardware and software to provide host communications for many users on a LAN. Because this hardware and software is centralized on the LAN, the communication services it can offer are usually more sophisticated. For example, most gateways to IBM mainframes support APPC communications, which allows for more efficient, faster, and more sophisticated data transfer.

When your research is complete, you should be able to draw a picture of your enterprise from the user's PC, radiating outward, showing all the resources you have available, where they are located, and how they are configured. Most organizations have a communications pipeline called a *backbone.* The network backbone is the physical network from which all other networks are hung. For example, in most IBM mainframe shops, an SNA network is usually in place. Static wiring and leased lines usually tie all an organization's locations together. At each location, there may be several LANs or a minicomputer/workstation with hardwired terminals attached. It is this backbone which allows us, in theory, to get from a workstation in New York to a server in Los Angeles. After determining where your users are located, what resources you have, and how they are interconnected, you can begin to consider the design of your client/server application.

One of the primary advantages of client/server computing is the ability to use the resources you have available through your organization's network and common communications protocols to hide the differences between the machine types.

What We Have So Far

What can client/server do for us? What's all the noise about? Let's take a close look at what we have now, and show how client/server can make it better.

Today, a vast majority of our programs are in 3GLs such as COBOL and FORTRAN. Client/server computing allows for the use of new 4GL technology to develop applications faster and better. Graphical design products, object-oriented products and others are the key to increased future productivity and are primarily available on a PC.

Relational database technology is undoubtedly a directional technology. The relational database got its start in a mainframe environment. The relational database will play an important role in breathing new life into the mainframe in a client/server environment.

However, requiring the services of a relational database no longer ties you to a mainframe platform. Client/server technology has allowed us to distribute the data we require across our network to other platforms. As a result, we can make use of the large capacity a mainframe has to offer when we need it, without absorbing the disadvantages the platform imposes.

In a traditional 3270-based environment, we are tied into the high cost of mainframe maintenance and support. To expand our resources and support the ever-expanding need for more access and power, shops had to incur the high cost of mainframe hardware.

At the same time, the cost of PC hardware has fallen exponentially while the power and sophistication available has skyrocketed. The idea of downsizing systems off the mainframe and onto PCs and LANs is more than fundamentally sound. Application downsizing can reduce costs by 25 percent or better. The issue has been this: What do we do with those systems that can't be moved off the mainframe because parts of the system require huge amounts of storage or the processing power of a mainframe? The answer is client/server. Client/server allows us to gain the advantages of the other platforms we have available in our enterprise without losing the advantages the mainframe has to offer.

Adding processing power to your network in the form of an appropriate platform addition can significantly reduce costs. Instead of being locked into a costly mainframe addition, you can add a midrange to enhance CPU processing power, or simply put another database server on the network to enhance storage, depending upon what you require. The point is you pay for what you want and you get what you pay for.

Client/server also allows you to add new processing power without recoding your application. Client/server applications should not be aware of the location of their data. As a result, if data has to be moved from one server to another, the application itself should not have to be modified to reflect the location change.

This translates into increased productivity. If your mainframe goes down, all processing stops. In a client/server environment, if one server goes down, only the users of that server are effected. And, the effect is temporary since processing can be quickly moved to another machine. Add to this concepts such as disk mirroring, data replication, and two-phased commits and you are left with an enterprise with no single point of failure. As we approach the age of 24-hour data access, this will become more and more important.

Cost aside, the mainframe has other faults. 3270 terminals are text-based terminals—no graphical user interface and no mouse. PCs have the superior interface modern applications require. MVS is a superior multitasking mainframe operating system. PCs have operating systems like Windows and OS/2, which allow for superior applications complete with color, pictures, and sound.

Learning by Example

You've had a lot to consider and absorb throughout this chapter. We've discussed all of the components of client/server and what you have to consider when entering into an enterprise-computing venture. At this point, it would be best to apply what we've learned in a practical example.

Client Tracking System

You work in a progressive data-processing department for a service-oriented organization. The primary function of the department you work in is dealing with customers by phone. Your department's personnel take calls from customers, log the calls, and track the results to their logical conclusion. At the moment, your users have an online CICS system, which puts up the screens your users require to collect the data related to each phone call they take (Figure 2.10). The data is stored on VSAM files and later used by batch programs to create and distribute reports to other departments in the company, which are responsible for responding and resolving the issues each call raises. All users who touch a problem are required to log the work they do and the results they achieve related to this call. As a result, access to this system is required across the organization.

Your management has made a commitment to attempt to scale back mainframe use and thereby cut their data-processing needs considerably. As a result, they have tapped you for suggestions concern-

Client Tracking System

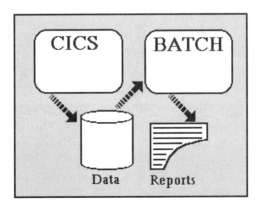

Figure 2.10   Client tracking system as it exists today.

ing a rewrite of the client tracking system which would improve efficiency, be easier for users to learn and master, as well as make better use of some of the less expensive resources your organization has available. They have provided you with the following constraints:

- They want to begin to explore using PCs as a more viable data-processing platform. Management is not prepared to make a full-scale commitment up front—this is unproven technology. The first phase of this project is to show what these machines can do.
- Management does *not* want to turn this into a full-scale, long-term development effort yet. They are looking for a maximum return with a minimal investment. (Aren't they always?) You have two months.
- You have been presented with a budget concerning the resources available for hardware and software upgrades. The users already have adequate PCs with LAN connectivity and a gateway to the host. At the moment, the PCs are being underutilized. In most cases, the users are using their expensive hardware as a dumb terminal for host access. However, they do require electronic mail, word processing, and other back-office functions. Management has set aside funds to bring all the users' machines up to a standard configuration of a 486 machine, 8 megabytes of memory, 120 megabytes hard drive, and Microsoft Windows. There are also funds available for a PC-based development package.

Because of the time constraints imposed, you do not have the luxury to completely redesign and rewrite the system on a new platform. You met with the users and did a short but thorough analysis on how they do business. You have some good ideas as to how to combine some of their processing together to allow them to work more efficiently.

Phase 1: Screen Scraping

You decide to take a small step into the client/server world by developing a Windows-based PC application that will primarily function as a screen scraper for the existing host system.

You develop a PC system (with any of several available PC-development packages) that presents a graphical user interface to the users (Figure 2.11). This interface will collect the data they have more efficiently and in a more logical form than the existing system. The user interface is better organized and easier to use than the old CICS screens. Furthermore, you can code some of the data edits which usually occur on the host on the PC. This allows for faster processing when the user needs it most, like when they are on the phone with a

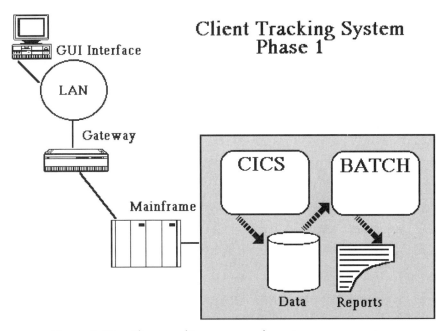

Figure 2.11   Client tracking system, phase 1: screen scraping.

customer, since the resources being used are on the local PC. More processing on the local PC also translates into reduced use of host resources.

Once the data is collected, a connection is made through the LAN to the gateway server to the host. Behind the scenes, your application starts the existing CICS system, drops the collected and other derived data on the CICS screens and simulates pressing the enter key.

Queries are processed in a similar fashion. The user fills out graphical screens on the PC. Upon pressing the enter key, the user must wait while the appropriate screens are filled out on the host and executed to retrieve the information. This process is not as quick as the data-entry process. However, this is a first cut at reworking this system and your budget and time are limited.

To the users, this looks like a whole new system. Basic functionality is the same. Their interface is faster and tailored more closely to their requirements. In addition, by simply moving the data collection piece of the application from the host to the PC, some cost savings have been achieved. You have reached your initial goals.

Phase 2: Moving Toward True Client/Server

Now that the users are operational and management is convinced of the advantages client/server theory can offer, you have been given more latitude. Management is looking to adopt client/server where possible in an effort to severely limit their reliance on the corporate mainframe. Your project has been chosen as a pilot for data processing.

With more time, more staff, and more money, you can implement a true client/server application. As a pilot application, yours must truly exploit the resources available to you and provide superior usability. Management is looking for a LAN-based PC solution.

Your first step should be data modeling. Your application is currently VSAM. You will likely move to a relational database solution. Data modeling will determine the number of tables, indexes, primary keys, foreign keys, and other relationships. Data modeling will also provide a forecast for the amount of data you will need to store. This information is required before choosing a LAN-based database management system.

Your second task should be to design a broad-based application. This design should be blue-sky stuff (Figure 2.12). Dream your best dream and make sure the DBMS can deliver. Since this application will be required to service several departments at different locations, your application database may have to be distributed across several different locations. Depending upon the size, some of it may have to stay on the mainframe. Make sure the DBMS you chose can handle inter-DBMS communication and host gateway communication if required. You will be living with this choice for quite some time.

Armed with a relational DBMS choice, you will need to purchase a database server. This is not an easy choice either. This machine must be fast and stable and fully loaded with memory, lots

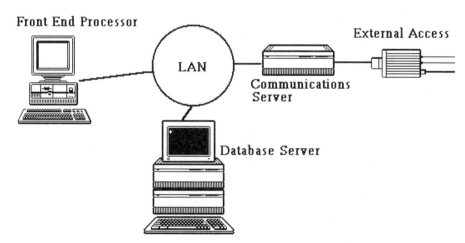

Figure 2.12   Client tracking system, phase 2: true client/server.

of disk space, and plenty of room for expansion. Furthermore, you may want to address issues such as disk mirroring to insure continuous operation.

With a DBMS and database server in place, and an application design on the board, you set to work. Creating tables, designing downloads and possibly uploads, establishing a data store. From there, significant application overhaul can begin. All of the existing windows must now include edit processing. All data must be verified and stored.

As design, code, and testing proceed, you may discover bottlenecks. For example, you may discover certain query types take a long time to process. Database tuning may alleviate some of these situations. If not, you need to reevaluate your resources.

Transactions can be split to allow for some processing to occur on different machines, making better use of available CPU resources. Stored procedures may speed up data access by pushing some transaction processing onto the database server. Other changes may include distributed database processing, where the centralized database can be split to allow for local as well as remote storage.

Remember the tools you have available to you and consider all the platforms at your disposal to make this a fast, efficient application. That's the goal of client/server.

What Does This All Mean to You?

The times are changing, and faster than you might think. Most of us got our start in corporate America. We were taught the stock-in-trade mainframe skills we would require to become productive cogs in the average IS machine. We were given the impression that, with a handful of those skills, we could go virtually anywhere in the country and find a job. Life was good.

Personal computers began showing up on everyone's desk, but very little was actually being done with them. A little word processing, some electronic mail, but mostly just 3270 emulation back to the host. Occasionally, you would here about some type of PC development but it occurred only in isolated areas and wasn't really threatening to your domain.

But, if you read the trade journals, you'll see that that's all changing now. Corporate America has gradually become convinced that its mainframes must disappear, having been told the mainframe is archaic and too expensive to maintain, and that there are better ways to run data-processing departments.

Some shops are outsourcing their work—they pay another firm to do their data processing. That firm is doing work for several clients and can charge each client less as they divide their mainframe costs up accordingly. Almost every shop is trying to downsize their operation. IS is attempting to change in two ways:

1. Automate anything that is currently manual to justify its existence and add savings to the bottom line. New projects can not be automated for the sake of automating, but they must be clearly justified and show real cost savings: personnel cuts, equipment savings, and so on.

2. Get rid of the corporate mainframe. The cost of doing business on a PC/workstation network is considerably less than that of supporting a mainframe. If a task can be moved to the PC/workstation arena, do it. If a task can be rewritten to make less use of the mainframe, do it. If you can find a way to move the development and maintenance of the remaining mainframe tasks off the mainframe, do it.

I don't think the corporate mainframe will be disappearing any time soon. While the mainframe is very expensive to keep, I believe most shops will find it is a necessary evil. The mainframe, after all, is just another server on your network and the most powerful resource you have at your disposal. Management will begin to realize it cannot bite off its nose to spite its face. Some tasks simply must remain on the mainframe, at least until a less expensive solution, such as MPP, comes along and becomes as stable and standardized as the mainframe.

The changes being made in corporate America are only part of the picture. The trade journals have been full of articles on new developments which will effect all of us.

The national data highway. This is a fiber-optic superfast network that will connect every business, every home, and every government agency. The proposed uses of this network are endless, including medical, financial, entertainment, and more. Interestingly enough, every application written to take advantage of this network falls into the client/server paradigm.

Advances in communications technology. The merger of communications giants such as McGraw Communications and AT&T will have an important impact. The wireless communication technology these companies are racing to provide will allow applications to reach out globally for data and information.

MPP technology. We talked about this earlier. Multiple parallel processing machines are here and they are beginning to stabilize and become useful. These machines offer processing capacity previously unheard of (with the possible exception of supercomputers) at a more than reasonable cost. These superservers will be required to support the kinds of data requests the next generation of applications will require.

Object-oriented operating systems, databases, and applications. All of these are either here or on their way. Those of us who had the foresight or luck to develop our PC skills during the past 10 years, and based our development on the prevalent operating system of the time, DOS, are also looking at a complete retooling in technology. The object-oriented paradigm is key to the future of data processing. You will begin to see it applied everywhere. Do not ignore it, for it will not go away.

All of these changes and many others add up to one simple statement. Things are changing. Fast.

Where the wage difference between someone who had no PC knowledge and someone who did once might have been a few dollars, now the PC illiterate is going to lose her job. The PC developer whose knows nothing about LANs, WANs, communications, servers, databases, GUIs, or other platforms is also going to be out of a job.

To stay employable, the average programmer must diversify. You must become knowledgable (if not expert) in all aspects of the new paradigm. You've made an excellent start with this book. Understand client/server. To do that, you need to understand graphical user interface development, local area networks, wide area networks, gateways and other communications. You need to understand database technologies and server requirements and begin to work with object-oriented design techniques. You should begin to explore the services offered by both Windows and OS/2. More important, get to know UNIX—its role in the future will increase dramatically. Don't give up your mainframe skills, they will be required as well.

You will have to spend considerable time developing these skills. To the average mainframe programmer, these concepts will not come easily. However, the writing on the wall would indicate you do not have a choice. IS shops, like everyone else, are scaling down. People are being laid off and the ones left are only the best of the best. If you rest on your current knowledge, you will become obsolete. Part of your job is to remain employable—to do this you must pick up the next generation of skills. The rest of your job is to keep up with the trade journals. One year after this book is published, all the choices may have changed. It is your job to keep up on that, too.

But, with all we've talked about, and all the new technology coming to a DP shop near you, it is apparent the concepts presented here about client/server will be important. Take the time to understand them and continue on your own. There is no doubt they will be part of your future.

3

Introduction to GUI and Microsoft Windows Application Development

In this chapter we will discuss the concepts of graphical user interface (GUI), and specifically, the GUI standards as they relate to Microsoft Windows, the current leader in commercially successful GUI products. We realize that there are some subtle but important differences between Microsoft's GUI standard (as set forth in *The Windows Interface: An Application Design Guide*) published by Microsoft Press, OS/2's GUI standard. There are even more pronounced differences between the Microsoft standard, and the GUI standards of Motif (OSF), Openlook (AT&T, Xerox, Sun), and other products that run on the Unix and VAX/VMS platform. However, the constraints of time and space have forced pragmatism upon us, and we have chosen to discuss GUI for the most basic reason—its commercial success. Most of what is presented in this chapter is portable to the other GUI environments (OS/2 and Unix), with a 10 to 15 percent difference. In other words, once you become familiar with one GUI, you can learn others relatively easily, as most of the concepts/facilities and even the terms have been ported from product to product.

What Is Windows Technology—and Why Windows?

Microsoft Windows represents a multitasking, object-oriented, graphically oriented platform for the development and delivery of contemporary PC-based applications. This platform (Figure 3.1) presents applications to users with a simple, consistent, and intuitive interface, based on a collection of standards published by Microsoft, Inc.

In Windows, the user interacts with an application using graphical constructs (boxes, buttons, pulldown menus, etc.) as opposed to operating system commands. These graphical constructs are con-

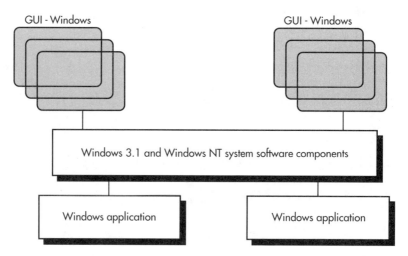

Figure 3.1 The Windows platform.

trolled by Windows applications working through the Windows execution system. Users access the graphical constructs with either the keyboard or (more commonly) the mouse. For example, when a program asks a user to enter a short piece of text such as a filename, it is typed into a standard graphical control known as an *edit box*. When a program displays a scrollable list it uses a graphical control known as a *listbox*.

Through these and many other standardized graphical interfaces to computer processing (such as a program manager; Figure 3.2), Windows and GUI technology in general, provide:

- A consistent user interface for both the operating system and application, so that user may more easily interact with a number of applications without needing to learn different interfaces.
- An intuitive interface for the end user, in order to make learning and using applications easier.
- A visually appealing interface, which has the effect of increasing the use of computers by the full gamut of end users (from the novice or casual user to the professional or power user).
- An integrated interface, with easy access (and often cross-access) to personal, workgroup, and corporate application systems.*
- An efficient communcations interface, so that typing errors and data entry errors are reduced, with a subsequent increase in efficiency and productivity.

*According to an August 1992 survey by Gallup, Windows users access an average of seven applications.

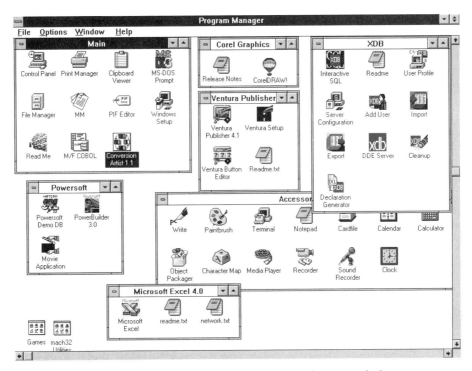

Figure 3.2   Windows Program Manager electronic desktop.

The Ever-Evolving Standards

While standardization and consistency are critical success factors in the overwhelming acceptance of Windows by the general computing population, this does not imply that standards of consistency and standardization cannot or do not evolve. Commercial Microsoft Windows applications have become so popular that a formal model of GUI-application design can actually be considered to be fashioned or derived from the latest releases of commercial software packages as Microsoft Excel* (Figure 3.3), Microsoft Word for Windows, and others.

As was discussed briefly in Chapter 1, formal software design principles driven by commercially successful products may not be as frivolous a concept as it sounds. This is because (at least in the case of Windows) the commercial software has become standard software for workstations and desktop computing. Packages like Excel, Word, and electronic mail are an integral part of the end-user computing world. They have, de facto, become standard production applications and so must be factored into the design equation for all other production

---

*As proof, witness the popularity of MDI (multiple document interface) frame, a type of window used in most of the major Microsoft offerings (including Excel—Figure 3.3); one that has evolved into the window type of choice for sophisticated, custom graphical applications.

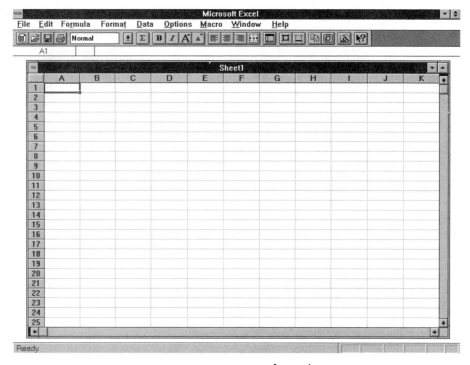

Figure 3.3   Microsoft Excel.

applications. And since custom Windows application developers have little hope of influencing the Microsoft design teams, it behooves designers to admit that these Microsoft packages are part of the real world of business computing in the 1990s and probably beyond. So rather than wait for the "the mountain to come to Mohammed, Mohammed must go to the mountain."

IBM and GUI—Somebody's Improbable History

Standardized graphical user interface (GUI) technology was designed by IBM (yes, IBM . . . stop hissing out there) in the early 1980s to simplify the efforts of the casual business-computer user. Casual users represent 80 to 90 percent of the computing world. They are business professionals who don't feel particularly comfortable dealing with computer technology on its own terms; that is, they don't want to have to remember operating system commands, would like a more relevant electronic desktop to work on, and prefer something a little more visually appealing than the black-and-white minimalism of standard DOS (disk operating system) computing. With SAA (systems application architecture), and, more specifically, CUA (common user access) IBM set forth a doctrine of graphical, object-oriented application design and development standards, that, while still in its adolecence, has established itself as the contemporary standard for state-of-the-art business-computing applications. This standard is based on the presentation of windows, icons, menus, and the use of pointing devices* (Figure 3.4).

Windows and Icons and Menus: "Oh, My!"

The Windows user interface is based on three graphical objects: menus, which are used to display lists of actions and options; icons, presented in a window, and which are used to represent the objects the user wants to use; and windows, which provide views of the contents of those objects (see Figure 3.2 for an illustration of Windows icons).

Icons: the graphical representation of Windows objects. What users see and work with in Windows applications are items on a desktop. These items—known to programmers as *graphical objects* and represented onscreen by little images known as *icons*—appear and behave in familiar ways; for example, to print a document Windows presents a printer icon. A user would probably guess that to print a document they could drag the document to the printer. With

*The "WIMP" interface: *windows, icons, menus, pointing devices,* a phrase coined by Jeff Tash, noted technology maven.

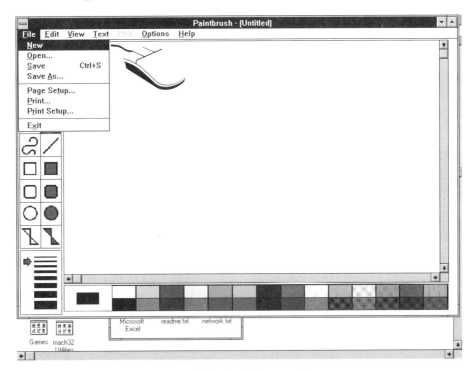

Figure 3.4   WIMP computing.

Windows, this is almost exactly what a user does. Having discovered that, the user might guess that moving a document to a mailbox might send it through e-mail, and so on.

In another example, within a Windows application an icon might represent a document that the user wants to modify; in order to do this she would open a view of the document in the form of a window displaying the text in editable form. To modify the document, the user would use action-oriented options organized in a set of pull-down menus (search, replace, spell check, and so on). When finished working on the document the user closes the document (the windowed view of the document).

Such conceptual real-world use of electronic computing lies at the heart of the PC-sales explosion of the past decade, as fewer and fewer users can come up with an excuse not to use these simple devices, which have become nontechnical, nonthreatening, and relevant to their noncomputing world.

Windows and Icons and Menus—and Toolbars

As Microsoft attempts to attract more Macintosh users into its camp, the designers of Microsoft standard desktop applications like Word and Excel have added a secondary menuing concept known as a *toolbar.* Toolbars are rows of icon buttons, generally situated directly below the menu on the left side of the screen, or at the very bottom of the screen. Many popular Windows packages also permit toolbars to be placed inside a window within floating squares, looking very much like a two-dimensional Rubik's cube. Toolbars generally activate the equivalent processing of some menu item (Figure 3.5). In fact, this is a fairly well-accepted Microsoft design guideline; that each major application Window should possess a menu and matching toolbar, which contain equivalent processing options between them. This standard allows some users, comfortable with pulldown techniques, to use the menus and others (notably ex-Mac users who may be more comfortable with icon-driven execution) to click on the graphical icons within the toolbars.

General Characteristics of Windows

Windows 3.1 applications revolve around the central theme of windows. A window appears as a rectangular area on the screen in which information may be displayed and user input entered. An application can create multiple windows, and multiple windows created by one or more applications may be displayed concurrently on the screen. However since Windows is a single-user system, the user provides input to only one window at a time. This window is said to possess the *input focus,* and is called the *active window.* The user may switch

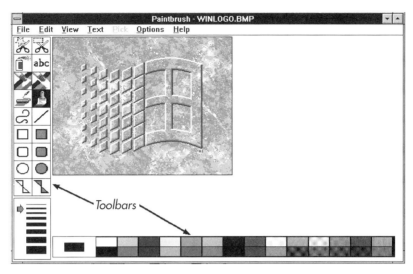

Figure 3.5   Microsoft paint toolbars.

input focus from one window to another by pointing to the desired window with the mouse and pressing the left mouse button, or with the keyboard by pressing Ctrl/Escape and selecting a different application or window to interact with from a task list.

Windows are displayed on the screen overlaying a background known as an *electronic desktop.* This desktop may be altered to any color, and text styles and font sizes may be adjusted using the Microsoft Windows Main Control Panel dialog. To avoid an overly cluttered desktop, you may minimize and close windows. When a window is minimized by clicking the minimize icon (Figure 3.6), it is displayed on the desktop (or within its parent window) in icon format. That is, its icon is placed on the desktop, rather than a view of the window displayed onscreen. To restore a minimized application, you may double-click the icon or access a Task List (Figure 3.7) of running applications by pressing Ctrl/Escape, and select the application name from the list of tasks presented. Windows may also be maximized, displaying a window to its full size as specified by the application.

Multiple windows may be visible on the screen at any time. However, the keyboard or mouse can only be associated with one window at a time. As mentioned earlier, this window is said to be the *active window,* or to have *input focus.* Windows automatically indicates active status by placing the active window on top or in the foreground, and changing the color of its sizing border and title bar.

Windows and Clients and Frames

Windows consist of two distinct areas: the frame area and the client area. The *frame area* allows a user to manipulate the window (move

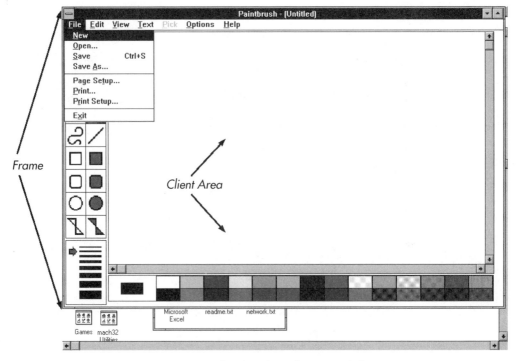

Figure 3.6   The Windows frame and client areas.

Figure 3.7   The Windows task list.

it, resize it, maximize/minimize), while the client area is used by the application to display information and solicit user input.

The window frame area. The frame area consists of a number of graphical controls such as the system menu, title bar, and menu bar. To a limited degree these controls adhere to IBM's original CUA standard (most of the 4GL tools permit all of the following window features in their development options).

Sizing border. A standard window has a *sizing border,* which allows the window to be sized (made proportionately larger or smaller) by using the mouse. When the mouse pointer moves over the sizing border, the pointer changes from the standard (arrow) to a special sizing pointer. The user clicks and holds the left mouse button while moving the mouse (dragging), and the window is sized accordingly.

Title bar. A standard window has a *title bar,* which performs two functions; it identifies the window to the user, and it acts as a moveable window *grip* (the user moves the mouse pointer over the title bar, holds the left mouse button down, and moves (drags) the window to a different location on the desktop). The title bar also contains a system menu and minimize/maximize icon (except for MessageBoxes and response windows, which may not be minimized/maximized).

Menu bar. Many shops have standardized on a common operational Windows look and feel (over and above the CUA standards) that utilizes a custom toolbar containing icons and a matching menu bar showing the same options. Each menu entry is associated with a pull-down menu (a list of actions associated with the entry). Pull-down menus often provide submenus (*cascading* menus; Figure 3.8) for further refinement of the options—although the number of submenu levels is generally limited for the sake of simplicity.

Minimize/maximize icon. In the top right corner of a standard window are the *minimize icon* (when it is selected, the application is reduced to an icon), and a *maximize icon* (when selected, this icon

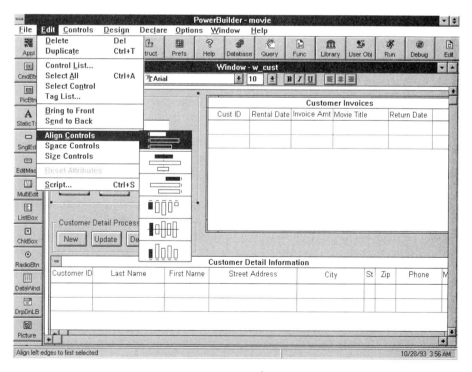

Figure 3.8   Cascading menus.

causes the window to be resized to the maximum defined in the application (window size is defined in the PowerBuilder Window Painter). When a window is maximized it may hide other windows (although they are still present, they are logically behind the maximized window).

Scroll bars. If information in the client area is too big to fit into the size of the screen, scroll bars may be selected in the PowerBuilder window painter to allow the user to scroll through the information. A scroll bar may be horizontal or vertical. It consists of a *slider* (sometimes called a *thumb slider*) with arrow icons at each end of the bar. Clicking the arrow icons moves the screen one line. Clicking *near* the arrow icon pages up and pages down the window (or pages right/left for a horizontal scrollbar). Dragging the slider moves the screen at the user's pace.

Client area. The client area of a window contains information specific to the application, and thus the contents and layout of the client area will vary from one application to the next. To preserve the ideal of consistent user interface, however, Windows (and the C/S-OO-GUI 4GLs) provide a number of standard window controls, which may be used to display and receive information to and from the user. The controls can be accessed via two methods: traditional keyboard access—tab, home, end, enter, and the program function keys; or by using a mouse.

Components of the Graphical Interface

Mouse Usage

Just ten years ago mouse navigation was in an embryonic stage. Little software supported mouse navigation, and early mouses were (in our experience) clunky and crude—one step higher on the technology evolution scale from the joysticks of the early 1980s video games.

However, the vendors of graphical interface software perceived the potential for this nontyping interaction to sophisticated applications, and they combined forces with the hardware vendors to refine and improve mouse technology, all the while embedding mouse functionality deeper and deeper into the commercial software product design and operations, until today it is hard to imagine poking through a GUI application with tab keys and combinations of Alt/Ctrl.

The simplicity and intuitive nature of using a mouse makes it appear as if mouse techniques and coordination can be taken for granted or ignored by sophisticated data-processing professionals. But such is not the case. For most people, mouse navigation mastery, mouse speed, and coordination skill is not simple to attain—yet it lies at the heart of most productivity benefits central to GUI technology.

Without mouse skills, developers (along with users) will forever be stumbling around in the windows, selecting options they do not want, canceling instead of saving, and so on. Mainframe developers making the adjustment to Windows-based technology would be well served to understand the importance of mouse skills, and to practice mouse navigation techniques with an eye toward the four basic operations whose descriptions follow.*

- Mouse speed—getting around the screens quickly and efficiently
- Mouse accuracy—clicking exactly the spot desired
- Text selection—mouse drag control within text-based panels
- Cut/Paste—a critical part of all text-based operation productivity

There are five basic mouse movements which represent valid user actions to GUI software. They include click, double-click, drag and drop, and right-click. Table 3.1 describes the salient characteristics of these mouse functions and associated activities.

Using the five mouse functions described in Table 3.1, users may: open and close windows (generally by single- or double-clicking, sometimes by combining drag-and-drop operations); minimize and maximize windows (generally by single-clicking); size windows (drag operations); cause windows to GetFocus and LoseFocus (generally by single-clicking anywhere within a window); display pop-up menus if built in to the application (single-click the right mouse button); access pulldown menus (generally by single- or double-clicking); and execute window functions and operations associated with window-graphics pushbuttons (generally by single- or double-clicking over the pushbuttons).

Because the five mouse operations represent (potentially) valid user activity, the actions described above must be trapped by GUI programs in a messaging cycle. This is known in windows programming terminology as the *message loop* and *event-driven programming.*

Message Loop

At the heart of graphical programming is the message-processing loop. Each application contains procedures to create and initialize windows, which are followed by the message-processing loop, and finally by some required closing or *termination* code. The message

---

*The authors have found that even time spent on the ubiquitous Windows Solitaire and Minesweeper programs will help develop mouse skills. (Just be careful about how you present that notion to your boss!)

Mouse Function	Accomplished by	Accomplishes
Click	Single-click left mouse button	Selection of menu item, action, graphic object
Double-click	Double-click left mouse button at preset speed (can usually customize double-click finger rate through Windows Control panel, Mouse rate option)	Perform task, combine with object selection
Drag	Press/hold down left mouse button	Move graphic object
Drop	While holding (dragging an object) let go of left mouse button	To a specific position onscreen
Right-click	Single-click the right mouse button	Invokes a popup menu, which generally allows access to additional options/functions

Table 3.1 Mouse function and operations.

loop is responsible for processing a message delivered by the Windows system to the main body of the program. Here the program acknowledges the message and requests the Windows system to send the appropriate graphic or procedural construct to process. This is done through the Microsoft Windows message processing system, and Windows/Custom Application message queues.

The native C-Windows/API programming to accomplish the processing involved with message queues and the message loop can be extremely complex and involved. It deals with Windows classes, object-oriented programming constructs, and literally hundreds or thousands of lines of code. However, the 4GL packages discussed in this book hide most of the Windows message loop coding complexity from developers. Still, developers must understand the concept of event-driven programming, as it is supported by their specific Windows 4GL development package.

Event-Driven Programming

One of the most difficult adjustments for many mainframe and 3GL programmers to make is the switch from application-driven to event-driven programming. In application-driven programming, the logic within the code dictates to users, and they are given limited choices based on predefined application processing paths. This is illustrated in Figure 3.9.

```
IF PF-1 THEN PERFORM PROCESS-INVOICE
ELSE
IF PF-2 THEN PERFORM PART-SERACH
ELSE
IF PF-1 THEN PERFORM SUPPLIER-LOOKUP
ELSE
IF PF-4 THEN PERFORM INVENTORY-ANALYSIS
ELSE
   MOVE INCORRECT-PF-KEY-MSGTO SYSTEM-ERROR
PERFORM SEND-MSG-TO-SCREEN.
```

Figure 3.9   Typical application-driven user-choice logic.

GUI Applications and Event-Driven Programming

Instead of rigidly attempting to control the user's actions, a quality GUI application is built upon the notion that the user is in control, that there is no predefined path the user must take, because there is no way to predict what the user will want to do. This type of application requires programming that is event-driven, in that specific pockets of code are defined for specific events that occur during the execution of the application, and drive the application.

Event-driven programming involves coding *scripts,* miniprograms that trap or handle applicable user actions within a window. The user actions that cause events are, of course, dependent upon the specific nature of the business processing, plus the graphic controls, menu options, and so on presented in each custom window. But the concept to focus on is that for each window, each menu, and each graphic control in the window, there are one-to-many events that could be triggered by virtue of a given user action (click, double-click, etc.). For each valid event, the programmer must code an event/script that handles the event with appropriate processing logic (open or close a window, perform a calculation, access the database, etc.).

The events themselves are often given permanent identifiers (they are given the status of reserved words) by 4GL vendors. Common event identifiers include labels such as Clicked, DoubleClicked, Drag-Drop, GetFocus, LoseFocus, as logical sections of the event/script—the 4GL code written to process the event. Besides accepting and handling external (user-generated) events, most Windows-4GL application packages also allow applications to trigger events through script functions, simulating the user's pressing a given button or selecting a menu option. This has the effect of executing the code within the script associated with the event triggered.

What Are Scripts?

Scripts are small programs, generally from 10 to 200 lines of code. Each script is attached to a window, menu, or window control. More specifically, each script is attached to a given event component or defined section of a menu or window control. In mainframe terms the concept of multiple, defined event/script sections within controls can be thought of as similar to the concept of paragraphs within sections of COBOL programs.

Windows and Event/Script Painting

Microsoft Windows supports a huge variety of conceivable events in its API language. Each of the vendors has chosen to directly support* a subset of the full range of Microsoft Windows events within its script painting facility. A *script painter* is part of the purchased 4GL software from Powersoft, Microsoft, Gupta, Digitalk, and others. It is generally a graphically oriented text editor, which allows nonprocedural specification (instead of typing the actual statements and commands, you select statements or statement skeletons from lists and paint your logic by responding to prompts and dialogs) of the 4GL language constructs and functions. Good script painters make it easy for developers to code event/scripts in all of the appropriate windows event sections within their application.

Script Languages and Function Calls

Scripts contain 4GL procedural logic, such as variable declarations, IF THEN ELSE, looping constructs, math statements, SQL, graphical, and database-related functions, custom functions, GOTOs labels, and calls to external routines such as 3GL business logic compiled into Micro Focus COBOL modules.

Most of the script languages are similar to the contemporary— mostly PC—languages: Basic, Pascal, and C. They are not very similar to COBOL. In fact, in many cases COBOL applications cannot be converted to script language due to differences in semantics. The languages are all proprietary (there is no standard Windows-4GL dialect from the ANSI committee), and all have different strengths and weaknesses. However, all have the necessary flexibility and procedural language elements to handle complex business-application logic.

We have found a general weakness of the 4GLs to be their compiler messages. Most of the script compilers leave a lot to be desired in terms of describing exactly what is wrong with a given statement. This is unfortunate, because after experiencing the glitz and glamor of working with the 4GL windows and database painters, it all still comes down to coding business logic. We have found that developers spend a good 60 percent of their time within a product working in the

---

*By direct support, we mean provide a software-facility-driven, nonprocedural way of associating a script with a given type of window event. Most of the packages provide for the establishment of custom events, which support all, or almost all, the Microsoft events.

script language, coding business rules, calls to graphics functions, and database processing.

All the 4GLs make heavy use of calls to functions (Power-Builder's PowerScript language contains over 500 internal functions and allows calls to custom functions, Visual Basic functions, and external functions coded in C, C++, Micro Focus COBOL, Pascal, and others). Mainframe programmers are generally surprised at the number of functions and their ubiquity in the event/scripts.

Actually this has a great deal to do with the C programming culture, which spawned the system code of these packages. C developers make extensive use of functions and libraries of reusable code. Hence, it comes as no surprise that the type of development products C programmers would produce reflect their tastes in development style and approach and application organization.

Functions, however, in a GUI-client/server world represent more than just nifty procedural language extensions. They represent the means of distributing application logic (see Chapter 2 in this book on client/server and distributed application logic), and the means to share and reuse business rules. A general design guideline for coding event/scripts into GUI applications runs as follows: Never tie your business logic directly to an event/script within a window control (such as a pushbutton or menu item). Code a call to the function library from the control instead. This way, if someone ever inadvertently—or deliberately, without understanding the consequences—deleted the control that contained the event/script logic from the application, the business rules which the function supported are still available from the function library.

The functions available from within these 4GL packages generally fall into one of four categories: window control and graphics functions, which allow developers to manipulate window items dynamically from within a script; database functions, which allow developers to process manipulation rows, columns, and, in general, data retrieved from a relational DBMS or flat file; text functions, which allow developers to process and manipulate text strings; Microsoft extension functions, which allow developers to interact with other Microsoft applications through DDE (dynamic data exchange), Ole (object linking and embedding), and Windows clipboard cut/paste operations.

Window Types

Microsoft has loosely defined a set of characteristics that describe certain basic behaviors and operations of windows. These characteristics have been redefined by the other three vendors, and in this next section we present PowerBuilder's definition of the basic window types and behaviors. These window characteristics define: parent/child window behavior, window movement on the desktop, whether a window type can get a minimize/maximize icon, window *modality* (whether the user must respond to a given window before continuing, or whether the user may access other windows within the same application), and window *independence* (what happens to associated windows when a window close event occurs, or when windows get moved around by the user on the desktop). The basic window types include: Main Windows, Child Windows, Pop-up Windows, Response Windows, MDI Frames, MessageBoxes, and Dialog Boxes.

Main Windows

Main windows are generally used as the base window for the first window in an application. They are also commonly used for the primary window in a given application, unless the application uses MDI Frames. You would choose to create a main window for either a standalone window within an application, or a top-level/main menu window. Main windows usually have a title bar and they are *independent*—If main window a opens main window b, b is unaffected by the state of a in terms of b's position on the desktop, opened and closed status (if a is closed, b remains open), maximized/minimized status (if a is minimized, b remains unaffected on the desktop). Main windows usually have minimize/maximize icons defined for them. Finally, main windows are *application modeless.* This means that while a given main window is the active window, you may access and work with other windows from the same application, and from the desktop.

Child Windows

Child windows are used to present information or processing derived from and directly related to a parent window—a window that opens another window is considered a *parent* window. You would choose to create a child window to display such things as detailed information relating to general information in the parent window, excepting conditions occuring within a main window and help messages. Child windows are *subordinate* to the parent window. They are *clipped* when moved beyond the parent window (Figure 3.10), they are *closed* when their parent window is closed, they move along with their parent window if the parent window is moved on the desktop. Child windows are never *active* (which means that although they may contain editable controls and operational pushbuttons, they are not registered to Microsoft Windows and you won't find them in the task list, and their title bar is not colored (which denotes active window status). In fact, child windows may or may not even have a title bar

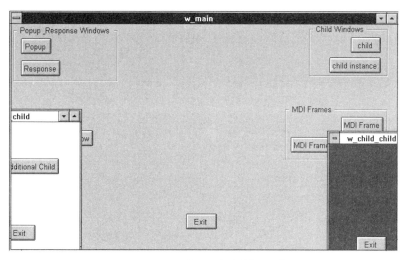

Figure 3.10   Clipped child windows.

(depending on what you are using them for). When child windows are minimized, they display as an icon within the parent window and not on the desktop. Child windows can open additional child windows, but any child windows opened from another child window behave like children of the original parent window (more like siblings than grandchildren). Like main windows, child windows are *application modeless* (you may continue working in other windows of the current application while the child window is active).

Pop-up Windows

Pop-up windows are used to present clarification or further explanation of specific items of interest. You would choose to create a pop-up window to display such things as help on a window function or control or to display a pop-up menu of additional options. Pop-up windows are semisubordinate to their parent window (the window that opened them). By *semisubordinate,* we mean that pop-up windows may move beyond the parent window and independently of the parent window, but they are closed automatically when their parent window is closed. Pop-up windows may or may not have a title bar and minimize/maximize icons. They can open any other windows of any type and are application modeless (Figure 3.11.)

Response Windows

Response windows are very similar to pop-up windows, with one notable exception. (Like pop-up windows, response windows are used to present clarification or further explanation of specific items of interest.) Response windows are often used to emulate the Microsoft standard Dialog Box window. You would choose to create

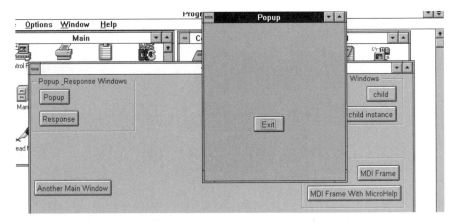

Figure 3.11   Independent pop-up window.

a response window to display such things as help on a window function or control, or to display a response menu of additional options, or error handling.

The one notable difference between pop-up and response windows is that response windows are *application modal*. This means that, unlike pop-up windows, the user must respond to a response window before doing anything else within an application. Users may access other Microsoft desktop applications, but may not access other windows within the response window's application. Like pop-up windows, response windows are semisubordinate to their parent window, in that response windows may move beyond the parent window and independently of the parent window, but they are closed with parent window. Other distinguishing features of response windows include the fact that while response windows may or may not have a title bar, they never have a minimize/maximize icon—you respond to their message, nothing else. Response windows can open child windows, and, once again, response windows are application modal: The user can go to another windows application while the response window is active, but the user may not go to another window in the current application while the response window is active.

Multiple Document Interface (MDI) Frame

MDI frames are generally used as a base application window. As such they are an alternative to main windows. Unlike the other window types we have discussed so far, an MDI frame is basically an *application shell* or a framework in which to open and manage other windows. The MDI frame was created to solve a traditional GUI problem—how to organize and present a single application which has many independent subapplications that may or may not need to communicate with one another. In other words, how to create a single controlling active application that allows other subapplications, one of which has the active status at the same time as the MDI frame. Microsoft Excel and Microsoft Word are examples of MDI frames.

To provide a method of having two windows active simultaneously within the same application, the multiple document interface defines two new window terms: the frame and the sheet (Figures 3.12 and 3.13). The *frame* is the application shell. It acts in a similar manner to the main window discussed earlier. MDI frames always have a title bar, a menu, a system menu, and minimize/maximize icon. Unlike main windows, however, MDI frames do not have any controls placed in the client area. In fact, the frame is only used to open and manage *sheets*—subapplications represented in the MDI frame as windows. All mechanics are driven from the MDI menu.

Considerations for Using MDI Frames in GUI Applications

You would choose an MDI frame for either a standalone window application, a top-level or main menu window, or an application that provides multiple document presentation. No window controls are allowed on an MDI frame. If MDI frame a opens main window b, b is completely controlled by the state of a, including b's position on the desktop, open and close status, and maximize and minimize states. Being able to manipulate an entire application with a single operation is is an important electronic desktop design benefit.

MessageBoxes

MessageBoxes are short-lived response windows, similar to a Microsoft standard Dialog Box, which are used to display a simple

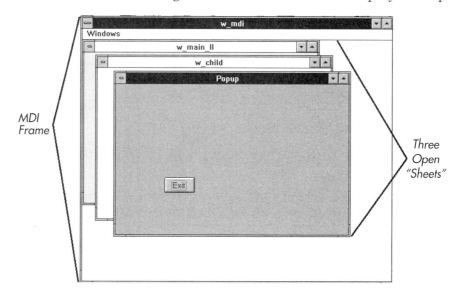

Figure 3.12   Simple MDI frame.

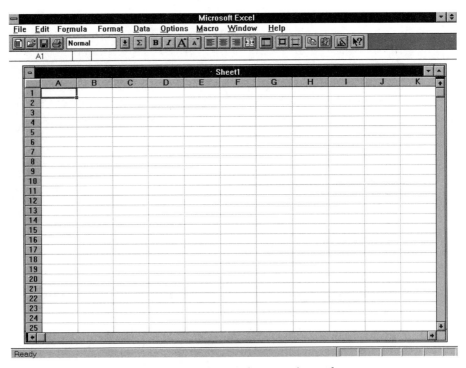

Figure 3.13   Excel, a sophisticated MDI frame.

message to the user, and to receive acknowledgement and a single decision from a one-, two- or three-part conditional expression. A MessageBox is used to inform the user of an event in situations where the information to be conveyed is relatively simple and the response returned by the user is limited to a single choice from a finite number of options. A MessageBox displays an application-supplied text string, along with one or more command buttons, (Figure 3.14) such as OK, Cancel, Abort, Retry Ignore, and so on. A MessageBox is a *modal dialog* with the user. This means that the user is required to acknowledge and act upon the messagebox before continuing interaction within the same application that generated the MessageBox.

Dialog Boxes*

A *dialog box* is a special type of response window for use in circumstances where an additional interaction with the user is required (Figure 3.15). A dialog box is created as a short-lived window to receive and/or display a particular set of information required by the correct performance of the application. Dialog boxes can be modal or modeless.

*Note to PowerBuilder users. PowerBuilder does not directly support Microsoft Dialog Boxes. You may utilize response windows or MessageBoxes for Dialog Box windows.

Figure 3.14   Typical MessageBox windows.

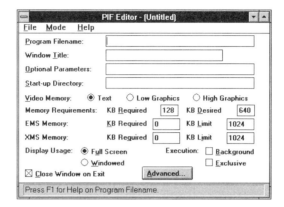

Figure 3.15   A Microsoft modal dialog box.

When using a modal dialog box, the user may not interact with another window in the application until the dialog is complete. PowerBuilder allows you to develop modal dialog box windows through the use of response windows and messageboxes.

With a modeless dialog box the user may continue to work with the primary application window before the dialog box has been fully attended to (while it is still visible). PowerBuilder allows you to develop modeless dialog box windows through the use of pop-up and child windows.

Window Controls

Window areas and dialog boxes contain a number of window controls to display and receive information. These *window controls* are in fact specialized classes of windows standardized by CUA, defined by Windows 3.1, and may be created with the help of the 4GL package's Window Object Painter. Some of the types of window controls offered by 4GLs include (note that most of these controls are illustrated in Figure 3.16):

Static text. This is constant text, displayed in the dialog box or window for information purposes only.

Entry box (single line and multiline). This is an area of defined size where are user may enter alphanumeric or numeric data. An

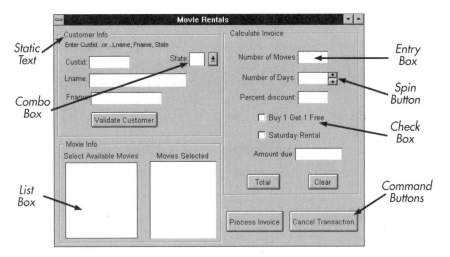

Figure 3.16 A window with assorted controls.

application may also place a default entry in an entry box to simplify the user's task of entering information. The user may then edit the existing data or replace it with new data.

Listbox. This is an area that contains a list of items, one or more of which may be selected by the user. If a list contains more information than will fit into the designated area, a listbox may display vertical or horizontal scroll bars.

Combo box. The combo box can be thought of as a prompted entry field—a combination of a listbox and an entry box. The user may enter data into the entry field, or select the data in the field from a listbox of items, which opens when the mouse activates a scrollbar icon. Not all vendors use the term *combo box.* For example, Powersoft calls combo boxes *drop down listboxes.*

Check box. This is a square area, surrounded by a border with accompanying text, which denotes an option that may be toggled on and off by the user. For instance, in a text search the option to ignore case may be implemented as a check box.

Radio button. These are small round areas usually displayed in groups; a group of radio buttons denotes a series of mutually exclusive options, from which the user may select one option only. Making a selection immediately deselects any previous choice. The selected option in a group of radio buttons is indicated by a dark center in the button.

CommandButton. This is a square or rectangular area containing some brief text and surrounded by a border. It indicates an option which may be selected for immediate action. Selections such as enter and cancel to complete or cancel a dialog are normally implemented this way.

Spin button. This is used to display a currently selected option from a finite range of options. The items displayed in the spin button control are textual, and may represent any alphanumeric item. It consists of a single line edit box, and up/down scroll bars or arrows that are stacked on top of one another.

Many of the 4GLs offer a complimentary set of window controls to the Microsoft and CUA standards in their window painters. The PowerBuilder complimentary controls consist of:

- PictureButtons and pictures—operationally the same as CommandButtons; in Windows terms, derived from the same basic Window Class
- Static graphics—oval, rectangle, and so on; the graphic equivalent of static text controls, used to display data results in color graphical displays
- Dynamic graphics—used to create 2- or 3-D full-color presentation graphics for data result/display
- DataWindows—operationally similar to list boxes, but much more powerful and sophisticated, DataWindows simplifies the process of client/server/SQL data access
- Edit masks—equivalent to single line edit boxes with picture clauses to format data in a readable fashion

4

Introduction to Object Orientation

The parameters of application development have changed dramatically in the last ten years. Substantial improvements in hardware, operating systems, and the emergence of graphical user interfaces have combined to present application developers with the tools to build applications that are easier to learn and implement at the user level.

So powerful are these gains that a whole new generation of programs have emerged, enabling business executives and administrators to have direct access to data that was formerly filtered through report programs generated by computer specialists. The most visible element of the applications that have extended this new computing power to the business community is the object-based graphical user interface (GUI), most notably in the form of Microsoft Windows and IBM OS/2—but this new power and ease of use comes at a price.

The developments of the last ten years, which have led to explosive growth in computers, have significantly complicated development cycles. The complexity of programming for new operating systems and GUIs, and the adoption of multiple operating systems and GUI standards in many corporations, create challenges that those grounded in traditional programming technologies and system design methods could not have anticipated.

Traditional System Design

Traditional top–down system design methods assume that information-delivery applications should be based on a series of steps starting with a topmost statement that is refined through a series of steps. Each step further refines the previous element down to simpler components in a process called *decomposition*. Decomposition expands all the elements until they are low enough to implement the step in the functioning programming language.

A design paradigm (archetype, pattern, ideal, or standard) is characterized by its approach to the decomposition process. The top–down, or traditional or procedural, paradigm uses a task-oriented methodology to decompose a requirement. After careful analysis, the proposed system is designed (decomposed) by breaking it into a series of tasks. These tasks form the basic building blocks of a procedural application.

The top–down paradigm logic usually flows from a controller that passes responsibility for tasks to lower-level modules through a series of case statements, as shown in Figure 4.1.

In top–down systems design, the requirements documented as part of the analysis process serve as input into the design phase. It is, however, in a dissimilar format and represents a different perspective that must be translated and migrated into decomposable information applicable to the design phase. For this reason, the traditional view of an application life cycle embodies what may be unnecessary boundaries that arise when shifting from the analysis phase to the design phase. In classic top–down design terms, we have just distinguished between the disciplines of *structured analysis* and *structured design.*

One of the legacies of development techniques using the traditional top–down approach is an absence of an enterprise consciousness where corporate goals should be established that provide for iteration of code and place a major emphasis on reuse of code. Each system is built from scratch with maintenance costs accounting for a prominent share of the system's total costs. A functional code inventory would result in the repetition shown in Figure 4.2.

Another legacy of the traditional top–down approach is the strangle hold it has on most computer programmers. They know the syntax of several programming languages, and most are familiar with a variety of programming techniques for representing design details. Most, however, know only the top–down approach to system design, primarily because learning a language involves memorizing keywords and syntax, while learning a new system-development technique requires a fundamental change in their thought process. It is much more challenging to learn a new system-development routine that utilizes a totally different set of terminologies than it is to learn a new programming language.

The need for enterprise to remain competitive, however, has awoken interest in new approaches to software design and development. Leading-edge development efforts are utilizing tools that are not task-based and, in many cases, remove the requirement of intimate knowledge of the hardware/software platform. These new approaches allow programmers and users to concentrate on solving business problems while building the enterprise reusable code repository.

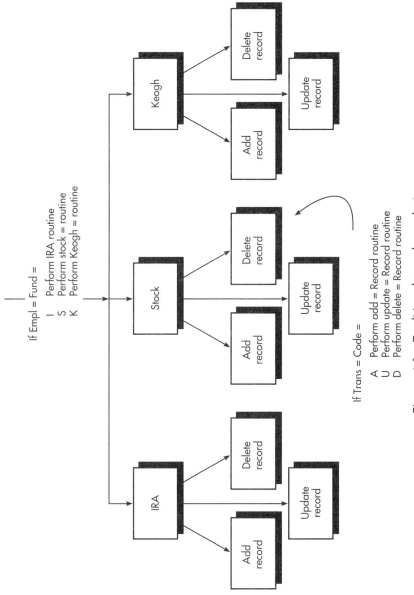

If Empl = Fund =

   I   Perform IRA routine
   S Perform stock = routine
   K Perform Keogh = routine

If Trans = Code =

   A Perform add = Record routine
   U Perform update = Record routine
   D Perform delete = Record routine

Figure 4.1 Traditional top–down design.

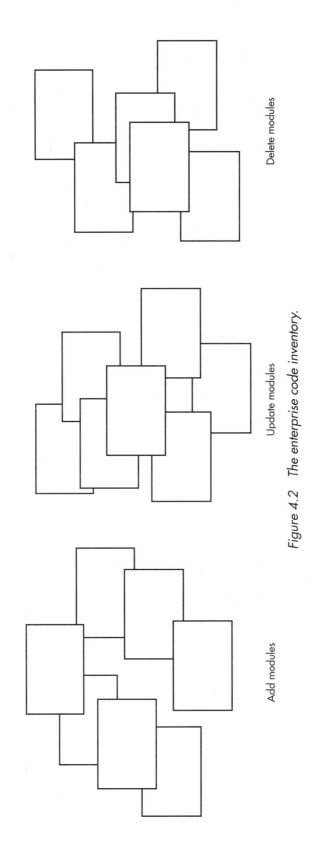

Add modules

Update modules

Delete modules

Figure 4.2   The enterprise code inventory.

Object-Oriented Programming (OOP)

Object-oriented programming is an approach to application development that allows applications to be built from defined, tested, separable components called *objects.* Object-oriented development environments typically contain large libraries of predefined, standalone, independent (*encapsulated*) objects that are combined to create applications. In simple terms, the job of the programmer is to decide which objects, grouped together, will satisfy the requirements of the application. The same logical principals of standalone encapsulation apply in most things we do and the system construction we encounter.

For instance, while many of our behaviors are routine they are not interdependent. If you get up in the morning, shower, have breakfast, jump in the car, and find that you've forgotten your keys, you don't go back to bed, get up and shower again, eat breakfast again, and make sure you walk out with your keys. You simply execute an independent capsule of behavior. You go back in the house, get your keys, and get off to work.

In terms of construction, consider an example whereby a PC is purchased to perform word processing and spreadsheet tasks. Some time later, it becomes necessary to transmit some of the resident data from that component to another PC in a remote location. To do this, modems that could be attached to any PC (and interchanged with other PCs if desired) are purchased. Without having to rebuild the PCs, each is connected to its respective modem, and the modems are connected by phone lines.

Why Object-Oriented Programming Makes Sense

The object-oriented design paradigm uses a different approach from the procedural (top–down) standard. The analysis and design phases of the object-oriented (OOAD) life cycle, while remaining distinctly separate activities, work closely together to develop a model that defines the problem domain (its province within the sphere of the overall enterprise requirements.) A *model* is constructed by viewing the problem domain as a set of independent interacting entities. The relationships among the entities are mapped, or assembled, to form the basic architecture of the application. The information developed in the analysis phase becomes an integral part of the design, rather than simply providing input into the phase. This smooth transition is made easier by the homogeneity of the entities being used by each process.

This homogeneity is in stark contrast to the difference in point of view between structured analysis and structured design. The pieces produced by the top–down design paradigm are procedures that perform interdependent tasks, while the pieces produced by the object-oriented paradigm are entity descriptions that can be reused in solving other problems.

Object-oriented programming provides an architecture for developing applications that has proven successful in other environments. In the design of computer hardware, for example, individual components are designed, built and tested, and can be used over and over again with confidence. If computer hardware were designed with the top–down approach, every PC system would be custom built for the application it was to serve, and would require rebuilding and testing to accommodate any required change. In the design and construction of buildings, prebuilt components like doors and sheetrock panels save construction time and still result in buildings of consistent strength.

This same approach can, and should, be applied to application development. Properly developed objects separate the object from the implementation in a specific application in the same way that properly designed building parts are not dependent on a specific type of house.

The separation of the nature of an object from its use in an application makes reuse practical. Although reuse is a popular topic, implementing it is frequently difficult, since most programming languages do not, by their nature, support the development of implementation-independent modules. Most attempts at reusing code require significant reengineering to make the "reusable" code function in the new application. When object-oriented methodology is implemented properly, the objects provide a framework for creating truly reusable code.

Object-oriented design methods also create a common, real-world, dialog through which developers and users can communicate about an application. The user and developer discuss the nature of an application in terms of the *entities* (things or materials) with which the user currently works and will need supported in the application. The developer then maps the user-defined entities directly to objects that will be required in the application. The result should be an application that more closely resembles the user's expectations, since the developer has spent development time immersed in the dialog and nature of the user's problems.

Objects are self-contained, or encapsulated—their logic and data are isolated from other objects. Each object is protected and can be modified without impacting other objects in the system. Some of the most insidious bugs in applications developed in traditional systems arise from changes made in a remote section of an application that has an unanticipated dependency elsewhere in the application. New development time that could benefit the enterprise is squandered as systems personnel are allocated for problem resolution. Changes to an object, however, even fundamental changes in an application, are encapsulated within the object, preventing such changes from having a catastrophic effect on other parts of the application.

This encapsulation also makes object-oriented programs easier to maintain, as it is no longer necessary to understand the processing requirements of an entire application and its design to understand how a given object does its job. Figure 4.3 illustrates this processing independence. All program functions are segregated into unique entities. There is no calling module with case logic to drive the functions. The process of add, update, and delete is the same for the three funds and is event driven, likely with a mouse, in simple point-and-click fashion. Click on the fund, click on the action. The resulting system requires far less maintenance, freeing investments to develop improved applications rather than baby-sitting old ones.

The following is a brief description of the key components of object-oriented programming, along with some examples of how they work in an application.

Objects

An *object* is a self-contained cell of data and the procedures needed to operate on that data. Objects are defined to represent real-world concepts. An application to model the workings of a banking system would include objects to represent accounts and ledgers, for example. The attributes of an account would include the balance (among other data items), and its *methods* (procedures) would include debiting, crediting, and balancing. This close relationship with the real world opens parts of the application development process to the ultimate end user, reducing the number of iterations between developer and user as applications are being developed. The end user can more clearly communicate requirements to the developer, since they both speak the same language at this level.

Objects are the basic runtime entities in an object-oriented system. Objects take up space in memory and have an associated address like a record in Pascal or a structure in C.

Encapsulation

The hiding of the internal details of an object, making it self-contained, is called *encapsulation.* Each object has a well-defined external interface for communicating with it, allowing the developer to deal only with the interface and not with the internal details of the object. Additionally, it is usually not necessary for the developer to intimately understand the internal workings of an object in order to use it.

Messages

Objects communicate with one another by sending messages. A *message* is an instruction to an object to do something, or may be a request for information. Every object has a set of messages that define its capa-

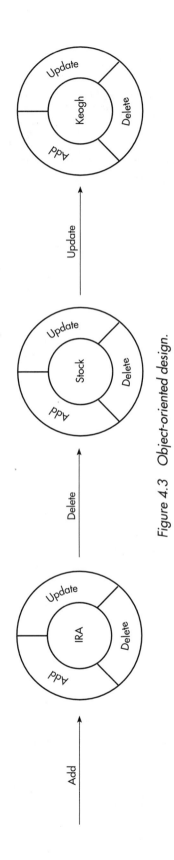

Figure 4.3   Object-oriented design.

bilities. Sending a message to an object triggers a method. In the banking example above, to get the balance of an account you send the account object a message to return the balance.

Method

A *method* is a unit of code that implements an action from an object. The method is the internal procedure that is encapsulated as described above.

Object Interface

The collection of messages to which an object will respond is called the *object interface*. As long as the object interface remains the same, a programmer can change the internals of how the object represents and operates on data without affecting the rest of the system.

Classes

A *class* is an object-oriented programming construct used to define data structures and procedures that control the behavior of similar objects (instances) by specifying their implementation (the variables they contain and the definition of the methods available for responding to messages sent to them) and enabling iteration. Classes are used as templates for creating objects that model real-world concepts.

Inheritance

Classes of objects are arranged in a hierarchy to maximize reuse. Most classes of objects are similar in some way to other classes. A new class can be created by taking an existing class and programming only the things that are different from the original. The rest of the behavior of the objects will be inherited from the original class. *Inheritance* not only supports reuse across systems, but directly facilitates extensibility within a given system. Inheritance minimizes the amount of new code needed when adding additional features.

Each object-oriented language has its own set of allowable inheritance mappings. At the language level, keywords are provided to indicate the kind of mappings desired.

The real appeal and power of the inheritance mechanism is that it allows the programmer to reuse a class that is almost but not exactly what he wants, and to tailor the class in a way that does not introduce unwanted side effects into the rest of the class. Furthermore, the object paradigm focuses on identifying and encapsulating commonality in higher level abstractions. If these higher-level classes are accumulated in a software repository, it would eventually be quite likely that for almost any desired class, a generalization of that class would already exist.

Polymorphism

There are many kinds of polymorphism, but, in general, *polymorphism* means the ability to take more than one form. In an object-oriented language, a polymorphic reference is one that can, over time, refer to instances of more than one class. For example, consider a graphics system having objects that represent squares and objects that represent circles. The methods for drawing squares and circles are different, but the display controller can send the message to draw a graphic object without caring what type it is. The receiver of the message will execute its own draw method.

Bringing It All Together in the Sample Application

So far we have presented the benefits of object-oriented programming and looked in detail at the terminology that defines this approach to systems development.

The following is a simple example, yet it should clarify the basics as to how these concepts relate to one other and how an object-oriented system is constructed.

Objects

Consider first the lowest-level component of an object-oriented system as a record in a file or a row in a table. Each record contains fields that hold variable information. If we were to use the example of an employee benefit application that handled investment fund options, we would see fields such as social security number, last name, first name, salary, and a variety of percentages that could be applied along with fund balances. In an object-oriented system, all the information captured in a single record could be wrapped into an object. The fields mentioned above are known as *variables* within the object. Fetching the next record changes the values of the variables.

Methods and Encapsulation

Remember that we learned that methods are embedded within an object. The method is equivalent to a procedure but it does not stand alone. Picture a jelly doughnut. The jelly is held within the dough. You cannot reach the jelly without biting through the dough. In much the same way, the variable data (jelly) is encapsulated and can be accessed only by going through the method(s) (dough).

Looking back at our benefit application, what might some of the methods be? Report current field values, modify salary/percentages applied, add a record, delete record, move funds from one investment type to another, and so on.

Logically, your next question might well be, "Who writes the method logic?" That depends on the object-oriented programming language (OOPL) and the development software that you are working with. For example, with PARTS Workbench, the programmer must first drop a push-button on the application screen. The next step is to create a link (message path) to the file. Finally, the programmer selects the message (keyword) *delete* or *write* to pass along the message path. Keep in mind that at runtime, the variable information that has been retrieved into our object variables matches the fields of the current record in our file.

Messages and the Object Interface

The next step is, how do we invoke a method, say, delete a record for simplicity? In procedural systems, you write a delete procedure. In an object-oriented system that method (procedure) is encapsulated in the object. All you need to do as a programmer is invoke it by sending a delete message (Figure 4.4.) In the runtime application, this would likely be accomplished by clicking on a delete button. You are, in simple terms, using a button to send a delete message.

The collection of all the messages to which an object will respond —add, delete, find, update, calculate—is called the *object interface.*

Polymorphism

Incidently, a similar button could be used to send the same message to any object in this or any other system/subsystem that has a delete method encapsulated. The encapsulated methods might be totally different, but the message that executes the method is the same. This reuse of messages is called *polymorphism.*

Classes

From our earlier definition, recall that an *instance* is a similar object within a class. The best way to understand classes and instances is to relate to procedural systems for a moment. Picture a table defined in a program with one hundred occurrences. In COBOL you are defining one hundred separate data items in about two lines of code that you access via a subscript. Now, imagine COBOL having no provision for table handling, requiring you to code each table occurrence as a separate item. Here object orientation would present the same dilemma were it not for classes. Without classes, each record would require its own object, variables defined within, and encapsulated by, methods.

As illustrated in Figure 4.5, a class serves much the same purpose as the table definition. The class contains the description of the variables and the methods required to process each instance occur-

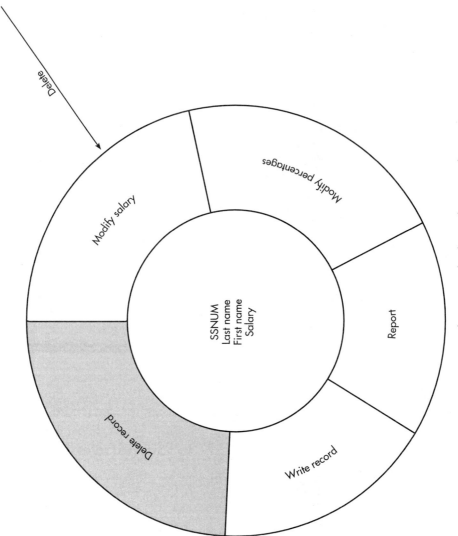

Figure 4.4 Objects, methods, and encapsulation.

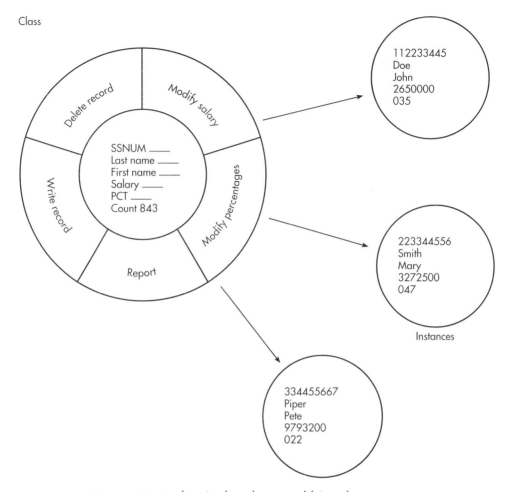

Class

Figure 4.5   A class (with a class variable) and its instances.

rence. The instance(s) of the class contain just the data. Remember, however, that object-oriented methods still label the instance as an *object,* and still consider the instance to have methods (instance methods) because it shares the same characteristics as the class (class methods). Referring to our benefit application, all variables and methods would be defined at the class level. The actual data is stored in the instance and the class definition serves as the template for accessing all or some of the data, enabling iteration.

Not to complicate things, but you need to keep in mind that a class-level object can also contain variable data. Known as a *class variable,* this would be information that should not logically be stored redundantly in an instance. If you wanted, for example, to store a count of all employees involved in a benefit program, it could be stored in a class variable.

Superclasses and Subclasses

Do you sense a hierarchy developing here? Our employee benefit application as defined above is a *class*. When viewed in relation to other classes in the corporate repository it can be further classified.

We can assume, that the enterprise has many specialized processing needs for its employees. In addition to the benefits application for profit sharing, there may be profile tracking, tax data, medical plan information, and so on. Each one of these classes would likely be defined as a *subclass* of the *superclass* employee applications (Figure 4.6).

Inheritance

Defining classes in a hierarchy also enables an important object-oriented mechanism called *inheritance*. Subclasses inherit all the variables and methods from the classes above it in the defined hierarchy. Can you see how this would eliminate redundancy? Variables and methods are defined once at the highest level at which they apply. In our continuing example, consider the general employee fields, such as employee social security number. Rather than including the method for accessing this information in the employee benefit subclasses and all other subclasses, it would be much more efficient to include this logic at the superclass level of employee applications.

Inheritance is not limited to single inheritance where a subclass inherits the properties of one superclass. A subclass may inherit properties from more than one superclass. This inheritance scheme is called *multiple inheritance* (Figure 4.7).

The Application Interface

An excellent standard for driving the operation of object-oriented systems is the *graphical user interface* (GUI). GUIs combine visual controls such as scroll bars, sliders, drop-down lists, spin buttons, radio buttons, and push-buttons with graphical controls such as folders, windows, menus, and icons. Activating a visual or graphic control sets an event in motion. An event is used to pass a message to an object to invoke a method.

What about our object-oriented employee benefit system in action? Many scenarios are possible. Note how the following flow makes objects directly available for user control (Figure 4.8).

• Double-click on the folder Employee Applications.
• Several icons would likely appear in the folder. Double-click on the icon Employee Benefits.
• A window is opened prompting you for User ID and Password.

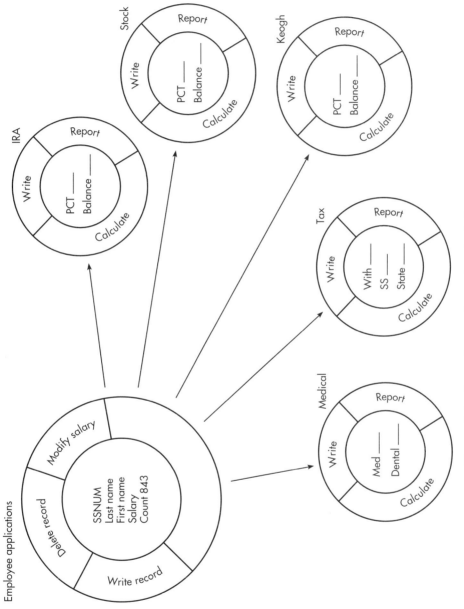

Figure 4.6 Superclass and associated subclasses.

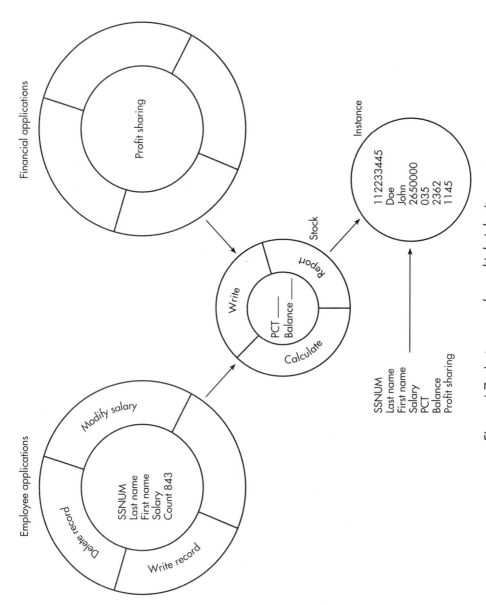

Figure 4.7   Instance under multiple inheritance.

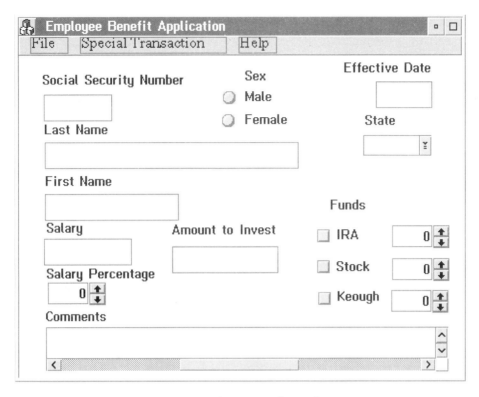

Figure 4.8   Employee Benefit Application.

- The prompts are filled in and a double-click on the OK push-button opens the Employee Benefit Application window (Figure 4.8).
- Across the top of the window is a series of pull–down menu options. One of the options, Special Transactions, will open the Special Transaction Menu.
- Radio buttons are used to indicate the gender of the employee rather than a M or F displayed on screen.
- Spin buttons enable selections from fixed ranges of percentages.
- A drop-down list is used for valid states.

You should consider all aspects of how the sample employee benefit application's GUI interface interacts with the objects of the corporate employee applications. For instance, the drop-down list for state will access the class object defined to pass back all the valid states to the list box. This state-object could be used for this and any other application requiring this information.

5

The Sample Business Application

The four product chapters (Chapters 6 through 9) will refer to the same application. The purpose of this chapter is to outline the details of the application in one spot, instead of discussing the application in each of the product chapters. The application is an employee benefits application that tracks information like employee social security number, employee name and address, salary information, employee sex, percentage of salary to invest, investment options, free-form comments, and effective date. The user for the application can add, modify, or delete employee information.

The Application Interface

The windows in the application are a logon window, employee benefit update window, employee select window, and a special transaction window. The logon window is used to connect the user to the database. The database connection gives the user the ability to perform database activities. The logon window has two data entry fields used for employee id and password (Figure 5.1).

The logon logic connects to the database using employee id and password. If the connection is successful, continue processing, otherwise open a dialog box with an error message.

The employee benefit update window is used for displaying, updating, and deleting employee benefit information (Figure 5.2). This window performs the major tasks for the application. There several types of controls on this window, such as data-entry boxes, listboxes, multiline text fields, check boxes, radio buttons, and combo boxes. Some of the applications used spin buttons instead of list boxes.

The employee benefits update window has a menu associated with it, used for controlling the application processes. The menu selection file is used for activities like new, open, select, save, delete,

Figure 5.1   Employee benefit logon window.

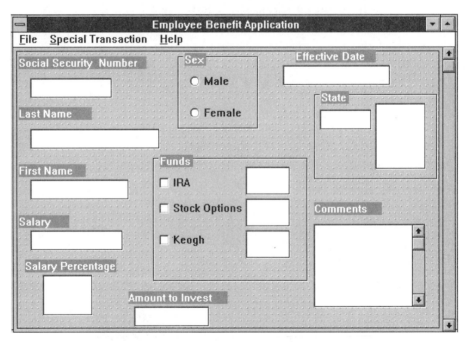

Figure 5.2   The employee benefits update window.

TBNAME	COLNAME	COLTYPE
EMP_SPEC_TRAN	EMP_SSN	DECIMAL
EMP_SPEC_TRAN	FUND_TY	CHAR
EMP_SPEC_TRAN	FUND_EFF_DT	DATE
EMP_SPEC_TRAN	FUND_AMT	DECIMAL

Catalog - EMPLOYEE:Column Catalog

Figure 5.3   Special transaction window.

logon, logoff, and exit. *New* clears the window, allowing a new employee to be added. *Open* retrieves the employee data based on the social security number entered in the social security number data field. *Select* opens the employee select window to allow the user to select the employee to display or update from an employee list. *Save* is used for saving the employee information. *Delete* erases employee information from all of the affected tables. *Logon* opens the logon window to connect the user to the database, and *logoff* disconnects the user from the database. The *special transaction* menu selection is used for add and history. *Add* opens the employee special transaction window. *History* prints a report on a history of employee special transactions. The help menu contains a selection called *about,* which opens a dialog box that displays the chapter's author.

All the controls on the employee benefit window are editable, except the amount-to-invest data field, and the data-field portion for employee state selection. The amount-to-invest field is calculated by the program by multiplying the employee salary by the salary percentage fields. The funds section of the employee benefit window displays three checkboxes labeled IRA, stock options, and Keogh. Checking one of these boxes opens a listbox or spin control for that fund, whereby the user can select the percentage of the investment that will be invested in that fund, with a choice of 25, 50, 75, or 100 percent. The total of the three funds must add up to 100 percent, or a dialog box will display an error message. The state combo box selects the state name in the listbox portion, and the state abbreviation is moved to the data field portion of the combo box.

Figure 5.4   Employee selection window.

Catalog - EMPLOYEE:Column Catalog		
TBNAME	COLNAME	COLTYPE
EMP_TABLE	EMP_SSN	DECIMAL
EMP_TABLE	EMP_LASTNAME	CHAR
EMP_TABLE	EMP_FIRSTNAME	CHAR
EMP_TABLE	EMP_STATE	CHAR
EMP_TABLE	EMP_SEX	CHAR
EMP_TABLE	EMP_SALARY	DECIMAL
EMP_TABLE	EMP_SALARY_PERC	SMALLINT

Figure 5.5   Employee table.

Catalog - EMPLOYEE:Column Catalog		
TBNAME	COLNAME	COLTYPE
EMP_FUNDS	FUND_TY	CHAR
EMP_FUNDS	FUND_EFF_DT	DATE
EMP_FUNDS	FUND_PERC	DECIMAL

Figure 5.6   Employee funds table.

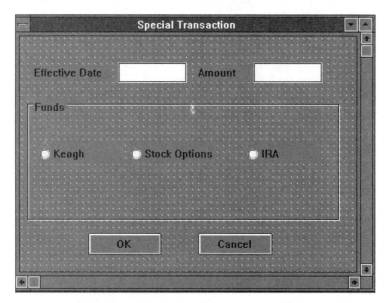

Figure 5.7   Special transaction table.

Catalog - EMPLOYEE:Column Catalog		
TBNAME	COLNAME	COLTYPE
EMP_COMMENTS	EMP_SSN	DECIMAL
EMP_COMMENTS	COMMENT_NUM	SMALLINT
EMP_COMMENTS	COMMENT_LINE	CHAR

Figure 5.8   Employee comments table.

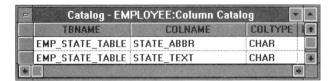

Figure 5.9   State table.

The special transaction window is used for adding out-of-the-ordinary transactions, such as when an employee wants to put a lump sum amount into a specific fund (Figure 5.3).

The last window is the employee selection window (Figure 5.4). This window is opened when the employee clicks the select option from the file menu. It is used for selecting an employee to display or update in the employee benefits window. Selecting an employee here populates the employee benefit window with the employee information.

Application Tables

The tables created for this application were employee data (Figure 5.5), employee funds (Figure 5.6), special transaction table (Figure 5.7), employee comments (Figure 5.8), and state table (Figure 5.9).

6

Building the Sample Application with PowerBuilder 3.0

"PowerBuilder!" Unless you've been marooned on some deserted island for the past three years, or have been "deep-sixed" with production abends you've probably heard of PowerBuilder—Windows' client/server development product extraordinaire. In the past three years PowerBuilder has swept into corporate America with a commercial vengeance, levelling such traditional methods of building C/S-OO-GUI applications as C or C++ with Windows API calls. As of this writing, there very well might not be a hotter, more popular software package on the market, anywhere, period, end of discussion! In this chapter we will look carefully at PowerBuilder, and show you how we used it to build our custom application in a step-by-step manner. Perhaps at the end of the chapter you may decide for yourself if the unabashed excitement over this product is reality or virtual reality, honest appraisal or hyperbole.

History

PowerBuilder, like many contemporary commercial data-processing (DP) products (including most of the other 4GLs discussed in this book) grew out of an enterprising consulting/software development firm's direct, real-life experiences building C/S-OO-GUI applications. Powersoft Inc., began as a standard time-and-materials application consulting company, specializing in building client/server-GUI applications for customers in the greater Boston area. In the late 1980s, Powersoft recognized that while GUI would provide the next generation of user-interface standards for business applications, and client/server would be the distributed RDBMS architecture of choice for the next decade of relational database applications, writing custom business applications in C, using remote procedure calls (*stored procedures*), and Window API graphical functions was well beyond the abilities of the programming culture of the MIS shops for whom it consulted. So, faced with the dilemma of providing rapid C/S-OO-GUI development tools to its own consultants for their use in the field, and sensing a vast potential market for a product that provided easy delivery of Microsoft Windows client/server applications, Powersoft developed the PowerBuilder 4GL toolkit.

PowerBuilder 1.0 (released June 1991) was a critical, commercial, and overnight success, and the company has never looked back. Building on the tremendous reception given version 1.0, PowerBuilder released version 2.0 in July 1992. Version 2.0 offered greater object-oriented features and improved SQL painting and database administration tools. Version 3.0, which shipped in the third quarter of 1993, has improved on virtually every component of the product, offering a more cohesive and fully functional developer interface into the tools, more advanced features (such as the ability to chart presentation graphics with point-and-click specification), real version control (through the InterSolv, Inc.'s PVCS Version Control Interface), more object orientation in the 4GL itself (PowerScript), and a more industrial-strength development platform, including the Powersoft Enterprise Series, an integrated product set that addresses the needs of power users as well as professional C/S-OO-GUI developers.

Installing PowerBuilder

The install process for this product was about as simple and straightforward as any we've done, and we have installed this product literally dozens of times on many different hardware platforms. Version 3.0 ships on five 3.5″ diskettes. To install the product, just launch Windows, access the run option from program manager, and type a:\setup at the prompt (standard install procedure for Microsoft Windows apps, or from the DOS prompt, type Win A:\Setup). There are three options you may choose during install:

1. Besides installing the core product executables and ancillary files, you may also install a sample application. This is a large and comprehensive collection of PowerBuilder objects, loosely organized into a window with sample miniapplications. The source code for all objects is provided. We highly recommend that you install the sample application for its tutorial and design uses.

2. If you are reinstalling PowerBuilder, you will be prompted as to whether or not you want to reinstall PB.INI and a few other custom files. The .INI files are analogous to DOS autoexec.bat and config.sys files (mainframe TSO and VM profiles). They may contain custom settings difficult to rebuild.

3. You can have PowerBuilder automatically update your DOS autoexec.bat, putting the PowerBuilder library search path in your boot DOS PATH statement. Whether you choose to do so depends upon your faith in electronic file manipulation, and level of comfort modifying your own DOS PATH command in autoexec.

Once you have installed the PowerBuilder product, you must repeat the install process of running setup for any/all DBMS interfaces to client/server database products you intend to work with. Power-Builder ships with Database Development and Deployment Kit disks, and you must install the necessary software drivers to allow your PowerBuilder applications access to the database systems of your choice. (See Chapter 1 for a complete list of PowerBuilder-supported DBMS products.) In this book, we have used the Watcom Database provided with PowerBuilder. To install both Watcom and the Power-Builder drivers we used the same setup command structure.

PowerBuilder Requirements

PowerBuilder requires that you install the systems and database software on a 386SX (or higher) microprocessor PC, with a minimum of 4Mb of RAM, and running PC or MS-DOS version 3.3 or above, Microsoft Windows version 3.1, a 3.5″ high-density diskette drive, and having approximately 18 Mb of hard-disk space (this is just for the Power-Builder software). EGA or VGA (recommended) display and a mouse are required.

On top of the basic requirements, we highly recommend a 486 PC, with fast disk access (seek time, ≤17 ms), and most definitely a VGA or, better, an SVGA-quality monitor. For group-based, large-scale development, we also recommend a printer because PowerBuilder provides quite decent GUI-application documentation through a print option from the development file menu in many of the painters.

Once you have successfully installed PowerBuilder, you would usually launch the product by double-clicking the PowerBuilder icon (Figure 6.1) in the PowerBuilder Windows group. This displays the PowerBar—a toolbar of icons that provides standardized access to the various PowerBuilder painter facilities.

The Components of PowerBuilder

So, what's inside PowerBuilder? Powersoft has provided a series of graphically driven, 4GL *painters* used to build C/S-OO-GUI applica-

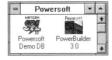

Figure 6.1   PowerBuilder icon group.

tions. These painters are specialized minitoolkits, which allow developers to program visually, that is, to accomplish much of the work involved with developing C/S-OO-GUI applications using point-and-click methods, instead of typing 3GL commands and keywords. For example, to change the color of a window you would double-click your mouse over the window and select the color from a listbox. To size and position a window on the Microsoft desktop, you would click the right mouse button over the window, select position from a pop-up menu, and drag the window, proportionately, over an area presented in a large subwindow. This visual programming provides for a more natural GUI rapid and dynamic development style consistent with today's development requirements.

Each PowerBuilder painter is customized for the purpose of providing simplified development procedures for a given component of a PowerBuilder application. The painters are represented within the product as graphical icons on the PowerBar (Figure 6.2), and include:

- Application Painter — A set of panels and dialogs used to define the overall defaults for a graphical application (application name, fonts, minimize/maximize icon, library search list, and so on), as well as to provide an open application event/script used to launch the initial window into the application, and do setup processing.

- Window Painter — A workspace plus multiple toolbars used to design, create, preview, and run custom GUI windows. The Window Painter includes screen painting facilities for 21 different graphical controls such as listbox and edit box, plus facilities for window and window control style handling, event/script editing, variable and function declarations, and much more.

- Menu Painter — A set of panels and specifications for defining pull-down and pop-up menus, toolbars, and MDI help for custom application windows.

- DataWindow Painter — A collection of multiple painters and workspaces provided to build custom client/server-GUI data access and to

Figure 6.2 PowerBar icons with text shown.

report windows in an easy, nonprocedural manner.

• Structure Painter	A simple graphical means of creating data structure copybooks for inclusion and use in event/scripts.
• Preferences Painter	A windowed dialog which provides point-and-click specifications for PowerBuilder configuration, DBMS, and application default settings.
• Help Facility	A robust, structured (indexed) and context-sensitive hypertext help system that ships with PowerBuilder, providing an extremely easy access to assistance on PowerScript coding techniques, statements, tool usage, PowerBuilder concepts, and product information, including the ability to annotate help and to copy sections of help text into your code through the Windows cut/paste buffer.
• Database Painter	A collection of multiple painters providing interactive facilities used to define client/server databases, tables, indexes, and views. This painter also provides the ability to define PowerBuilder column edit/validation extensions to tables, and to manipulate test data within tables.
• Query Painter	A prompted dialog graphical point-and-click specification method for developing and testing SQL statements for DBMS access.
• Function Painter	A visual method of painting custom logic functions, used to store common business-processing routines at the application (global) level, and called from event/scripts inside PowerBuilder objects such as windows, window controls, and menus.
• Library Painter	An application administration tool that provides library administration facilities such as object check-in/check-out, library creation, export/import, reorg, and copy/move/delete.
• User Object Painter	A graphical facility for building application-specific, encapsulated, reusable ob-

jects such as reusable window controls and external objects such as stored logic, Visual Basic .DLLs, and combinations of controls and logic.

- Run icon

  Executes the current specified application's open event/script from within the PowerBuilder environment for testing purposes.

- Debug icon

  Executes the current specified event/scripts in debug mode, providing visual source-level script execution, break points (stops), variable monitoring, and edit capabilities.

Along with the standard toolbar items it is fairly easy to customize the PowerBuilder toolbar, adding icons for oft-used features (such as DOS file editors and icon editors), showing text for the icons in the toolbars, and modifying where the toolbar sits within the product (top, bottom, right, left, or as a floating square). This is accomplished by pressing the right mouse button over the toolbar and selecting an option from a pop-up menu. For most of this chapter we will be presenting screen captures of the icons with the text enabled. Occasionally we will need to turn the text mode off in order to fit all the icons into one screen capture.

What Is a PowerBuilder Application?

Before we tackle the step-by-step process of building our sample application with PowerBuilder, it will help to set the stage by describing briefly the components of a PowerBuilder application. It will actually help to think of two separate definitions for a PowerBuilder application: the user's (external) definition and the developer's (internal) definition.

External Definition

A PowerBuilder application is a Microsoft-standard GUI application which serves some defined business purpose and executes from the Windows 3.1 desktop. PowerBuilder applications typically access data stored in relational databases using client/server access technology.

Internal Definition

A PowerBuilder C/S-OO-GUI application is an organized collection of various graphical and nongraphical objects, including all of the different graphical and nongraphical objects described below, and shown in Figure 6.3.

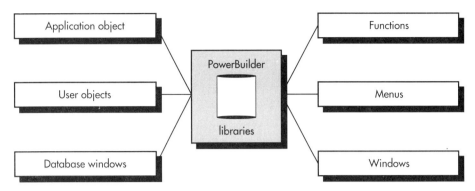

Figure 6.3   *PowerBuilder application components.*

- Window objects

  Graphical objects that present data and processing information to end users through menus and subwindows (sometimes referred to as *window controls*).

- Functions

  Nongraphical objects that contain Power-Script 4GL statements (processing logic, database access routines, window handling, etc.).

- Menus

  Lists of processing options presented to end users in either pull-down or pop-up form.

- User objects

  Graphic or nongraphic objects used to enforce consistency and provide shared, reusable application components.

- DataWindow objects

  A complex window control consisting of data access (SQL), database result-data customization (report window), and the associated PowerScript transaction processing commands (Retrieve, Update, GetClickedRow, etc.).

- Event/scripts

  PowerScript statements coded to handle defined actions of end users within an application (open window event/script, clicked commandbutton event/script, double-clicked listbox item event/script, close application event/script, etc.).

- Application object

  A defined, nongraphical object that sets application-wide defaults for text style and PowerBuilder (internal) library usage. Application objects also include application-level event/scripts, such as an open event/script, which contains the processing that is to occur when the end user initially invokes the application.

- PowerBuilder Library (.PBL)   A DOS file used by PowerBuilder to organize and manage the above graphical and nongraphical objects.

You should note that this definition of a PowerBuilder application is a bit simplified. PowerBuilder applications are, in fact, built using many different subcomponents of the defined objects, and may include many different external objects such as DDE and Ole access to other Windows applications.

You should also note the close tie between the PowerBuilder Painters and the various application objects. Each application object is developed using its own custom painting facility.

In line with the other three products discussed in this book, let us continue our discussion of the process of developing a PowerBuilder C/S-OO-GUI application, starting with the database/table creation.

Database/Table Creation Using PowerBuilder

The first step in creating a C/S-OO-GUI application is often the act of designing and developing the relational database objects. As discussed in Chapter 1, PowerBuilder provides database support for the following popular client/server DBMS products: ALLBASE/SQL, Database Manager and DB2/2, Informix, Micro Decisionware Database Gateway to DB2, ODBC, Oracle, SQL Server, SQLBase, Sybase, WATCOM SQL, and XDB. Except for the ODBC interface, all the DBMSs are supported through API calls generated by PowerBuilder. Because of the internal differences in the above products (support for various SQL extensions, remote procedures, and so on), there are major differences in the way the products are utilized throughout the PowerBuilder programming world. For example, many shops have chosen as a standard access to Sybase/SQLServer databases through stored procedures (defined remote procedure calls (RPCs) to 4GL SQL, which exists on the server). RPCs are not directly supported in DB2 and DB2/2, so they would not be used (standard static and dynamic SQL is used, instead). There are also major differences in the SQL object syntax, and even the database objects themselves (DB2 supports the use of table aliases for distributed processing. Aliases are not widely used objects outside DB2—DB2/2 does not even support them). However, despite all the above-described differences, the interface to the various RDBMS products for database, table, view, and index definition and manipulation is the PowerBuilder Database Painter. Before we look at the specifics of this tool, let's spend a moment on the client/server DBMS we have chosen to develop our application with—WATCOM SQL.

The WATCOM SQL DBMS

WATCOM SQL is a Windows-based, relational DBMS that supports the ANSI SQL89 standard SQL dialect, plus many extensions to ANSI SQL89, which are part of IBM's DB2 relational DBMS. WATCOM SQL can run as a standalone (local) or networked (server) DBMS, providing completely seamless portability of your applications. Other features of WATCOM SQL include support for binary large objects (BLOBs), referential integrity support through primary/foreign keys, security access, row-level locking, and 32-bit processing support. Applications built using WATCOM SQL can ship without a deployment fee (although the user must be connected to a WATCOM DBMS for database access).

PowerBuilder 3.0 includes WATCOM SQL in its packaged product deliverables. And, to underscore their faith in WATCOM SQL as a legitimate C/S-OO-GUI development platform, Powersoft, Inc. purchased WATCOM SQL in the third quarter of 1993.

WATCOM SQL Usage

In spite of Powersoft's blessing, as of this writing WATCOM SQL is not used extensively as a production-quality DBMS engine, and is not about to replace Sybase/SQLServer, Informix, Oracle, XDB, and other RDBMS products with large and established production install bases, as the client/server relational DBMSs of choice. WATCOM SQL does not provide two phase commit, nor does it provide much in the way of distributed database features such as support for distributed unit of work. However, due to the simplicity of development, rapid startup time, and adequate performance (at least for small amounts of data), many shops are using WATCOM SQL to develop PowerBuilder applications, and then later, to port those applications to their production client/server DBMS.

The Database Painter

The facilities of WATCOM SQL (and all of the other DBMSs, for that matter) are accessed through the Database Painter. By clicking the icon for the Database Painter (Figure 6.4) you invoke the Database Painter window, which causes PowerBuilder to automatically connect you as a Windows client to the DBMS of choice. This choice is established and read in through the use of the PB.INI file, which you

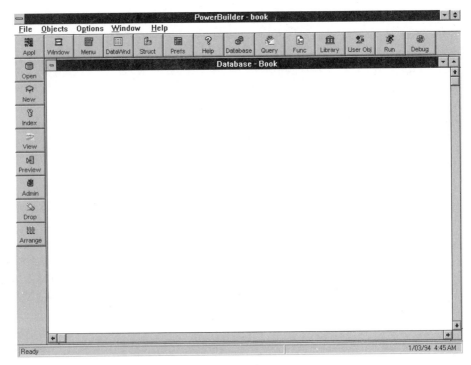

Figure 6.4   Database Painter.

may configure through the graphical Preferences Painter.* If the DBMS you are connecting to requires a logon/password combination (such as Oracle/Sybase SQLServer) you will be prompted for one at this point in time, unless the *connect string*—a text literal containing DBMS parameters found in PB.INI—supplies one.

Once past the logon/password screen, you are presented with a response window from the Database Painter asking which defined tables you wish to work on (Figure 6.5). You may select one, several, or simply click on the Cancel command button, which drops you into the Database Painter without selecting any tables (you may select tables later, if you wish).

The Database Painter is a good example of a standard Power-Builder graphical development environment. This environment is divided into four areas:

1. The menu bar provides dropdown menu access to all of the Database Painter facilities.

2. The toolbar (icons on left side of window) provides point-and-click (quick) access to certain facilities.

---

*You may also simply edit PB.INI using a standard DOS text file editor, provided you understand the various parameters, fields, and keyword usage throughout the file.

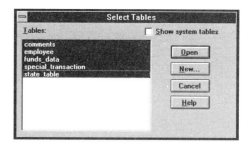

Figure 6.5   Table Select window.

3. The workspace provides the work area for viewing and manipulating database objects.

4. The powerbar (icons on top of window) provides point-and-click access to other PowerBuilder painters from within the current Database Painter session

Working with the Database Painter

The Database Painter provides development capabilities through one of two standard PowerBuilder methods: Select something to do by clicking on an icon (see left toolbar items), such as create a new table, or create view definition; or select something to do by opening a drop-down menu, and selecting an option from the menu, such as create a new table, view definition (same as icons), or maintain column validation rules (an option not available on the toolbar).

All of the available something-to-do options exist on the drop-down menus. Not all available options are found on the toolbar icons. Because all options are available through the menus, some developers find it more comfortable to learn the PowerBuilder painters by using only the menus at first. Then, later, they memorize and use the icons. This problem is slightly exacerbated by the size and quantity of the icons. In the DataWindow and application Window painters there are so many defined icon options that you cannot display the icon buttons in text mode on the left (nor can you scroll down through icons hidden from view in text mode). You must either change the style and usage of the painter toolbar (from showing on the left to showing on top/bottom, or floating where there is more room), or, if you prefer to see the toolbar on the left, you must change the icon presentation from text mode on to off by clicking the right mouse button over the toolbar, and selecting Show Text (an off/on toggle).

In spite of this, most developers find the painters consistent, intuitive, and relatively simple to learn. In fact, for the entire product a three-to-four month learning curve is estimated for mainframe developers following the appropriate training, and a one-to-two month learning curve is estimated for C, C++, and PC programmers familiar with products such as Microsoft Visual Basic, Access, or FoxPro.

The Database Painter Icons

Each of the Database Painter toolbar icons introduce extended dialog processing to enable a certain phase of Database Administration processing.

- Open — View a complete table definition in graphical or native SQL syntax format
- New — Define a new table (from scratch)
- Index — Define a new index on an existing table
- View — Access the View Painter to define a relational view on an existing table or view
- Preview — Access the Data Manipulation Painter, which acts as a live table edit and/or browse window
- Admin — Access the Database Administration panel, which allows you to edit and execute native SQL statements, including running SQL files through in batch mode to create and/or populate tables
- Drop — Delete the selected table and any associated subordinate objects (indexes, views, etc.)
- Arrange — Electronically rearrange the current workspace for optimal viewing

The standard course of events in designing and implementing your Client/Server relational DBMS objects would consist of:

- Define the database
- Define the relational tables
- Define indexes for the relational tables
- Define Referential Integrity constraints (*triggers* in some DBMS products) to establish the relationships among the tables
- Populate the tables with test rows

Creating a Database

A WATCOM SQL database is similar to most PC/server-product databases (and completely unlike a DB2 database). A WATCOM SQL database represents a physical, operational structure and location which governs most of the legal access allowed against tables, views, and indexes defined within the database. A DB2 database is a logical object, used only to organize authorizations and the hierarchy of dependent physical objects like (tablespaces, tables, etc.). DB2 databases do not (for the most part) represent physical boundaries of any kind. WATCOM SQL databases very much do. With DB2, the tables you access may be in any one of several different databases. With WATCOM, you connect to a single WATCOM SQL database with a PowerBuilder control block (an SQL communications area) to establish unit of work processing and data access. You may connect to other WATCOM databases with multiple communications areas, but that is a discussion for a later section of this chapter. The points to stress here are that WATCOM SQL databases have little in common with DB2 databases and in fact are more like DB2 locations or subsystems, each with its own separate data dictionary catalog, and that you primarily access all tables from a single database, although there are ways around this restriction.

To create a new WATCOM SQL database, you follow a standard PowerBuilder dialog, filling in window entries with specifications, and clicking OK to signal "okay to create the database." From the File menu, select Create Database (the Create Local Database window is displayed). For your new database, specify the database name (the first one to eight characters of the filename: dbname.db) and the database path (the DOS filepath in which you want the database to exist). After you click OK, PowerBuilder creates your database.

During this process, it creates the physical database files <<dbname.db>> in the DOS path specified and creates a set of system tables which become the database catalog. PowerBuilder also upates several .INI (initialization) files: ODBC.INI, PB.INI, adding the name and location of the database to the PB.INI connect string, and adding several other parameters. Finally PowerBuilder automatically connects you to your new database.

Connecting to a database is a process whereby PowerBuilder issues the appropriate Windows and DBMS API calls to allow your PowerBuilder development system (acting as a client), to electronically link to the DBMS (acting as the server), begin a logical unit of work (*transaction*), and enable database access and manipulation (in our case, we will create tables, views, and indexes in our new database). The actual details of this process will vary from DBMS to DBMS, but the overall steps and procedures will not.

Local- versus Remote-based DBMS Development

The biggest actual difference will be between using local and remote databases. In using WATCOM SQL for this book, we created the application using a local database. In working with local databases you typically have complete authorization access to all areas of database administration: create, alter, and delete object. In many shops working via a remote database, a central DBA group composed of individuals with experience in the arcane world of relational database design, performance, and tuning are assigned the task of the design and creation of database objects. While this concept of centralized design teams and development groups runs somewhat counter to the notion of distributed client/server development, centralized design and development teams developing database objects can go a long way toward managing the complexity of a large-scale development effort and can help reduce eventual bugs and problems with a C/S-OO-GUI application.

Deleting a WATCOM SQL Database

When you are finished with a development effort, or even a phase in the development cycle, you may need to delete a database. To do so you follow steps similar to those used in creating your database.

From the File menu, select Delete Database (the Delete Local Database window is displayed). Select the database name to be deleted, and click OK. This will cause PowerBuilder to remove the physical database files (dbname.db), and update ODBC.INI (in the case of WATCOM databases) and PB.INI (in all cases). You should note that in the release we used PowerBuilder did not issue a delete confirmation window. This prompts us to add the explicit warning: Choose the database to be deleted carefully. Deleting the wrong database—particularly in a shared server-based development environment—can be hazardous to your popularity among the members of your project team.

After you have created a database for your application you will want to create tables, indexes, and views within the database. To do so you use the Database Painter, Create New Table window (click the New Table icon, or select Objects, New, Table from the dropdown menu). The Create Table window is then displayed, prompting you to enter a valid WATCOM SQL table name, column names, column datatypes, and null specifications. Much of the table specification may be painted using items selected from dropdown listboxes (Figure 6.6). After painting your table specification, add primary and/or foreign key specifications if it is appropriate to your design. If the foreign keys must be added later in a table create series, you may use the Alter Table window, or the Objects, New, Foreign Key dropdown menu option.

In addition to the standard relational table definition specifications, you may add extended table and column display criteria, utilized through PowerBuilder custom controls, called *DataWindows*. These extended table criteria include: table display fonts, table comments for amplified documentation, column justification, column format masks and editing style characteristics, and column data validation rules, which can be used for front-end data entry edit process-

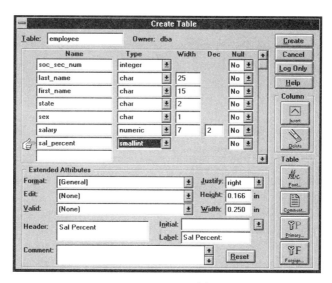

Figure 6.6   Create Table window.

ing. Note that these extended criteria do not apply to tables accessed through standard SQL, only those accessed through PowerBuilder's DataWindow controls. However, in most PowerBuilder applications DataWindow control access to relational data is the rule (90/10), not the exception.

Maintaining and Viewing Tables Using the Database Painter

To view table definitions using the Database Painter click the Open icon, which displays the Select Tables window. Then select the table(s) you want to work with by highlighting the table names and clicking Open, or by double-clicking on the table names within the Select Tables window. Each table opens in the Database Painter workspace as a simple rectangular graphic, identified by the table name. To expand the details of the table graphics, click the right (maximize) icon in the table graphic. This has the effect of expanding the table display to provide a detailed relational view as shown in Figure 6.7. Note that primary/foreign key relationships among tables are displayed through connecting lines in the graphics, and that index (primary, unique, and nonunique) information is also displayed in the detailed graphic table views.

The *current* table (most recently selected) is identified by a dark icon. The current table may be indexed (select a table and click the Index icon, and build a Create Index specification), deleted (select a table and click the Delete icon to issue a Drop Table statement), and edited (select a table and click the Preview icon). The table editor (called Database Manipulation Painter by Powersoft) allows you to add, delete, or change rows in the table in graphic display mode.

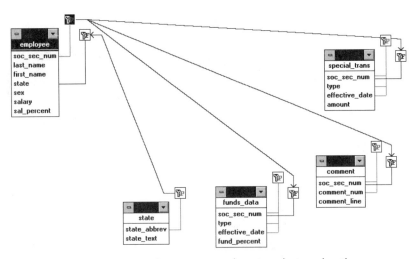

Figure 6.7   Database painter showing design details.

An Overview of the Window Painter

Once you have built your data structures, you are ready to create the application object, window objects, and script portions of the application using other PowerBuilder painters. There are many different approaches to designing and developing a complex piece of C/S-OO-GUI software.* And while this chapter can not hope to explore most or even many of them, a good generic step-by-step implementation process follows. We will continue this chapter with a detailed look at each separate procedure in the process.

Building a Simple PowerBuilder Application

1. Define the Application Object
    - Define the Application Properties
    - Define the Application Event/Scripts
2. Define a Window
    - Define the Window Properties
    - Define the Window-level Event/Scripts
    - Define the Window Controls:
        - Define the Window Control Properties
        - Define Window Control Scripts
3. Define a Menu
    - Define the Menu Properties

*In fact, during our procedures, we defined the application windows before coding the Application Open event/script.

- Define the Menu Event/Scripts
  - Define the Menu dropdown items:
  - Define the Window Control Properties
  - Define Window Control Scripts
4. Associate a Menu with its Window

Define the Application Object

Each PowerBuilder C/S-OO-GUI application is defined within the context of its own single nongraphical application object. This application object names the application, and also serves to define certain overall application properties and any application-level event/scripts. By defining application properties, we mean: application text font defaults for all windows, window controls and DataWindows defined for the application, the application library search list (which allows you to specify one or more PowerBuilder libraries as repositories for window, function, menu, DataWindow, and UserObject libraries), and the application icon, a bitmapped graphic displayed on the desktop when the running application is minimized by the end user.

For the Employee Benefits application we set the default PowerBuilder fonts to Arial, font size 10, with no extra font attributes such as bold, underscore, or italic. It should be noted that you may override the application-wide defaults for text both during the development of the individual objects, and programmatically—during the application execution. We did just that in many of our GUI components.

Selecting fonts can be important in ways that go beyond application look and feel. For example, if you choose a specific font (or font attribute) for your application and do not ship that font with the executable, at runtime Windows will attempt to match your font's characteristics with one of the available fonts on your users' systems. Sometimes Windows does not do such a hot job of matching fonts—with deleterious results. Font sizes also come into play if you are developing in super VGA mode but shipping your applications to users running standard VGA (or even EGA). You will find that the differences in font appearance can be less than attractive.

For an icon, we have chosen a standard PowerBuilder-supplied icon called emp.ico. This icon is one of only four that ship with PowerBuilder. To enlarge your cache of available icons, you may ferret some away from the hundreds that ship with Visual Basic (provided you get all the necessary permissions, of course), create your own icons with either the Windows SDK (Software Developers Kit) icon authoring package, or use some shareware icon authoring tools.

Coding the Application-level Event/Scripts

Powersoft has predefined anywhere from six to approximately twenty* discrete events as common to a given component of an application (events common to windows, to actions involving Command-Buttons within a window, to menu actions, etc.). By *predefined,* we mean that Powersoft has provided readily accessible event slots or sections within a graphical object through the PowerScript Painter facility. Each of these event/script sections can contain an event/script (PowerScript 4GL code), which is invoked if/when the event activity occurs during the execution of the application. Application-level event/scripts typically include scripts coded to perform some type of processing when the user opens and closes the application. An application open event/script might contain a series of Power-Script statements including database logon, setting the pointer to the hourglass during database logon, and opening the main or first window in the application. An application close event/script might contain client/server commit or disconnect commands, report printing, or other typical shutdown functions.

---

*PowerBuilder also allows you to define and utilize a sizable number of custom user events beyond the default events embedded in the painters. These events may be invoked by one or more Microsoft Windows messages.

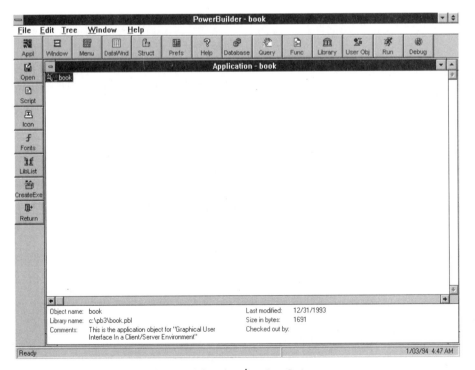

Figure 6.8   Application Painter.

To define these application properties and the application open or close event/script, you must access the Application Painter (Figure 6.8). This painter is used in the same fashion as the Database Painter we looked at. You select something to do by clicking an icon or selecting an option from the dropdown menu, and then engage in a series of dialogs with PowerBuilder windows (such as to create a new application, add libraries to the search list, or specify an icon for the application).

To code the application-level event/scripts, you would click the Script icon, and enter the PowerScript painter. From within the PowerScript painter you would code the 4GL statements and functions to satisfy your GUI-client/server requirements using standard typing, cutting and pasting from statement template blocks, importing external DOS file text, or even copying HELP file text from the PowerBuilder online Help screens. We will discuss the PowerScript painter, the PowerScript language, and this specific application open event/script in more detail in an ensuing section. For now, the script we coded in our application Open event is as follows:

```
SetPointer(Hourglass!)
Open(w_logon)
If logon_successful="y" Then
    Open(w_main)
Else
    MessageBox("Error", "Database Connection Failure")
    Halt
End If
```

Having constructed our database and application-level components, it's time to turn our attention to the actual Window painting, and processing of the application.

Define a Window

A window is the graphical interface between your application and your user. As arguably the most prominent characteristic of this technology when compared with nongraphical (character-based) interface applications, windows development tools under PowerBuilder are rich and powerful. There are many different features and approaches available, allowing developers the ability to create virtually every type and style of Microsoft-standard window. The basic window development toolset is located in the Window Painter (Figure 6.9). Before looking at the use of the Window Painter in the process of building our application, we should briefly review the concept of the composition of windows.

Application windows under PowerBuilder consist of a window object, which is stored in a PowerBuilder library (.PBL). A PowerBuilder window object is defined with a unique name and a specified

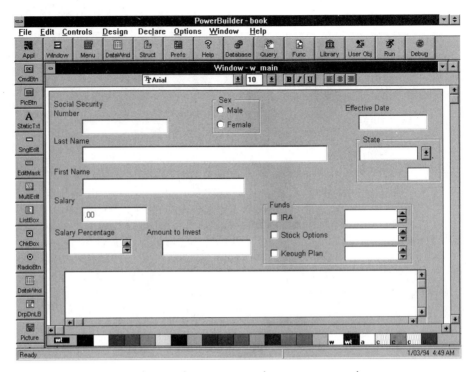

Figure 6.9   Window Painter with w_main in work area.

set of window properties (attributes) such as size, color, position on
the desktop, whether the window contains a Microsoft-standard system menu, title bar, minimize/maximize icon, and so on.

Each window object is also derived from one of six base window
categories or *types*. The window types are a Powersoft, Inc. formal-
ization of the Microsoft's loosely defined standard window catego-
rizations (MDI frame, modal windows, dialog boxes, etc. See Chapter
3 for a more comprehensive discussion of this topic). Each Power-
Builder base window type has its own set of consistent characteristics
and behaviors which dictate, among other things: style—the use of
the Microsoft-standard controls, addressing such issues as whether
this this type of window should have a system menu, title bar, mini-
mize/maximize icon, and so on; independence—what happens to the
window when its parent window is manipulated on the desktop (for
example, if window a opens window b, how is b affected by the state
of a in terms of position on the desktop, meaning does b move with a,
can b be moved outside a); open/close state—does b automatically
close when a is closed; maximize/minimize state—does b automatically minimize when a is minimized; and modality—each of the six
window types has a predefined modality. Recall from Chapter 3 that
windows may be either *application modeless,* in which case the user
may access another window in the current application while the

response window is active, or *application modal,* in which case the user may *not* access another window in the current application while the response window is active.

The six PowerBuilder-supplied basic window types include: main, child, pop-up, response, multiple document interface (MDI) Frame, and MDI frame with MicroHelp. The windows in our application were defined as follows:

Employee Benefits Window:	Main type
Logon Window:	Response type (a modal window that cannot be minimized to the desktop)
Special Transaction:	Response type
Employee Selection:	Pop-up type

All of these windows have title bars and system menus. Note that the Logon and Special Transaction windows were defined as response (modal) windows, without a minimize/maximize icon. This was made necessary by the application's hierarchical processing requirements, meaning the user must respond to their options/choices before continuing the process from which the window was invoked.

Besides window style, each window may have one or more window event/scripts to handle application/user activities such as window open/close, maximize/minimize, and others. Windows may also have menus assigned to them, which drive the mechanics of using the application from a menu bar or toolbar. Menus for windows are created using a separate Menu Painter, which will be covered a bit later in this chapter. Finally, each window may have one or more window controls. Window controls are custom graphical subwindow objects that accept user interaction or display application-specific information to the user. Controls include Static Text and Edit Boxes, List Boxes, Check Boxes and Radio Buttons, CommandButtons, DataWindows, and Graphs, as well as drawing objects like lines and colored-in rectangles. All window components described on this page are handled by features of the Window Painter.

The Window Painter

By clicking the window icon on the PowerBar from anywhere within PowerBuilder you invoke the Select Window dialog, and, after choosing a window name to work on an existing window or selecting New from the Select Window panel, you are presented with the robust graphical development toolset that is the Window Painter. This painter complies with the PowerBuilder standards as defined to date in this toolset: PowerBar, with access to all additional PowerBuilder painters; Window Painter toolbar, with access to the most common window controls; a custom Window Painter menu, with access to all window controls plus several additional development options; a text ribbon that allows you to manipulate selected text items on the window, such as changing size and font, and adding bold or underline. Finally the Window Painter allows you to make use of a color bar (shown at the bottom of Figure 6.9). This color bar works in a manner similar to that of the color bar option in Microsoft Paintbrush, and allows you to change the color of the text or background for a selected window control. Besides the toolbars and text ribbon, the Window Painter displays a large workspace which contains the current window design within the active work area. New windows are initially gray, and drawn as a 3 × 5 rectangle. This workspace extends down and to the right, so you can paint extremely large windows if necessary (the workspace is scrollable). The workspace shows only certain elements of the current window design, including size, shape, and window controls. To view the window as it would be seen during application execution, select Design, Preview from the Window Painter. This option leaves you in the Window Painter, but removes the workspace, and in its place displays the current application window, its position relative to the desktop, the window's title bar, system menu, application menu (if defined), and all other controls. Design, Preview is extremely useful in that it allows you to see the appearance of your window work and the effects of design changes to a window immediately (no compiling or scripts necessary).

Window Size, Shape, and Position

To change the basic size, shape, and position of a window you would (without having selected any window controls), click the right mouse button over the window itself. This action will result in the display of a pop-up menu from which you then select Position. This option displays a window-position panel which allows you to size, shape, and position the application window relative to the Microsoft Windows desktop. This position window is displayed in Figure 6.10. To save your size, shape, and position settings select OK, which returns you to the window painter.

Working in the Window Painter

The basic operational mode of select something to do and select what to do with it is continued with the Window Painter toolset. For example, to place a control on the window, you would:

- Select something to do by selecting the control type to be placed by either clicking the control's icon in the toolbar, or selecting the control name off a dropdown menu option.
- Select what to do with it by positioning your cursor in the window at the approximate area of control placement and click once.

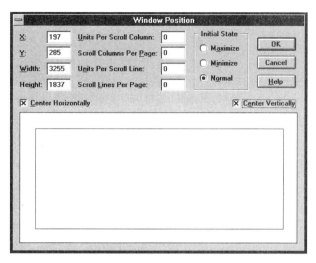

Figure 6.10   Window position panel.

This places a default control in the window (default in terms of size, name, and style attributes). After successfully placing a control in a window the control remains *selected.* This means that you can drag the control—moving, sizing, and shaping it, and modifying all other control attributes. This is done in one of several ways, the most popular being the use of the right mouse button.

The right mouse button (as we have seen for window size, shape, and position) opens a context-sensitive pop-up menu for selected objects that provides the ability to change virtually all attributes of the selected object. Each window control has a different set of attributes, and perhaps the best way to discuss the specifics of window controls and their attributes is to describe the process of building the Logon (w_logon), Employee Benefits (w_main), Special Transaction (w_trans), and Employee Selection (w_select) windows.

Creating the w_logon Window

To build the w_logon window we began by selecting New from the Select Window panel, which provided us with a new empty window panel. We then designed the window's basic size, shape, and position by clicking the right mouse button, and following the steps described previously (see the section titled Window size, shape, and position). We then set the rest of the window style characteristics by double-clicking the left mouse button over the window. This displays the Window Style panel (Figure 6.11). Window Style allows you to set most of the window's basic attributes. You select/deselect options as necessary, scroll through color choices, type the window title bar, and associate menus with windows through this panel.

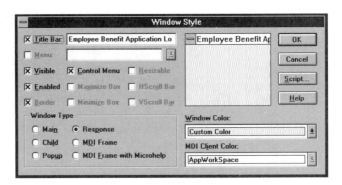

Figure 6.11   Window style panel.

From the Window Style panel you may access the various event/scripts.

Conspicuously absent from the list of options presented in the Window Style panel for a window is an area in which to name the window. PowerBuilder typically allows you to select a new (unnamed) object, and work on it until you are ready to quit, at which point Power-Builder prompts you to name the object. Note that you may explicitly name the object at any point by selecting File, Save as . . . from the dropdown menu.

After defining the basic form and structure of the window, we add six window controls: two StaticText controls, two SingleLineEdit controls, and two CommandButton controls.

StaticText Controls

StaticText controls are passive controls, usually used to display liter-als, labels, and other presentation aids such as hardwired instructions on how to use the window. To add a StaticText control: Click the Stat-icText option from the Controls dropdown menu (the list of controls is *not* alphabetized in the menu—it follows the order of the icons in the toolbar—ostensibly most common to least common options), and click your cursor over the window approximately where you want to place the control, which places a default StaticText control on the window, with a default name (st_n), default attributes, and the word *none* as the StaticText itself. To modify these defaults double-click over the newly placed StaticText control in the window, which will display the StaticText style panel (Figure 6.12). I generally adhere to the naming conventions defaulted by Powersoft (a prefix that describes the object type, an underscore, then a meaningful and unique name for the object*).

*PowerBuilder object (including variables) names may be up to 40 characters, must start with an alphabetic (a through z), are case insensitive (powerbuilder = PowerBuilder = POWER-BUILDER), and may include alphanumerics and certain special symbols: – $ # % _.

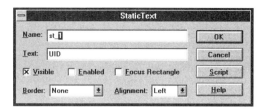

Figure 6.12   StaticText style panel.

Besides the StaticText control name, you might modify the text itself (what is displayed on the window), the text alignment (left/center/right justified), the control border (no border, the default, works well with most StaticText controls). To completely customize the control presentation, you may change the color of the control itself (a rectangle surrounding the text) and the text. You may also override the application text font and size by using the text-ribbon options.

SingleLineEdit Controls

SingleLineEdit controls are used as edit boxes for one line of input/output to the user. They are created in a manner consistent with StaticText controls: Click the SingleLineEdit option from the Controls dropdown menu, then click your cursor over the window where you want to place the control. This places a default Single-LineEdit control on the window, with a default name (sle_n) and default attributes. To modify the defaults, double-click over the newly placed SingleLineEdit control in the window—this will display the SingleLineEdit style panel (Figure 6.13).

Besides the SingleLineEdit control name, you might modify several additional options depending on the needs of your application: Case forces all entered values into upper/lower case, or accepts the text as entered (any); Border—boxes are used in our application, but 3D-raised in gray on a gray background has a terrific three-dimensional look and feel (Figure 6.14), Display Only creates a read/only nonenterable output field on the window. Finally, by checking the Password

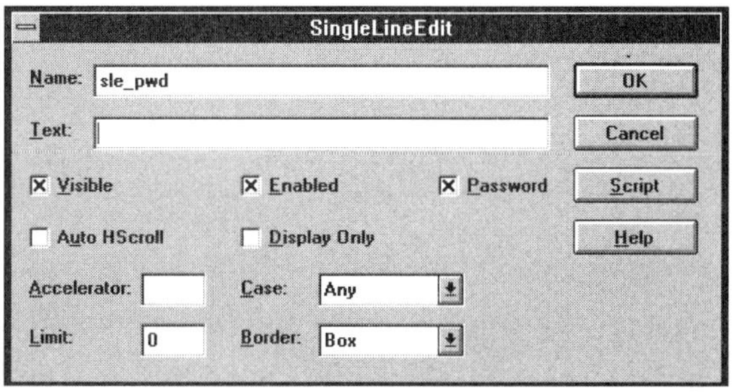

Figure 6.13   SingleLineEdit control style panel.

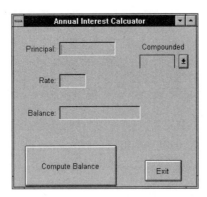

Figure 6.14   Auxiliary window displaying 3-D look-and-feel controls.

CheckBox, PowerBuilder automatically masks the letters typed by the user in standard password-no-display style (it turns the keystrokes into asterisks).

CommandButtons

CommandButton controls are used in place of, or in addition to, menu options as active controls, which almost always contain event/scripts to do something within the application (open or close a window, logon to the database, edit some fields, invoke a function, etc.). To modify the CommandButton defaults for each new control, double-click over the newly placed CommandButton control in the window, which will displays the CommandButton style panel (Figure 6.15).

CommandButton Style

In this panel, in addition to the CommandButton control name (cb_n), you may modify several other options, depending on the needs of your application, including: Text—what you type here is what is displayed on the CommandButton itself. Using the ampersand (&) character will force an underline character in the next letter within the CommandButton text. It also activates the Windows shortcut key feature, used to comply with CUA standards. Shortcut keys allow users to press an Alt/letter combination, which is substituted for single-clicking the mouse over the CommandButton.

Figure 6.15   CommandButton style panel.

You may optionally select a particular CommandButton to be a default or cancel key. By checking default for a CommandButton, the clicked event/script for that control will be executed if the user presses enter. By checking cancel for a CommandButton, the clicked event/script for that control will be executed if the user presses escape.

Unlike StaticText and SingleLineEdit controls, most Command-Buttons have event/scripts and ours is no exception. However, in the interests of continuing our discussion on window controls, we will move on to the creation of w_main, and its bevvy of controls, and get back to the event/scripts in w_logon a bit later.

Defining the w_main Window

After saving our work on the w_logon window, we returned to create a new window for our employee benefit application. This window, named *w_main,* is shown in Figure 6.16, and consists of nine StaticText controls, six SingleLineEdit controls, four EditMask controls (spin buttons), three CheckBoxes, two RadioButtons, a MultiLineEdit control, a DropDownListBox, and three GroupBoxes.

Edit Mask Controls

Edit Mask controls are alternatives to SingleLineEdit boxes for one line of input/output to the user. Edit Mask controls provide simple data formatting for data entry/data presentation (similar to COBOL picture clauses, except that it is available to control input as well as output values). Edit Mask controls also enable the popular Microsoft

Figure 6.16   w_Main window running.

spin button control used in this and in many other GUI applications and code table presentations. Code tables provide a means of translating an encrypted stored value to an ostensibly more meaningful presentation value. For example, you might denote employee status as I for inactive, A for active, V for on vacation, and T for terminated. Through the use of an Edit Mask code table you could they have I, A, V, and T presented as inactive, active, vacation, and terminated.

Edit Mask controls are created in the same manner as the command buttons described in the preceding sections. Click the Edit Mask option from the Controls dropdown menu, click your cursor over the window where you want to place the control, and so on. The default Edit Mask name (em_n) and style defaults may be modified by double-clicking over the newly placed Edit Mask control in the window—this will display the EditMask style panel (Figure 6.17).

To create a spin button through an Edit Mask control, check the Spin Button CheckBox (Figure 6.18). This extended style window allows you to specify low and high values for the spin button, and the value with which to increment/decrement the spin button for each mouse click on the up/down icons. As you can imagine, spin button Edit Masks may only be defined for numeric datatype fields. To scroll through lists of nonnumeric values, utilize ListBox and DropDownListBox controls.

ListBox and DropDownListBox Controls

One of the proven gains of GUI technology is the impressive drop in end-user data-entry errors through the use of point-and-click specification instead of manual typing. ListBox and DropDownListBox controls are a centerpiece of this feature, as they allow you to set a

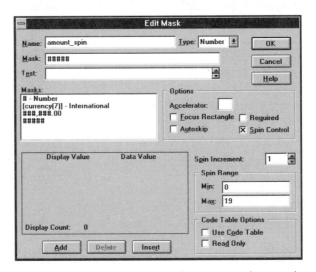

Figure 6.17   Edit Mask style panel—note spin button elements.

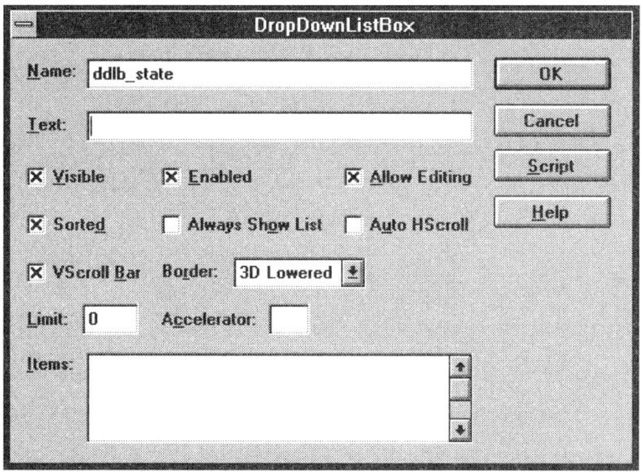

Figure 6.18   DropDownListBox style panel.

scrollable list of valid data responses which may be selected rather than keyed. ListBox and DropDownListBox controls are derived from the same basic class of window control. ListBoxes provide read/select-only scrollable lists of values. DropDownListBoxes provide scrollable lists of values, plus the option of typing an explicit value (much like a SingleLineEdit control), instead of selecting a value. In this way DropDownListBoxes enable the Microsoft combo box control.

To create a DropDownListBox control, follow the same procedure as with the controls discussed earlier: Click the DropDownListBox option from the Controls dropdown menu, click your cursor over the window where you want to place the control, and so on. The default DropDownListBox name (ddlb_n) and defaults may be modified by double-clicking over the newly placed DropDownListBox control in the window—this will display the DropDownListBox style panel (Figure 6.18). The DropDownListBox style panel has quite a few more entries than the style panels for StaticText and Single-LineEdits, and is worth a closer inspection.

DropDownListBox Style Panel

The DropDownListBox style panel allows you to specify some key behaviors for the control: Sorted, if checked, your DropDownListBox entries will be sorted (ASCII sort) alphanumerically; Allow editing, if checked, allows users to enter values in the SingleLineEdit portion of the DropDownListBox; Always show list, if checked, will display the list of values (as many as permitted by the control size within the window) like a ListBox; Auto HScroll, if checked, permits you to enter values in the SingleLineEdit portion of the control and scroll to the right, and most important, the Items area. In the Items area of the style panel you type in values one line at a time—these values make up the scrollable list from which the user may select the appropriate value for their purposes. To enter multiple lines, press Ctrl/Enter—a plain old enter equated to the OK CommandButton, and exits the specification dialog abruptly.

Using Scripts to Populate ListBoxes and DropDownListBoxes

The concept of hardwiring listbox entries into the item list, as described above, will only go so far in the real world. Often items to be displayed are dynamic and come from sources external to developers (such as databases and files on servers). To add entries to ListBoxes dynamically, you write a script (embedded within the appropriate event in the application) which references a PowerBuilder-supplied built-in function, *AddItem()*.

Scripts and Functions

Most script statements that manipulate screen objects (such as ListBox entries) do so using window-graphics functions. PowerBuilder version 3.0 ships with over 500 (that's not a typo—five hundred) predefined functions that expedite coding requirements for procedures such as ListBox item population. Actually, if you are a C or Visual Basic programmer, you probably aren't a bit surprised that PowerBuilder ships with 500 canned functions. However, if you are a COBOL mainframe programmer (or ex-COBOL mainframe programmer), the heavy use of functions will be part of the initial culture shock that occurs when you begin to work within a PC-client/server development environment. The PowerBuilder architecture is based heavily on the architecture of C programming shops—small, discrete functions (as opposed to large COBOL monolithic, standalone modules), and modularization. And the use of functions is encouraged as a means of leveraging the client/server architecture (functions represent a sort of nondatabase remote procedure call) and reusing code.

In our application we coded a script called *wf_state* which follows:

```
string     st                //temp variable
ddlb_state.Reset()            //clear dropdownlistbox
declare st_crs cursor for select state_text from state_table;
open st_crs;
fetch st_crs into :st;        //see if there are any rows
do while sqlca.sqlcode = 0    //if rows exist...
   ddlb_state.AddItem(st)     //   add them to the listbox
   fetch st_crs into :st;     //get the next row
loop
close st_crs;                 //release server resources
Return(0)                     //set return code OK
```

As we have not talked much about the PowerScript procedural language yet, an analysis of this code is a good place to start.

To paint the graphical components of your GUI screens, you use the PowerBuilder painters. But to actually glue the application together internally, to specify business processing logic, to respond to the relevant events in your application, and to manipulate many elements of the C/S-OO-GUI environment, you will be writing code, as your programming forebears did. Instead of COBOL or C, in Power-Builder you utilize a language called *PowerScript.*

PowerScript is a 4GL (albeit a low-level 4GL with a lot of procedural flexibility), very similar to Pascal, less similar to C and Basic, and not much at all like COBOL. PowerScript contains the standard procedural elements necessary for robust logic development: variables or variable structures (also known as Copybooks/DCLGENs); statements such as computations and assignment, For/Next, Do/While, If-Then-Else; functional references to windows, window attributes, or window controls (Open window, AddItem() to List-Boxes, and so on); statements that reference relational tables, either DataWindow Functions, Stored Procedures, Embedded SQL; Comments for code maintainability; and literals embedded within the scripts.

What is not in the PowerScript Language are many of the formal trappings of 3GL code, like predefined program divisions (data division, identification division, environment division, and so on); predefined program sections (working-storage section, linkage section); predefined or reserved coding margins (A margin, B margin). There are also no terminators or statement delimiters in PowerScript such as periods and semicolons, etc.).

This lack of formal structure in the language allows developers to code PowerScript statements in a manner similar to SQL coding. We highly recommend that PowerBuilder development shops formulate their own coding standards and procedures to add some discipline to the PowerScript components of their applications, otherwise they may be faced with a maintenance problem, as developers could code unique and creative solutions into their scripts which might be difficult for the next generation of application developers to modify.

The following list covers the elements of the PowerScript event/script from the wf_state function script, line by line.

1. string   st   //temp variable
1. A standard declaration of a string variable length. Note that the variable datatype (string) is on the left, and the variable name (st) is on the right. PowerBuilder supports over 16 standard datatypes, including Blobs (binary large objects, used to represent bit-mapped graphics and large files), strings (all variable length), numbers (integer, real, long, decimal, etc., date, time, date/time, and others). PowerBuilder also supports what are termed *enu-*

merated (abstract) datatypes. Enumerated datatypes are used to reference and graphic controls, and modify Windows processing.

2. ddlb_state.Reset()   //clear dropdownlistbox

2. The function of initializing a ListBox or DropDownListBox to zero items. Note the syntax of this function: object_name.Function(arguments)*. This more message-oriented function syntax is new with version 3.0 of PowerBuilder. It is provided (in addition to) the original PowerScript function calling syntax of: Reset(ddlb_state), used in versions 1.0 and 2.0.

3. declare st_crs cursor for select state_text from state_table;

4. open st_crs;

5. fetch st_crs into :st;   //see if there are any rows

3.4.5. Standard embedded SQL statements to: 3. declare a cursor name (st_crs) for a multirow table retrieval. (COBOL/DB2 programmers note: no EXEC SQL/END-EXEC, as the semi-colon [;] acts as the delimiter on SQL statements.[†]) 4. the open activates the defined cursor. 5. the fetch is used as a *priming read,* an initial retrieval to determine if rows exist in the table prior to entering the AddItem loop. Note that while DBMS-dependent, most database return codes adhere to the industry standards of; 0 = success, +100 = no more rows, <0 = database error. Also note that a control block called the *SQLCA* (SQL Communications Area) is also supported, and in fact, is built for each and every PowerBuilder application so you don't even have to declare it (see item 1 on declaring variables). You simply reference the fields of the SQLCA with qualified syntax (sqlca.sqlcode—the sqlcode field of the sqlca control block).

6. do while sqlca.sqlcode = 0   //if rows exist . . .

6. PowerBuilder supports five iteration or looping constructs; Do While . . . Loop, Do . . . Loop While, Do Until . . . Loop, Do . . . Loop Until, and For/Next. The five are virtually interchangeable, and are provided to satisfy the coding and logic specification preferences of a wide range of individual tastes. do while sqlca.sqlcode = 0 says, "Check to see if the field sqlca.sqlcode = 0 . . . if it does, execute the statements between this statement and the next subsequent loop statement at this logical level" (you may nest Do While loops within Do While loops in PowerScript).

---

*In the case of Reset() there are no arguments, you still must maintain the argument-placeholding parentheses.
†SQL statements are terminated with semicolons. PowerScript statements are not terminated with semicolons.

7. ddlb_state.AddItem(st)   //   add them to the listbox

7. Another function, this one is used to fill ListBox and DropDown-ListBox controls with external values, in this case, the data fetched from the SQL statement in line 5. The items are added to the named ListBox, which (if you checked Sort Entries) on the ListBox style panel is subsequently sorted by PowerBuilder before being presented to the user.* Again note the version 3.0 object-oriented messaging syntax to the function call.

8. fetch st_crs into :st;   //get the next row

8. The fetch-row standard SQL cursor-processing statement, a continuation of the cursor block begun in 3, 4, and 5 above.

9. loop

9. The Do While . . . Loop scope terminator. This PowerScript statement is necessary to complete the iteration statement begun in line 6.

10. close st_crs;   //release server resources

10. The close standard SQL cursor-processing statement, the completion of the cursor block begun in 3, 4, 5, and 8. above. Note that with many relational DBMSs close is optional, but recommended, as it acts to release system resources such as buffers and temporary work areas.

11. Return(0)   //set return code to OK

11. An optional but recommended element of all PowerBuilder functions. The Return(value) function sets a global return code, which is accessible to the script statement that invoked the function. In our case we are returning zero, the (almost) universal value which signifies successful process completion. In other cases, the function would set its Return() to a nonzero value, appropriate to the outcome of the function's processing. For example, if the state_table was empty (for whatever reason), and there were no rows to AddItem to the ListBox, the wf_state function might have set return to −1 designating some sort of database problem, and the script which invoked wf_state could make some sort of decision about continuing the application or not, depending upon the severity of the problem.

Since we have opened the door on discussing script statements, let's go back and discuss the event/scripts found in the Application Open event, and in the CommandButtons in w_logon.

---

*This concept of the flexibility surrounding where and when to sort hints at the potential for client/server access to offload central processing requirements by distributing the sorting cycles to local PCs, performing sorts when/if called for, and relieving the central (host) processor.

The Application Open Event/Script

Every PowerBuilder application will require an event/script coded for the Application Open event. This occurs when the user runs the application either using the Windows Run command prompt (Windows Program Manager, File, Run option), or by double-clicking the application's icon within a program group. The open event/script can be either very simple (a one liner opening the main window in the application) to complex (a script which communicates to other running Windows applications, or does some database access prior to displaying the first window). Ours is moderately small.

```
SetPointer(Hourglass!)
Open(w_logon)
If logon_successful="y"
    Open(w_main)
Else
    MessageBox("Error", "Database Connection Failure")
    Halt
End If
```

This simple script opens the w_logon window, which attempts a connection to the ODBC database (see the w_logon connect script). If the connection succeeds w_main is opened, if it fails the application is terminated using the halt function. An annotated version of the application Open event/script is shown below. Note that a global string variable (logon_successful) is used in this script to communicate the success/failure of the logon attempt in the w_logon window.

SetPointer(Hourglass!)	Sets the Windows pointer to an hourglass style. This is done to conform to CUA standards and should be coded at the top of virtually every Window Open and database access request.
Open(w_logon)	Opens the w_logon window (next topic), which prompts for userid and password, and attempts to connect to the DBMS using the specified text.
If logon_successful="y"	w_logon assigns the *global variable* (a variable that may be referenced throughout any event/script in the entire application) logon_successful a y or n
Open(w_main)	Open the main Employee Benefits window
Else	. . . otherwise . . .
MessageBox("Error"	Describe the problem to the user . . . and . . .

| Halt | Terminate the application and return to the Windows desktop. |
| End If | If-then scope delimiter |

Once w_logon is invoked from the Open application event/script, the user would type in their userid and password, and click either the logon or cancel CommandButton. Both CommandButtons contain scripts, and we will start with the easier of the two, the Cancel CommandButton.

Cancelling (Closing) a Window

Although any window that is defined with a system menu can be closed thorugh the standard (double-click) close technique, generally you will want each custom window to have its own custom method of closing. This is accomplished typically through a CommandButton set up as an *E*xit key, and/or through an *E*xit option from the File menu. The PowerScript command to close the window depends on where within the window the command is issued. If the command is issued from within a CommandButton, you would code: Close(Parent) which means "close the parent window of this control."

If the command is issued from within a menu, you would use the command Close(Parentwindow), or you could close the explicit window name which is the parent of the menu option: Close(w_main).

Logging On to the Server

Each PowerBuilder application that accesses relational DBMSs must connect to the DBMS server through a network and attach the client (your application) to the server (the centralized DBMS running on the LAN). PowerBuilder uses some fairly straightforward script statements to do this.

```
string uid
string pwd
uid = sle_uid.text
pwd = sle_pwd.text
SQLCA.DBMS='ODBC'
SQLCA.DBParm = "DataSource='BOOK', &
    ConnectString='DSN=BOOK;UID=" + uid + ";PWD=" + pwd + "'"
Connect;
if sqlca.sqlcode = -1 then
   MessageBox("Error","Logon Password Problem")
   Close(Parent)
Else
   logon_successful = "y"
   Close(Parent)
end if
```

This script represents a few new concepts. Please take a minute and study this script line by line in the description that follows.

1. string uid
    string pwd

1. Two declarations of string variables to be used to pass userid and password values to the DBMS.

2. uid = sle_uid.text
    pwd = sle_pwd.text

2. Assignment statements used to value the declared variables with values entered by the users through the w_logon window controls sle_uid, and sle_pwd. Note the references to the field's text attributes.

3. SQLCA.DBMS='ODBC'

3. This statement initializes the values of the the SQL control block field SQLCA.DBMS with the name of the database management system we are connecting to (in our case, we are using ODBC protocol to link to the WATCOM SQL DBMS). Other PowerBuilder supported DBMSs include XDB, SQLServer, Oracle, and others. See Chapter 1 for a complete list of DBMSs supported by PowerBuilder as of the writing of this book.

4. SQLCA.DBParm = "DataSource='BOOK', &
    ConnectString='DSN=BOOK;UID=" + uid + ";PWD=" + pwd + " ' "

4. This statement is a DBMS-specific set of keyword (as opposed to positional) parameters which describe the database we wish to connect with (DataSource='BOOK'); the physical DOS files, which hold the database (DSN=BOOK); the userid and password values entered by the end user (UID=" + uid + ";PWD=" + pwd + " ' "). Note that because of a predetermined set of single and double quotes, the actual syntax for this statement is fairly complex, requiring an exact specification of plus signs (+) the concatenation operator, and single/double quotes. Having valued our SQL Communication Area control block (SQLCA) with the necessary entries we may now

5. Connect;

5. This statement attempts to link the client application to the executing ODBMS server through the values specified in the SQLCA.DBPARM.

6. if sqlca.sqlcode = –1 then
    MessageBox("Error","Logon Password Problem")
    Close(Parent)

6. If the connection is unsuccessful, the sqlca.sqlcode will be valued as a negative one by WATCOM. If such is the case it is generally considered polite to inform the user of this problem.

7. Else
   logon_successful = "y"

7. However, if the logon is successful, this statement assigns the global variable logon_successful a "y" value, which is evaluated in the previous script (application Open event/script).

8. Close(Parent)

8. Whether or not the logon was successful, our application no longer needs to present the w_logon window, so close it.

9. end if

9. Terminate the scope of the above If-Then-Else.

While it is not our purpose in this chapter to enter into an in-depth tutorial on every aspect of the PowerScript language, suffice it to say that the language is well suited to GUI, object-oriented, client/server-based development, with most requirements of C/S-OO-GUI coding techniques directly covered by functions and statements.

Script Language Problems

I did run into several problem areas during the development of the application that required help from the Powersoft Tech Support staff. They provided me with workarounds in a timely fashion (often faxed within the hour). These workarounds were usually coding routines that employed little-used functions (or common functions used in little-known ways). The areas of difficulty I encountered and worked around included accessing multiple lines in a MultiLineEdit control (Figure 6.21), multiple listbox entries (determining/resetting), Data-Window transaction control, and occasional low-level syntax.

The one large area Powersoft could improve is their compiler diagnostics. Very little information is given regarding the nature of many syntax errors, thus the learning curve is increased dramatically for apprentice product users. For example, the diagnostic messages for several common problems simply state that there is a syntax error on a given line of your script. Exactly *why* a given line returns a syntax error remains a mystery (until you solve it—and solve it you must, or you cannot save your script, although you may use comments to save a script). In contrast to the almost overabundance of high-quality help throughout the rest of the product, there is no syntax or runtime error help available through the online facility. And, in spite of the incredibly good documentation that ships with version 3.0 of this product, there is no explicit messages and codes reference manual (or even a section of the massive documentation set). Given that Power-Builder developers spend between 40 and 80 percent of their time coding and maintaining event/scripts,* it would behoove Powersoft to work on this one area of concern with their product.

Other Window Controls—RadioButtons and CheckBoxes

If you glance back at Figure 6.16 (the Employee Benefits Application window), you will note that there are several other controls that we haven't discussed. We shall start with the options controls, RadioButtons and CheckBoxes.

CheckBox controls. CheckBoxes are employed in a window to allow end users to select one or more options for a given processing choice. In our example, the operator could specify that, of the available investment fund types, employees should be able to break their savings down into IRAs, stock options, or Keogh plans, or any combination of the three. To present this choice scenario in a GUI world you utilize CheckBoxes.

CheckBoxes are defined in the standard fashion as described in earlier sections (see sections on defining StaticText and Single-LineEdit controls). The CheckBox style panel is shown in Figure 6.19. After modifying the default CheckBox name and displayed text (what winds up being presented next to the CheckBox), the only other option that you may wish to modify is the three state option. Power-Builder CheckBoxes are able to present checked, not checked, and third state (identified as a gray box, instead of a checked box) conditions, for complex true/false options which would be better served with true/false/other specification.

RadioButton controls. RadioButtons are employed in a window to allow end users the option of selecting only one choice (*exclusive or* selection) from a series of two or more options within a given processing group. In our example, the operator could specify that a selected employee was male or female. To present this exclusive choice scenario in a GUI world you would utilize RadioButtons. RadioButtons are defined in the standard fashion in all earlier sections, and the only modifications typically made to their style are the RadioButton name and accompanying text.

RadioButton exclusivity. RadioButtons are controls that present the opportunity to select only one possible choice out of many to the user.

---

*Statistics gathered through an informal survey of 25 PowerBuilder consultants taken by the authors in 1993.

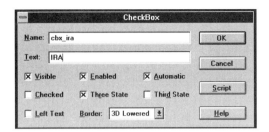

Figure 6.19   CheckBox style panel.

If RadioButton a is clicked, all others are clicked off by PowerBuilder. However, the scope of a group of radio buttons is determined by where the RadioButtons are placed. If they are placed within a GroupBox, then the GroupBox delimits the on/off mutual exclusion of RadioButtons. This is why you almost always find RadioButtons defined within a GroupBox.

GroupBox controls. GroupBoxes act to physically and logically segregate a window into separate groups of RadioButtons, Check-Boxes, CommandButtons, and so on. GroupBoxes are for the most part passive controls (they may not be selected and have no PowerBuilder-designated user events). However, they are not entirely passive, as they are often used to functionally isolate groups of RadioButtons.

To define a GroupBox, simply follow the same procedures that we have been using. Select GroupBox from the Controls menu. Place the GroupBox in the window (click over the approximate spot). Size and shape the GroupBox by dragging its edges, and define a name and text display for the GroupBox by double-clicking over the GroupBox control. Because GroupBoxes are such passive controls, their style window is so simple that it doesn't even bear displaying in this chapter. However, recall that most windows use GroupBoxes to organize RadioButtons, so they are logically segregated appropriately for their use in the application. Thus, clicking one RadioButton does not turn off all other RadioButtons on the entire window (the alternative to using GroupBoxes to control RadioButton behavior).

Checkpoint

At this point, we have defined a WATCOM SQL database for our application; built five small tables (comments, employee, funds_transfer, special_transaction, and state_table), defined an application object (book) and a library with which to maintain all of the nondatabase objects for our application (book.pbl); defined two windows (w_logon and w_main), defined the complete set of controls for both windows, defined an application Open event/script, defined a database connect event/script complete with logon/password checking for our database, and opened w_main upon successful logon to the DBMS.

Except for the script coding, this has all been accomplished with point-and-click style development, using the Database Painter, Application Painter, and Window Painter. One of the nicer features of Power-Builder, and event-driven programming environments in general, is the dynamic nature of the development process. PowerBuilder has several facilities built in to its toolset that allow you to prototype your design, run your application, and interactively test your application.

Prototyping Your Design

By clicking the Design, Preview option anywhere from within the Window Painter, you will see the current window design as it will appear on the desktop when your application is finished. This Preview feature emulates all windows features and behavior, stopping just short of event/script execution. This means that when you preview your window, its size, proportions, and position on the desktop are revealed, all window controls may be tabbed and activated (no event/scripts behind controls), all ListBox and DropDownListBox items are functionally depicted (scrollbars and all), all graphics are shown, and the system menu Close function is operational.

Aligning Controls

During the course of prototyping and previewing your window, you will probably notice one or more controls which are not lined up, sized proportionately, or spaced correctly on the window. PowerBuilder provides a modest amount of desktop-publishing style electronic justification and sizing for window controls. By selecting two or more controls and then selecting the Edit, Align, Size, or Space options, you may align objects top, bottom, left, right, and so on; size multiple controls to a selected control size; and space three or more controls to the spacing between two controls. This is a very useful feature of graphical development tools, and the only improvements I would suggest to Power-Builder are the inclusion of an *object-anchoring* option, which would permanently anchor controls within a window when you are satisfied with their position, and an *object-grouping* option, which would allow you to define a set of controls as permanently belonging to a given group, thus allowing you to manipulate a group of controls more easily.

Running a Window

To test the event/scripts within your application, PowerBuilder supports three separate methods: running the window, running the application, and debugging the application. By pressing Ctrl/W from within the Window Painter, you are prompted to save changes made within your current window edit session, then presented with the list of windows available in the current application, and allowed to run, or execute, the window as if it was being launched from the desktop. This quick exit into application test is very handy as it permits developers to, in an iterative fashion, code/save/test discrete components of their windows with very little effort.

Running an Application

In our case (at least at this point in the project), we took advantage of the PowerBuilder Run option. By clicking the Run icon from the PowerBar (recall that the PowerBar can be displayed from within any of the PowerBuilder painter facilities) you are prompted to save any outstanding changes you have made within the painter; the Power-Builder product minimizes itself to the desktop and your original Windows desktop is displayed; and the application Open event/script is executed. This quick access to application testing further extends the iterative code/save/test development procedures discussed previously, and is extremely useful for prototyping and rapid application development efforts.

Debugging an Application

If your script contains any significant level of logical complexity (most do) and you wish to view the code interactively during a run session, PowerBuilder provides a reasonably good graphical debugging facility. By clicking the debugging icon which looks a "just say no to bugs" button (Figure 6.20) on the PowerBar, you are prompted to set up a debugging session for your application. (Note: application-level, not window-level, debugging is required. The debugger allows you to set breakpoints, called *stops,* within your application event/scripts, to step through your code line by line, to view the contents of variables within a script, and to modify the contents of variables within your event/scripts. The debugger is simple to use, following the same consistent point-and-click mouse-driven development mechanics we have seen in all of the painters. The debugger also represents a central repository through which you can browse all event/scripts within all objects throughout your entire application.

Utilizing the various painter facilities, PowerScript coding panels and the dynamic run/testing features of the product we can continue to build and test all components of our application in a discrete,

Figure 6.20 Debug icon.

controlled, and iterative process. There is not much in the way of graphical objects and painter techniques to point out, but there are a few new script features which deserve mentioning.

The Remaining Scripts in the w_main Window Controls

Because we are driving the mechanics of w_main primarily from the custom menu, which we will discuss later, there is little in the way of significant event/script logic in the actual w_main window or its window controls. There are, however, a couple of small PowerScript elements.

Dynamically Checking and Unchecking Controls

To refer to or modify the state of RadioButtons and CheckBoxes within an event/script, you reference the checked attribute of the control with a true/false test. The syntax of such statements are as follows:

```
rb_male.checked=false
If rb_female.checked=true Then
   . . .
If cbx_ira.checked=true Then
   . . .
etc.
```

Code that references the state of RadioButtons and CheckBoxes is often found in CommandButton and Menu event/scripts, which launch some sort of active process (write to the database, print a report, calculate a total, etc.). However, sometimes you must initialize, or set, the state of window controls due to a clear function on the window, or perhaps when the window is first Opened. The Power-Script statements necessary to dynamically uncheck the RadioButtons and CheckBoxes in w_main follows:

```
rb_male.checked=false
rb_female.checked=false
cbx_ira.checked=false
cbx_stock.checked=false
cbx_keogh.checked=false
```

Enabling/Disabling Controls

Along lines similar to checking and unchecking, it is sometimes necessary to dynamically hide/show/enable and disable controls. Hide/show are functions which are fairly self-explanatory. When you dynamically hide a control using Hide(sle_lname) the control is not visible on the window, although it is still there. To show hidden controls you use the show function, Show(sle_lname). Show displays hidden controls. Hiding and subsequently showing controls is a somewhat less common GUI programming technique. Enabling and disabling controls is more usual.

When a control should be visible on a window but inactive unless/until the user selects certain options or enters certain values, you disable the control. When a disabled control must be subsequently enabled, you programmatically enable the control. The PowerScript statements to enable/disable controls are shown here:

```
Enable control: em_ira.enabled=true
Disable control: em_ira.enabled=false
```

In our application, we have decided to disable the three spin buttons (em_ira, em_stock, em_keogh) unless or until the user checks the associated CheckBox to open that type of account. To disable the three spin buttons from within the w_main window Open event/script you would code:

```
em_ira.enabled=false
em_stock.enabled=false
em_keogh.enabled=false
```

To subsequently enable the spin button associated with a CheckBox control when the user clicks the CheckBox, you would proceed as follows.

From within the clicked event/script section of the cbx_ira control:

```
em_ira.enabled=true
```

From within the clicked event/script section of the cbx_stock control:

```
em_stock.enabled=true
```

From within the clicked event/script section of the cbx_keogh control:

```
em_keogh.enabled=true
```

Event-Driven Programming Consideration

Note that for the above enabled logic, it is not necessary to test whether or not the cbx_ CheckBoxes have been clicked, with logic such as If cbx_ira.checked=true. The only possible way for the above scripts to execute—since they are coded within the clicked event/script slot/section of the cbx_ CheckBoxes—is when or if the user actually clicks the CheckBoxes. This element of graphical controls containing discrete event/script sections wherein programmers code small units of logic to handle specific user events, forms the basis of event-driven programming and is key to understanding the use of products such as

PowerBuilder and Visual Basic. For the rest of the scripts in the Employee Benefits (w_main) window, we must turn our attention to menus, scripts within menus, and the PowerBuilder Menu Painter.

Menu Review

Recall from Chapter 3 that menus are vertical lists of choices, commands, functions, and options that users select from for a given active window. One of the CUA and Microsoft standards suggests that all windows, except for child and response windows should contain menus, although for many windows the basic system menu (upper left window icon containing restore, move, size, minimize, maximize, close, switch to . . .) is sufficient.

Other standard menu design guidelines include the concept of grouping related menu options and partitioning them with a separator line; restricting cascading menus (menus of menus of menus) to one level due to the complex mouse movement and coordination needed to navigate; and any menu option that opens an additional window should be followed by an ellipsis (. . .), like: Run . . . or Search . . . Once again, we strongly recommend that if you are going to be responsible for designing windows and menus that you read a book such as the Hix and Hartson *Developing User Interfaces* (John Wiley and Sons) or attend a GUI design class in order to fully understand the nuances and issues surrounding graphical application design.

The Menu Painter

PowerBuilder has provided a simple facility to develop drop-down and pop-up menus. By clicking the Menu Painter icon on the Power-Bar you invoke the Menu Painter (Figure 6.21). The steps in building a menu using the Menu Painter are as follows:

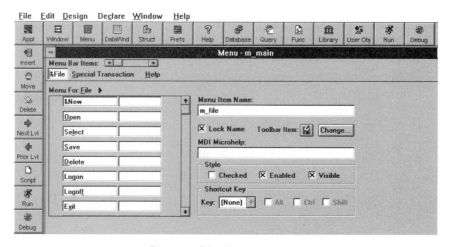

Figure 6.21 Menu Painter.

- Create the menu bar by defining each highest-level item, from left to right in the menu (this typically includes categories of options)
- For each option on the menu bar, add:
  - Help
  - Shortcut keys
  - A toolbar (optional)
- For each option on the menu bar, create the dropdown option list (the menu or action items):
  - Name the menu item
  - Assign accelerator/shortcut keys
  - Create separator lines
  - Define MicroHelp (if MDI Frame with MicroHelp base-window type)
  - Write event/scripts

Finally, you must associate the menu with a given window. This is done within the Window Painter. By opening the base-window style panel (see Figure 6.11), you may select a menu for the current window through a DropDownListBox.

Note that this concept of explicitly associating menus with the windows they control implies that, in PowerBuilder, menus are considered reusable, shared objects. In fact, menus may be inherited and reused like windows and user objects. In practice we have rarely seen menu/window independence in action, however, perhaps with a bit more standardization of surrounding menu options and their meaning throughout the industry, the notion of menu independence may come in handy.

Using the Menu Painter

You can see the Menu Painter in Figure 6.20. As you can see, it is a standard PowerBuilder specification painter interface, with custom toolbar options and a custom menu. The Menu Painter offers a fairly intuitive style of development. To add menu bar items, click the Menu Bar Items area of the painter, the Insert icon, or select Edit, Insert from the dropdown menu. To add action items (which hang off a menu bar) you click in the Menu For: xxx section of the work area, and follow the same procedure.

Each menu item gets its own unique name, which is generated by PowerBuilder, and, in the case of duplicates, text edited to avoid problems. You may also custom name the menu option entries. According to Microsoft/CUA standards, each menu option (including the menu bar options) should have its own defined accelerator key(s), allowing a user the flexibility of pressing Alt/letter or some alternate key combination to access a menu option directly through the keyboard. Actually, PowerBuilder provides for both shortcut and accelerator keys, the difference being that accelerator keys, which are identified by underlines in the menu option and on controls, provide direct access to the text of the menu item list. Shortcut keys, defined only in the Menu Painter, are typically used to invoke a menu item option (fire off its clicked event/script). Both serve the purpose of allowing keyboard access to the mechanics of a window.

Contiguous groups of related menu options should be separated from others in the menu list by a separator line. By simply typing a single dash in the Menu For: xxx entry area, you create a separator line at that level in the menu list. Once you've defined the basic menu layout, you may change your mind. Move items around, delete items, add new items, and so on by selecting options and using the Edit menu, or by using the editing icons in the toolbar.

Menu Scripts

Like the controls, windows, and most everything visible in GUI applications, menu items* in PowerBuilder menus contain predefined event sections, which may be used to hold PowerScript logic to invoke processing. The most common event against a menu item is the clicked event. This event generally contains an event/script relating to the processing text in the menu-item option.

In our menu, the script to open an employee benefit follows. This is one of the longer scripts you will see, and it breaks down into several sections.

```
//1. Variable Declarations
integer  sal_pct, account, fundpct, ira, stock, keogh, i
string   lname, fname, sex, state
long     socsecno
dec      salary,, amt_invest
date     eff_date
//
//2. Select Customer Row
//
If Not IsNumber(w_main.sle_soc_sec_no.text) Then
    MessageBox("Error","Bad Social Security Number")
    SetFocus(w_main.sle_soc_sec_no)
    Return
Else
    socsecno = long(w_main.sle_soc_sec_no.text)
End if
//
```

*Menu bar entries themselves (as opposed to their dropdown list of items) may also contain event/scripts, but this is atypical. Menu bar entries are generally high-level descriptions of related dropdown items, and rarely fire off processing when merely selected with a mouse.

```
select soc_sec_num, lname, fname, state, sex, salary, sal_pct
into :socsecno, :lname, :fname, :state, :sex, :salary, :sal_pct
from employee
where soc_sec_num = :socsecno;

if sqlca.sqlcode < 0 then
   MessageBox("Error",SQLCA.SQLErrtext)
   Return
End If
if sqlca.sqlcode = +100 then
   MessageBox("Warning","Employee Not Found")
   Return
End If
//
//3. Assignment statements to send database fields to window controls
//
w_main.em_sal_pct.text=string(sal_pct)
w_main.sle_fname.text=fname
w_main.sle_lname.text=lname
w_main.em_salary.text=string(salary)
w_main.sle_state.text=state
//Calculate amount invested
amt_invest = salary * sal_pct
w_main.sle_amt_invest.text = string(amt_invest)

If sex = "F" Then
    w_main.rb_female.checked = true
Else
     w_main.rb_male.checked = true
End If
//
//4. Select Funds_Data Rows
//
Select eff_date, fund_pct into :eff_date, :fundpct
 From funds_data
Where soc_sec_num = :socsecno and
   type = 'I';
if sqlca.sqlcode = +0 then
   w_main.em_ira.text=string(fundpct)
   w_main.cbx_ira.checked = true
   w_main.sle_eff_date.text = string(eff_date)
End If

Select eff_date, fund_pct into :eff_date, :fundpct
 From funds_data
Where so_csec_num = :socsecno and
   type = 'S';
if sqlca.sqlcode = +0 then
   w_main.em_stock.text=string(fundpct)
   w_main.cbx_stock.checked = true
   w_main.sle_eff_date.text = string(eff_date)
End If
```

```
Select eff_date, fund_pct into :eff_date, :fundpct
 From funds_data
Where soc_sec_num = :socsecno and
    type = 'K';

if sqlca.sqlcode = +0 then
    w_main.em_keogh.text=string(fundpct)
    w_main.cbx_keogh.checked = true
    w_main.sle_eff_date.text = string(eff_date)
End If


string st_abbrev
string st_text
st_abbrev = w_main.sle_state.text
select state_text into :st_text
    from state_table where state_abbrev = :st_abbrev;
w_main.ddlb_state.text = st_text
//
//5. Routine to populate MultiLineEdit control
//
string     txt, textline
Int        countrow
select count(*) into :countrow from comments where soc_sec_num = :soc-
secno;
If sqlca.sqlcode <> 0 Then
    Return
End If
declare comnt cursor for select comment_line from comments
        where soc_sec_num = :socsecno;
open comnt;
If sqlca.sqlcode <> 0 Then
    Return
End If
for i = 1 to countrow
    fetch comnt into :txt;
    textline = textline + txt + ";tdr;tdn"
    next
w_main.mle_comments.text = textline
```

Sections of the Event/Script

//**1. Variable declarations.** This section describes the host variables necessary to access the database. There is nothing special about these declarations. They conform to the PowerBuilder standard datatypes (dec for decimal data, string for character data stored as variable-length strings, date for valid calendar dates, etc.).

//**2. Select Customer Row.** The second section is a static SQL singleton Select, a retrieval database access which returns either one row or zero rows based on where criteria. This statement is standard fare for programmers who have used embedded SQL in other languages such as COBOL, PL/I, C or Fortran. Powersoft has adhered closely to ANSI standards for SQL in the majority of their SQL statement delivery.

Of course the critical component of the database access for embedded SQL is the DBMS you are using. There are many vendor-specific SQL dialect extensions permitted by the various DBMS products. As long as you conform to the vendor's syntax you will be able to compile and run your code. It does bear mentioning, however, that the more that developers rely on proprietary SQL dialect extensions (Outer Join operators, extended column mathematical functions such as standard deviation and variance, etc.), the less portable the application becomes.

//3. Assignment statements to send database fields to window controls. These statements are similar to ones we have seen previously in this chapter. The only contributions of these examples are in the number and variety of graphical functions used to translate nontext data into text data for use in the text-only world of window controls. The other interesting element of the assignment statements is the example used to check the appropriate RadioButton based on male/female data.

//4. Select Funds_Data Rows. This lengthy and cumbersome SQL and script language sample is used to set the funds_data controls to the appropriate values and states. Its repetitiveness is unfortunate, but not atypical in the 4GL world (or 3GL world for that matter). Note the last routine to read state information from the state table based on the state abbreviation.

//5. Routine to populate MultiLineEdit control. This final routine displays several interesting aspects of PowerScript. First are new variable declarations. Unlike COBOL and other sectional languages where the programs are divided up into defined sections, Power-Script allows you to define variables at any point in the script language (provided that the definitions occur prior to any references made to the variable). The first SQL statement determines the number of comments/soc_sec_num, and is used as the eventual loop counter in the For/Next construct. Thereafter begins a standard cursor Select block. Cursor Selects are retrieval operations, which are defined in four sections: declare, which states the logical SQL data access requirements; open, which executes the statement in the declare and places results rows in a data buffer; Fetch, which returns one row at a time into host variable(s); and close, which signals end-of-fetch-operations and frees the cursor's DBMS resources (buffers, temporary storage, etc.). These four standard parts of cursor operations can be found in virtually all SQL-DBMSs' third and fourth generation languages, from IBM-mainframe assembler/DB2 to SAS/SQL operations. Once again, the details and specifics of the allowable SQL dialects will depend upon the DBMS you are using, but in all cases PowerBuilder has adhered to industry-standard embedded-cursor processing.

The final piece of number 5, a routine used to concatenate text lines, is interesting. In this routine two line break characters, ~r and ~n, were necessary to provide the new line function, and to break the fetched comment lines out over multiple lines of the MultiLineEdit-Box. Without the inclusion of these characters, all of the text lines fetched in the previous example would be concatenated onto a single line in the edit box.

PowerBuilder DataWindow Controls

While we have used embedded SQL so far in this application to accomplish database access, it is now time to turn our attention to the technology that has set PowerBuilder apart from its competition—DataWindows. DataWindows are complex GUI controls that provide SQL data access painting, vastly simplified and nonprocedural report specification, and greatly simplified data access and update coding (automated scrolling, one-line-function Delete/Update processing, and much more). DataWindow technology is so powerful, in fact, that many PowerBuilder shops have chosen DataWindow data access and presentation in favor of embedded SQL for the preponderance of their applications.

We will use a DataWindow as the basic data-access mechanism for the Employee Selection window, which is invoked when the user clicks the Select option from the Employee Benefits window's File menu. The basic process will be: the user clicks Select from the File menu, which opens the w_emp_list, window; w_emp_list then populates a DataWindow control (dw_emp_list) with employee names. The user may then click an employee name from the list, and the social security number associated with that particular employee will be used to Open the benefits information on the Employee Benefits window.

What Is a DataWindow?

A *DataWindow* is actually two separate objects: the graphical control, which is placed in the application window (actually called the *DataWindow control*), and the database-access and data-manipulation object (referred to in the Powersoft literature as the *DataWindow object*).

The DataWindow control is a simple graphical object created like all of the other window controls—select DataWindow Control from the Controls menu on the Window Painter, and click in the Window workspace over the spot you want to place the control. DataWindow controls define the size/proportions, scrolling capabilities, defaults, event/scripts, and name for the DataWindow within the application window.

DataWindow objects are defined using the DataWindow Painter. The DataWindow objects are named independent client/server database access and reporting components. DataWindow objects are created using the DataWindow Painter (Figure 6.22). The DataWindow Painter itself is composed of two separate elements: data-access specification and report specification.

The data access specification painter (Figure 6.23) allows you to build robust SQL statements including table joins, computed fields, subselects, outer joins, GROUP BY/HAVING, ORDER BY, and select-through arguments (host variables in the Where clause). Most of the Select statement components are built with graphical specification techniques: select something to do—add a computed column to the Where clause by clicking the Computed Column icon and select what to do with it—build the computed column's mathematical or statistical function. This is compliant with the rest of the PowerBuilder operations we've looked at so far. Besides SQL syntax creation, the data access specification painter allows you to view the SQL you've created, edit, and export the SQL.

It should be mentioned that the data access painter does not in any way remove or lessen the necessity for a strong SQL programming background on the part of Powerbuilder developers. SQL is a complex, relational-mathematics-oriented data access language from IBM. (Need we say more?) The data access specification painter merely creates the SQL syntax you supply with your graphical development

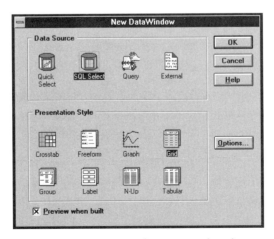

Figure 6.22   DataWindow new style selection.

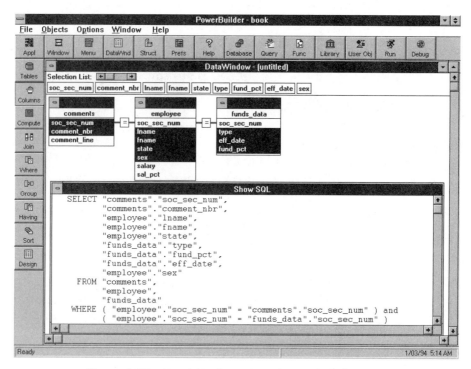

Figure 6.23   DataWindow—DataAccess (SQL) Painter.

tools. It does not in any way, shape, or form guarantee the logical accuracy of the SQL you have composed. In fact, a case could be made for the notion that the further removed one gets from the details of any imperfect technology (say, SQL for example . . .), the easier it gets to introduce bugs that are incredibly resistant to detection because you aren't used to thinking at the low level of specification native to the [SQL] language.

Once you have successfully painted the SQL for your data access request, you invoke the report painter (Figure 6.24). This toolset breaks all reports* into four areas: the Header, where you would typically place literal page headers, date/time, and page numbering information; the Detail area, representing the detail rows of your report (this is where your column specifications are placed); the Summary area, usually where you place report totals and final calculations; and the Footer area, an area displayed at the bottom of each page, available for page totals, calculations, and other end-of-page report statistics.

The report painter treats all elements of data presentation as distinct graphical objects. Each individual element (each specific column, each column header, etc.) may be selected, moved, sized, aligned, deleted, undeleted, expanded, and combined using point-

---

*By *reports* we refer to all data presentation, through window controls and batch (paper) reporting.

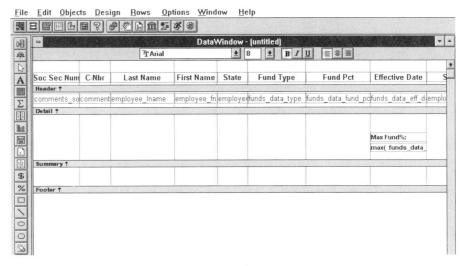

Figure 6.24   DataWindow—report painter.

and-click manipulation. To this end, the report painter is very easy to learn but, like many desktop publishing packages, it requires a high degree of mouse coordination and precision to master. There is a lot of of flexibility in the report painter. You may add computed fields, group rows, suppress duplicate values in columns, add full color/data dependent graphics, modify text fonts with total control over individual fields, retrieve only one page of data at a time from the data buffer, and do many other user-friendly development procedures with this tool. However, to position a significantly complex production report *exactly* alignment/spacing and other precision specifications can take a bit of time. This is due to the electronic desktop-publishing aspects of the tools and interface.

Assigning DataWindow Objects to DataWindow Controls

Once you have successfully painted and tested the SQL data access portion of a DataWindow object and painted the report presentation of the data, you save the DataWindow object and return to the Window Painter, editing the window that contains the DataWindow control in which you want to place the DataWindow object. When you double-click your mouse over the existing DataWindow control, you are then prompted for the name of a DataWindow object to place in the control (you choose one from a DropDownListBox full of DataWindow object names). After you have selected the DataWindow object for your DataWindow control, you will see the DataWindow (without data) within the DataWindow control (Figure 6.25). At this point, you may need to adjust the DataWindow control's size and shape, due to the look and feel of the DataWindow object. You also may need to return

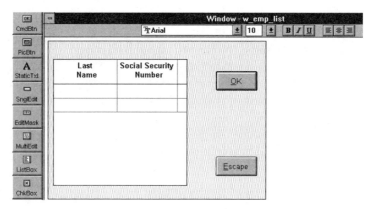

Figure 6.25 DataWindow object after association with DataWindow control in Window Painter.

to the DataWindow Painter in order to customize the size of the report header, detail, or other aspects of the report presentation.

DataWindows and Database Access

To invoke a DataWindow from within a PowerBuilder application, you need to add a few PowerScript statements to the event/script responsible for accessing the database through the DataWindow. These statements follow:

```
long  ret_code
// Tell the DataWindow about DBMS parameters
dw_emp_list.SetTransObject(SQLCA)

// Load the DataWindow
ret_code = dw_emp_list.Retrieve ()
If ret_code = 0 then
   MessageBox("Sorry","No employees available")
   Return
end if
```

The new functions and concepts in this event/script include dw_emp_list.SetTransObject(SQLCA) and calling a function with a return code. The SetTransObject function is a PowerBuilder data access function, which connects the DataWindow control (and the associated DataWindow) to the client/server DBMS using the parameters specified in the SQLCA global control block (see "Logging on to the Server"). A SetTransObject call is required for each DataWindow prior to attempting to access data through the DataWindow.

Invoking a Function with a Return Code

Most external functions will be declared with some sort of success/failure indicator—a return code that is addressable by the calling routine. In order to access the information in the return code, you must declare a variable which matches the datatype of the declared return code variable, then invoke the function, placing the variable name at the beginning of the call as follows: ret_code = dw_emp_list.Retrieve(). This statement says, "Use the Retrieve function to populate the dw_emp_list DataWindow with rows. Value the ret_code field with a standard value showing success/failure of the call." After the Retrieve function is issued, the script may then evaluate the status of the mission by testing ret_code (see earlier). It is interesting to note that DataWindow return codes have little in common with the fast-becoming industry standard SQLCA.SQLCODEs (note that 0 denotes no rows returned).

Printing DataWindows

Our application requires a report (hard copy) against the special transactions table. You may write the report the old-fashioned (3GL) way with line counters and procedural logic to specify the totals, page breaks, and so on or you may—and most often, will—utilize the DataWindow technology, specifically the report painter features of the DataWindow technology to create professional reports. To create sophisticated reports with the DataWindow Report Painter, paint the necessary headers, footers, page numbers, and calculated fields throughout the report page (for control break processing, select the Rows, Create Group... option. This allows you to select one or more control break columns). For each control break, the report painter subdivides the page window into grouping sections, allowing you to place columns (including calculated fields) in group section headers and footers for subtotals. When you are finished with your DataWindow you may print the object directly from a running Windows application with the Print() function.

The Print function is very easy to specify. Simply code:

```
Print(dw_control_name)
```

inside the event/script designated for printing (typically a print command or picture button), and the entire contents of the DataWindow are routed to LPT1, or some designated Windows print queue.

Accessing Values within a DataWindow

One of the more popular GUI design techniques is to allow users to select (with a mouse) information displayed in a DataWindow by clicking on the row of choice, and having the clicked or double-clicked event, fire off some additional processing associated with the selected information. In other words, the application passes values from window to window, or window control to event/script. This is accomplished in PowerBuilder by using one of the twenty or so DataWindow data access functions. In our case, we utilize the GetClickedRow and GetItemNumber functions that follow.

```
real rownum
rownum = dw_emplist.GetClickedRow()
If rownum > 0 Then
    glb_soc_sec_no = dw_emplist.GetItemNumber(rownum, 2)
    Close(parent)
Else
    MessageBox("Warning","Must Select Employee First")
End If
```

GetClickedRow returns a numeric value equal to the relative row number within the DataWindow which most recently received a mouse click from the user:

```
rownum = dw_emplist.GetClickedRow()
```

This relative row number can then be used in a lookup within the row for a specific item (value). This is accomplished with the GetItem-Number function:

```
glb_soc_sec_no = dw_emplist.GetItemNumber(rownum, 2)
```

As shown, the previously obtained row number (rownum) identifies the row most recently clicked. From there GetItemNumber allows us to access a relative column number (from left to right) within the dw_emp_list DataWindow, and assign that value—in our case to a global variable: glb_soc_sec_no. Note that in our script we must test for a rownum of zero (0). This is because if the user is not terribly accurate with their mouse coordination they may click or double-click over the border of the DataWindow, thereby firing off the event/script containing GetClickedRow and GetItemNumber, but may not have selected a valid row within the DataWindow control. This causes a Power-Builder invalid DataWindow row error, and should be trapped with an application specific MessageBox as shown in Figure 6.26.

The Application Events for Employee Selection

At this point, we have populated dw_emp_list with employee names and allowed a user to select a given employee out of the DataWindow control using point-and-click (GetClickedRow/GetItemNumber). We have assigned the selected social security to a global variable, and now we close the window—Close(Parent)—and return to the menu selection option under File/Select. At this point in the process we may Open the benefits information on the selected employee, but how? The code for Open is stored in the File/Open clicked event/script in the m_main menu. This is not a trivial piece of code.

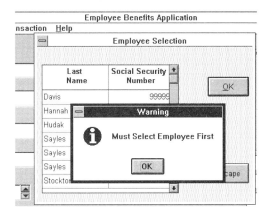

Figure 6.26   Message Box for 0 rows selected.

Our options in terms of invoking it are to physically copy the code into the File/Select clicked event/script, or somehow invoke the original File/Open clicked event/script. We choose the latter.

Triggering External Events

PowerBuilder supports a special function called: TriggerEvent, which allows you to name a particular event/script external to the current event/script and invoke it in a manner similar to that of a called function. The code to use TriggerEvent is follows. As you can see, it is not a difficult operation.

```
If glb_soc_sec_no > 0 Then
    w_main.sle_soc_sec_no.text = string(glb_soc_sec_no)
    m_file.m_open.TriggerEvent(Clicked!)
End If
```

The basic (annotated) logic flow follows.

1. If glb_soc_sec_no > 0 Then
1. If the w_emp_list window has returned a valid social security number . . .
2. w_main.sle_soc_sec_no.text = string(glb_soc_sec_no)
2. Value the social security number in w_main with the returned global value
3. m_file.m_open.TriggerEvent(Clicked!)
3. Execute (trigger) the clicked event/script defined for the File/Open option in the m_main menu.

Finishing the Application

Once we had worked out the specifics of the individual routines, we continued to build the application, one procedure at a time. We tested the application by running it, and by occasionally using the Debugger to determine problem areas (almost always involving event/script logic). Once we were satisfied with our efforts, we built an executable by generating the application, a simple matter of entering the Application Painter (Figure 6.27), clicking the CreateExe icon, and naming the application to build.

Finished PowerBuilder applications contain three basic components: .EXE files—compiled and linked executables; .PBD files—PowerBuilder dynamic libraries containing compiled, but not linked, executable code; and resource files—separate object files containing dynamically called graphic objects (such as .BMP, .ICO, and .RLE files, etc.). Because of the diverse nature of GUI applications, Power-Builder provides many ways to build and distribute an application, ranging from the simple to the complex.

The simplest method of building and executable is to link everything in the application into a .EXE file. This is what we did with our sample application, and is window driven (Figure 6.27). Other applications may be too large or too dynamic to ship as a single, statically linked .EXE, or they may contain programmatic and dynamic references to external resources (such as .BMP, .ICO, and .RLE graphics files). For these types of applications you would create .PBD libraries (PowerBuilder dynamic library files), populate these .PBD files with components of your application (compiled windows, menus, DataWindows, etc.), and generate your application referencing the .PBD files. These .PBD files will then have to be distributed with .EXE file. This same basic process is used with external resource files.

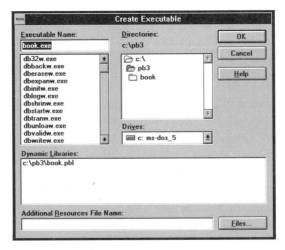

Figure 6.27   Application painter—generate .EXE window.

Distributing Your Application

After a successful build (application generation), you may distribute your application. In order for user to invoke a PowerBuilder application, they will need the .EXE file for the application, any .PBD files—if dynamically linked, and any additional resource files (such as .BMP, .ICO, .PTR, .RLE files), and the database deployment kit for the client/server database for which you have developed the application. There are no Powersoft runtime fees associated with distributing an application, but the user must have the necessary DBMS attachment modules supplied from Powersoft for connecting to the client/server database of choice.

The PowerBuilder Perspective

In this chapter we have only scratched the surface of this powerful product: its features, facilities, options, and operations. Powersoft has done a remarkable job with the tool, improving it dramatically with each new release, adding functions, painter facilities, script language options, and other productivity-enhancing elements. As far as 4GL, Windows-development packages go, PowerBuilder can be considered second to none. The DataWindow feature, consistent (point-and-click) graphical development procedures, database access, and administration facilities, as well as product integration has made PowerBuilder the darling of the C/S-OO-GUI industry. The product and company deserves all the attention it is receiving. The documentation and technical support are outstanding, the product is easy to install and migrate from version 2.0. And the company is being proactive about the distribution of its technology, as evidenced by its commitment to external consulting (the Powersoft Certification Program), the quality of its documentation, the commitment to technical support help, which we found to be excellent, and the overall attitude of the company.

Powersoft seems to be that rarity among modern corporations: a big company with a small company attitude. In other words, Powersoft is a company with enough resources to do things the right way (a big-company virtue), but still small enough to be concerned about customers opinions, and dynamic and flexible enough to address them (a small company's responsive attitude). It is our opinion that Powersoft and the PowerBuilder product will stand the test of time, withstand the challenge of the new products on the market, and survive and flourish well into the 21st century.

7

Visual Basic 3.0

Basic. Usually, that's as far as most people get. How can you take a product seriously if it has the word *basic* in the title? Basic has long been known and accepted as the easiest language to start with when learning computer programming. More important, Basic was (and still is) the only programming language that comes with the MS/DOS operating system right out of the box. Most of us had a brush with Basic in high school or college and, today, I suspect elementary-school students are as fluent in Basic as they are in English.

So there you have it. Here's a language that is widely known and understood. And yet, the further average programmers evolved, the further away most of us got from Basic. We developed skills in COBOL or C, FORTRAN, ADA, or even Assembler. Virtually anything but Basic. Why? Well, because it's *basic!* Somehow, by definition that must mean its power is somehow limited. Microsoft is here to tell you it's not. Basic is, in fact a very powerful and versatile language—one that is more than suitable to build a graphical development environment around.

Visual Basic is a graphical development environment for Microsoft Windows client/server applications. What does that mean? Well, you have all the tools required at your disposal to develop an application with a graphical user interface (GUI) front end to run under Microsoft Windows. Visual Basic provides an intuitive screen painter used to paint windows with a variety of controls (entry fields, check boxes, list boxes, push buttons, and so on). Each control has properties (characteristics such as background color and starting text). By painting a window and setting each control's properties, you can lay out the foundation for a single- or multiple-windowed GUI application. From here, it's just a matter of writing the code to tie all these controls and windows together, and that's where Basic comes in. With Microsoft handling the specifics of window-control display and action, that simple, easy to learn, and easy to use language—Basic—becomes a versatile, powerful script language more than adequate to control the flow of your application. And, in the event you are creative enough to dream up an application which needs more power than Basic has to offer, VB provides access to dynamic link library (DLLs) functions written in such languages as C, C++, and COBOL as well as access to object linking and embedding (OLE) calls, and dynamic data exchange (DDE) calls. All this and more—if you can get past the word *basic* in the title.

Database Access and Network Considerations

It is fair to say the success of a GUI development tool depends on many things, including ease of use, programming language versatility, speed and optimization of the finished executable. However, while the GUI front end is more than half of your finished product, back-end database access is critical to a client/server application's success.

Microsoft, by publishing their database interface specifications and supporting third-party vendors, has succeeded in creating an impressive list of relational database support. With the aid of middle-ware packages from a variety of vendors such as Pioneer Software and Novelle, Visual Basic can communicate with virtually any database on the market, including Oracle, Sybase, Ingres, Database Manager, and many others. Furthermore, with version 3.0, Microsoft included the Microsoft Access Database Engine providing for the creation and use of local databases in Access, Paradox, or DBASEx formats.

As if this weren't enough, Microsoft developed open database connectivity (ODBC). ODBC is a clearly documented structure that allows for click-in support for external database management systems that conform to the ODBC standard. ODBC allows the developer to select an ODBC driver during or after install time, making database access a snap. Visual Basic is distributed with the drivers for SQLServer and Oracle connectivity. However, database vendors are quickly embracing the ODBC standard and new drivers, for a wide variety of databases are imminent.

When discussing database interfaces, the subject of network access must be addressed as well. Third-party drivers are available to support a wide variety of network protocols including TCP/IP, NET BIOS, and APPC/LU6.2, providing access to LAN-based databases, wide-area network access, and UNIX solutions. The plethora of drivers available makes database access and network protocol choice a decision based more on requirements than availability.

For the purposes of our discussion, our application will be written in Microsoft Visual Basic 3.0, Professional Edition, running under Microsoft Windows 3.1, interfacing through ODBC to Microsoft SQLServer Version 4.20 database located on an IBM LAN Server 2.0 server.

Requirements

Visual Basic Version 3.0 comes in two flavors—Standard Edition and Professional Edition (Figure 7.1). The standard edition contains all the tools necessary to develop Windows based GUI applications. The professional edition includes 18 additional controls, the help compiler, ODBC access, the Access Database Engine, Crystal Reports, and the documentation required to create your own custom controls. The difference in price is often between two and three hundred dollars. The difference in versatility is incalculable.

Visual Basic requires DOS version 3.1 or higher and Microsoft Windows 3.0 or better—running in either standard or enhanced mode—on an Intel 80286 or better processor, with at least one megabyte of memory. A hard drive is required, as Windows will consume approximately nine megabytes and Visual Basic up to another 40 megabytes. The client machine will also require the IBM LAN Server 2.0 DOS/Windows client and the Microsoft SQLServer client applications.

The server machine will require OS/2. Microsoft recommends OS/2 version 1.3, and bundles a version of the operating system with its SQLServer product. Developed as a 16-bit application, SQLServer can run under OS/2 version 2.x, since 2.x can support 16- as well as 32-bit software. However, Microsoft claims OS/2 2.0 is still bug riddled and unstable. Furthermore, Microsoft claims performance is actually better under OS/2 1.3. Our application was developed on a 486 server running at 33 MHz with 16 meg of ram running OS/2 2.1. We did not experience any problems or degradation of performance.

Since dissolving their partnership with IBM and OS/2, Microsoft has reworked their vision of the future. With the introduction of the

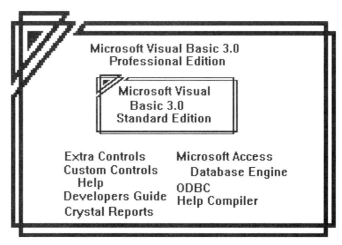

Figure 7.1   Standard edition versus professional edition.

next generation of Windows—called Windows NT, Microsoft's first 32-bit operating system—Microsoft intends to abandon OS/2 altogether and support only Windows products. The next generation of Microsoft SQLServer will run only under Windows NT.

To support OS/2 and SQLServer, a server with a 386 CPU or better and at least eight megabytes of memory is required. OS/2 requires between 18 and 30 megabytes of disk space with SQLServer software requiring another five megabytes and data space chewing up a minimum of 15 megabytes more. IBM LAN Server and other support software require additional resources.

Installation

Although the documentation is a little hard to follow, installing SQLServer on the LAN Database Server is relatively simple. Run the SETUP program to install SQLServer (Figure 7.2). Choose a LAN installation and the rest will happen on its own. The SQLServer installation guide includes a checklist of information for first-time installations. Aside from the obvious required information (install drive, amount of memory available, do you want to modify config.sys, etc.), you will also need to choose a sort order and specify the amount of disk space to reserve for the master database device. The master database is responsible for controlling and keeping track of user databases and SQLServer administration information. Minimum installation is 15 MB. Depending on the number of database objects and users, you may have to increase this amount.

The sort order chosen will effect how data is stored and retrieved in SQL queries. More important, sort order cannot be changed with-

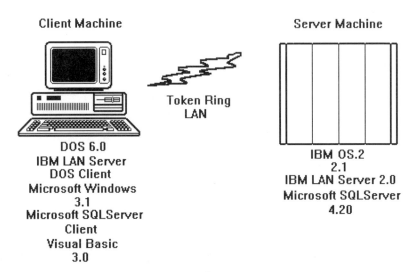

Client Machine

DOS 6.0
IBM LAN Server
DOS Client
Microsoft Windows
3.1
Microsoft SQLServer
Client
Visual Basic
3.0

Token Ring
LAN

Server Machine

IBM OS.2
2.1
IBM LAN Server 2.0
Microsoft SQLServer
4.20

Figure 7.2   Visual Basic requirements.

out reinstalling SQLServer. The choices available are all described in appendix A of the installation guide.

Installation of Visual Basic on the client machine is very straightforward. Simply execute the SETUP program on the install disk. SETUP will prompt you for all required information, and copy all system files to their proper location. The autoexec.bat file is automatically updated and a Visual Basic group is automatically created under Windows. Once the basic VB install procedure finishes installing Visual Basic, it will ask if you want ODBC installed. To use ODBC, simply choose the driver listed for SQLServer.

Once the Visual Basic install is complete, you need to install the SQLServer client software. Executing the SETUP program from a DOS prompt will load all required software and modify your autoexec.bat file to load the terminate-and-stay-resident DBNMPIPE executable at startup (Figure 7.3). This will allow the Windows client to communicate with the database server.

The Visual Basic Windows Group (Figure 7.4)

Microsoft Visual Basic. This icon represents the Visual Basic Workbench. Most of your work will be done here, including screen painting, coding, menu creation, testing, and debugging.

Read me. This icon will display the read.me file in the windows file viewer. Do not underestimate the importance of the read.me file. This file contains tips, corrections, and useful information that never made it into the product documentation at release time.

Visual Basic Help. The online help for Visual Basic is extensive. The VB help facility can be accessed via this icon or by pressing F1 at any time with the VB workbench. In fact, by highlighting an object in VB

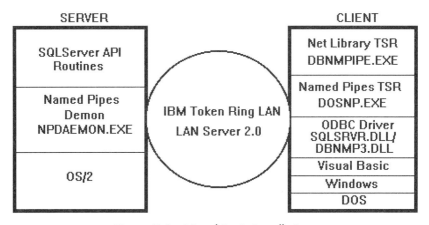

Figure 7.3   Visual Basic installation.

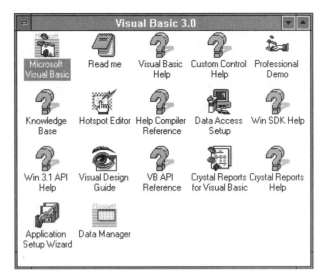

Figure 7.4   Visual Basic Windows group.

and pressing F1, the help facility figures out which help library (VB Help, Custom Control Help, WIN SDK Help, etc.) to bring up and will give you an answer accordingly. The search button is very useful for looking up the specifics of a particular topic or for scanning available information.

Custom Control Help. Visual Basic version 3.0 includes 19 custom controls. Add-ons to the original product, these custom controls were designed by third-party vendors and compiled as an enhancement to the original product. The custom control help facility provides comprehensive help with these custom controls in the same depth and format as standard VB help.

Professional Demo. This icon runs a program to demonstrate or provide overview information on all of the extra features provided with VB 3.0 Professional Edition. Many of the custom controls are demonstrated here to give you a better idea of what the custom controls can do. An overview of such concepts as ODBC and the help compiler are also available.

Knowledge Base. This icon represents a new level of customer support. Microsoft has compiled a selection of articles and information about Visual Basic. Everything from programming tips to third-party vendor support information is available online. Knowledge Base can be an exceedingly helpful and useful tool when you need some help or can't figure out how to do something.

Hot Spot Editor. A hot spot is an area on a graphical image that is associated with an action. For example, you may wish to write an application that displays a map of the United States. When an area of the country is clicked on, the application might put up a window with statistics pertinent to that area of the country. The Hot Spot Editor is used to place hot spots on an image and create the associations required for code or macros.

Help Compiler Reference. This icon represents help on the Help Compiler. The Help Compiler allows you to create context-sensitive help that has the same format and style as all the help available in Visual Basic. This can add a high degree of professionalism and user friendliness to your application.

Data Access Setup. This icon runs ODBC setup routine used to install an ODBC (online database connectivity) driver. You will need this icon if you choose to use a different database with Visual Basic, which is supported by ODBC.

WIN SDK Help. Visual Basic has an interface available to DLL functions. By using this interface, you can write code to talk directly to Windows 3.1. The Windows System Developers Kit (SDK) Help library provides information about how to work directly with Microsoft Windows API functions for more complicated programming functions.

WIN 3.1 API Help. This help guide gives more detailed information on the Windows 3.1 Application Program Interface (API). Declares, header files, and function information are available and can be copied directly into your VB application.

Visual Design Guide. One of the advantages a GUI environment offers is the ability to develop applications with an interface that is intuitive and looks, acts, and smells virtually the same as the interface on your word processor, spreadsheet, and database. This guide is required reading for Windows developers. It describes, in detail, how to create an application under Windows 3.1 that subscribes to the most common interfaces' standards. By subscribing to this standard, you give your application the same look and feel as any other application running under Windows.

VB API Reference. This reference provides low-level API information on all documented Visual Basic APIs. This information is particularly useful when you are writing your own .VBX controls or attempting to accomplish something unusual in Visual Basic.

Crystal Reports for Visual Basic. Visual Basic 3.0 comes with the Crystal Reports Report Painter and a Crystal Reports Custom Control (.VBX). The utility allows you to create slick, professional reports graphically. Crystal Reports is both easy to use and very sophisticated. Furthermore, once you've created a report template, you can use the Custom Control to tie the report to your application.

Crystal Reports Help. This icon gives online help for Crystal Reports. Help can also be activated directly from Crystal Reports with the F1 Key.

Application Setup Wizard. After writing an application, the developer must begin to be concerned with distribution. Writing a setup or install program, and creating distribution diskettes used to be a considerable assignment. Setup Wizard takes some of the mystery and work out of this process. Setup Wizard will create a setup program, create diskette layouts, and generate distribution diskettes. Pretty slick, huh?

Microsoft SQLServer—Database Creation

SQLServer is one of the most robust client/server databases on the market today. SQLServer supports all the major database features including data locking on all levels, two-phased commits, and very large data storage. Built to run on an OS/2 database server, SQLServer is the database of choice when building a large client/server application. The only downside to SQLServer is that it does not allow for localized development and testing.

First, since SQLServer runs only under OS/2 and Visual Basic runs under Windows, it should be apparent that the two cannot coexist on the same machine. Even with OS/2 2.1, VB cannot communicate with SQLServer on the same machine. As a result, application-development tasks are forced into a LAN environment from the start.

Second, although it gets high marks for stability, SQLServer does not make database, table, and index creation an easy task. SQLServer comes with several tools to help administer databases but none of them are easy to use or very straightforward. As a result, most shops have turned the administration of SQLServer over to the same database administrators who currently manage the shops' mainframe DB2 databases.

The most basic way to interact with SQLServer is through the interactive SQL utility (ISQL). ISQL gives you a command-line interface to SQLServer. With ISQL you can perform all functions including database, table, and index creation all the way through to SQLServer shutdown. We used the ISQL interface until we discovered the SQL Administrator for Windows.

Database Administration under SQLServer

SQL Administrator is a graphical tool that allows you to perform most administrative functions. There are buttons that allow you to manage connections, devices, database users, remote servers, remote users, database backup and recovery, and configuration and performance. SQL Administrator also allows you to execute queries against a database, including running the SQL necessary to create database objects.

When SQLServer is installed, it comes with a master database and a system administrator login id. To accomplish data-administration tasks, you need to login to SQLServer using the system administrator login id and attach to the master database.

The first task to be accomplished under SQLServer was to create a device. A device is a file that holds databases, transaction logs, and backups. Before a database can be created, a device must be created on which to store the database. A single device can be used to store multiple databases. Typically, one device will be created for one or more databases and another will be created to hold the database logs. These devices will be in different physical locations (this insures that if the database device fails, the logs are not lost as well).

By choosing Manage from the menu bar, and choosing Device and Create, we were able to get the create device window. We gave our device a logical name, a physical name, and a size of five megabytes (The minimum for a database is 2 MB). With a device in place, we can move on to creating a database.

Database creation under SQLServer requires an accurate forecast of the amount of disk space the database will require. When you create a database, you must tell SQLServer how much space the database will consume. If you overestimate this number, the disk space will be wasted and cannot be easily reclaimed. If you underestimate this number, the database can be expanded to another device. This expansion can lead to performance problems over time.

By choosing the Manage option from the main menu bar, and choosing Database and Create Database, you will get the Create Database Window. Here you can enter the database name and size. You can also assign the database to a device, and assign the database log to another device. The database name we chose was bk_ebadb (Book—Employee Benefit Application Database). We made this database two megabytes in size with a one megabyte log.

With a database in place, we thought we were ready to create tables. We were wrong. The next task, which must be performed, is managing users. Managing users can be split into two logical categories. First, each user must have a login user id and password registered with SQLServer. This give the user access to SQLServer. Next, each user must be granted access rights to specific databases. Without these rights, a user can get into SQLServer but cannot access any data.

To add a user (instead of using the system administrator's login id) we chose to manage users and choose the Add Login option. Using the System Login window, We entered a login ID (sdkarlen) and a password. We also assigned the default database to bk_ebadb.

Now that we created an active user ID, we needed to give that ID access rights to the bk_ebadb database. This is a two-step process.

First, we had to create a group. A group is a management device that allows you to assign common access rights to all users who are part of the group. To create a group, choose the database box to get the Database Management Window. From there, we chose the bk_ebadb database. To create the group for that database, we chose Manage from the main menu and users, Users/Groups from the sub menu. We gave the group a name and put our user id in the group.

Next, we had to assign permissions to the group. To do this, we got the Command Permissions Window by choosing Permissions from the Manage/Users menu. We gave our group all permissions to the bk_ebadb database.

Database Object Creation under Visual Data

By now, we have created a database and a user ID that has appropriate access rights to that database. The next task was to create the tables and indexes to meet the application's needs. The only way to do this through SQL Administrator was to write SQL queries and execute them through the query facility. We were in the middle of this task when we came across Visual Data.

Visual Data is a sample application that comes with Visual Basic 3.0 (Figure 7.5). This application will allow you to create database objects using either the Access Database Engine included with VB or ODBC, which gets you to SQLServer or Oracle. We compiled the application into an executable and used it to create all our database objects.

Creating and managing objects is very straightforward in Visual Data. Clicking on New in the tables window gives you a window, which allows you to create tables and indexes in your database. Once the tables are created, data can be inserted and viewed by simply double-clicking on the table name. Our only complaint about Visual Data was that it should allow you to generate standard DDL for a table after it was created. This way, the DDL could be saved and, if the table had to be modified or restored, the DDL could be used to speed those modifications. The good news is, you are given all the source code for the Visual Data application. A few modifications and Visual Data can have this feature, too.

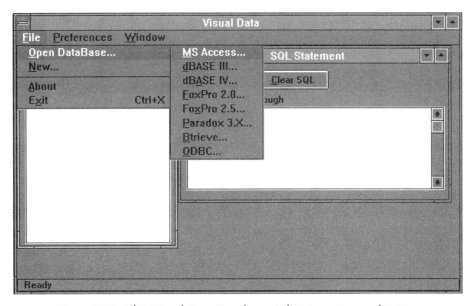

Figure 7.5   *The Visual Data Database Administration application.*

Creating the EBA Application

Having created the tables needed for this application, our next step was to paint the necessary windows and develop the code around them. All of this work will be done within the Visual Basic icon from Windows. Before we jump into the Visual Basic Development Environment, let's talk a little about how development is done within Visual Basic.

An Overview of Visual Basic Development

Development of a user-interface application in any language is a combination of presenting screens or windows and writing code to respond to user interaction with these screens. The central element in GUI application development is the control. A *control* encapsulates a specific set of data elements and coded procedures together into an object. The primary control in Visual Basic is the screen itself—called a *form.*

A *form* is the equivalent of a window frame (Figure 7.6). The form control has specific characteristics associated with it. A form can have a system menu, minimize button, and/or maximize button. When the form is first displayed, it will open to a set position on the screen occupying a specified area. All of these options for a form (or any control) are called *properties.*

Properties are a list of the options a control has available and how they are first set. All of a control's properties are set initially during application coding and many of a control's properties can be mod-

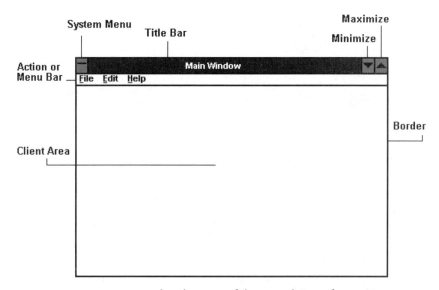

Figure 7.6   The elements of the Visual Basic form.

ified programmatically during execution. Along with predefined properties, a control has predefined methods.

A *method* is hard-coded procedure which is part of the control. A method procedure is used to perform some kind of predefined action on the control. For example, every form has a show method. The show method will cause the form to become visible and active to the user. The application developer does not have to code these methods; they are precoded subroutines embedded in the control and available for use.

Along with predefined methods, each control has a series of predefined events. An *event* is an action to which the control is capable of responding. An action might be the user clicking on a control. An action could also be input or stimulus from an outside source. For example, an event might be an OLE link established by another executable (suffice it to say the stimulus for an event is not necessarily an action taken by the user).

Each predefined event has a predefined default response (usually ignoring the stimulus). Coding in Visual Basic is a matter of writing procedural code to respond to an event in a manner specific to your application. In other words, Visual Basic provides you with the controls themselves. Each control knows how to display and hide itself, and so on. These methods are provided. Each control also comes with a set of hooks or events. By writing application code for the events you wish to respond to, you create an application. You can ignore the events to which you do not choose to respond. All you have to do is place the controls on the screen where you want them and code how the application should respond to user interaction with those controls. This is called *event-driven application development*. If this entire concept is not clear, stay tuned. We are going to put these concepts into practice soon enough.

Now that we have some understanding of controls, methods, and events, let's put all of this together into some kind of plan for application development.

In Visual Basic, all development is managed and coordinated by project (Figure 7.7). A *project* is a file (.MAK extension) that contains a reference to all the files required to produce an executable (.EXE). If a single application has multiple executables, it will have multiple projects—one .MAK for each .EXE. The files that make up an application fall into one of the following categories: form, control, or module.

Project File Example (VBBOOK.MAK):

```
EBAFORM1.FRM
C:\OS2\MDOS\WINOS2\SYSTEM\GRID.VBX
C:\OS2\MDOS\WINOS2\SYSTEM\OLECLIEN.VBX
C:\OS2\MDOS\WINOS2\SYSTEM\ANIBUTON.VBX
C:\OS2\MDOS\WINOS2\SYSTEM\CMDIALOG.VBX
C:\OS2\MDOS\WINOS2\SYSTEM\GAUGE.VBX
C:\OS2\MDOS\WINOS2\SYSTEM\GRAPH.VBX
C:\OS2\MDOS\WINOS2\SYSTEM\KEYSTAT.VBX
C:\OS2\MDOS\WINOS2\SYSTEM\MSCOMM.VBX
C:\OS2\MDOS\WINOS2\SYSTEM\MSMASKED.VBX
C:\OS2\MDOS\WINOS2\SYSTEM\PICCLIP.VBX
C:\OS2\MDOS\WINOS2\SYSTEM\SPIN.VBX
C:\OS2\MDOS\WINOS2\SYSTEM\THREED.VBX
EBAFORM2.FRM
EBAFORM3.FRM
ProjWinSize=152,402,248,215
ProjWinShow=2
```

The project file listed above describes all of the elements required to create an executable. The primary form (EBAFORM1.FRM), the

Figure 7.7   The Visual Basic Project window.

controls available to the executable (.VBX files), the other forms and modules (.BAS) in this executable and any project level defaults are all listed here. This project file is entirely generated and maintained by Visual Basic.

Form Files (.FRM)

The primary object in a project is the form or forms the executable will display. The information defining each form is stored in an .FRM file. The .FRM file contains the properties and event code for a particular window. It also contains the properties and event code for each control living within the form. For each control on the form, the type of control, user-defined name, controls initial property settings, and the code written for any event to which the programmer chooses to respond are stored in the .FRM file. Only programmer-modified properties are listed for each control, and only code the programmer wrote to respond to specific events is stored here. The control itself knows what its default properties are and what its default actions are in response to events. There is no need to duplicate that information in the .FRM file.

Forms versus MDI Forms

Most of the forms in your application will be standard forms. Visual Basic has a control called *MDI* (multiple document interface) *Forms.* Each project can have only one MDI form. An MDI form can have multiple standard forms, which act as children to the parent MDI form. The MDI form is a desktop that provides workspace for the children forms. All children forms are confined to the parent MDI form's space. MDI forms are used to provide a centralized menu or toolbar to the user. The menu or toolbar causes action-specific forms to open within the MDI. For example, an MDI form may have a new menu pick. Choosing this menu option may cause a form to open to allow for entry of new text. In MDI fashion, with one form open, the user can choose the new menu pick again and open a second occurrence.

All forms in an MDI application do not have to be children to the MDI form. The use of MDI forms can allow for the creation of some very slick applications.

```
Sub mnAboutEBAFORM1_Click ()
    Dim szMsg As String * 75
    Dim szTitle as String * 35
    Dim iType As Integer
    Dim iResponse As Integer
    szMsg = "      Employee Benefit Application" + Chr(10) + "
Written By Steven D. Karlen"
    szTitle = "About Employee Benefit Application"
    iType = MB_OK + MBICONINFORMATION + MB_APPLMODAL
```

```
    iResponse = MsgBox(szMsg, iType, szTitle)
End Sub
```

In this excerpt from a form file (.FRM), you can see the definition for any event the programmer wrote code to respond to. That code is stored here. Notice the name for the subprocedure. The first part of the name (mnAboutEBAFORM1) is the name of the screen control to which this code is attached. After the underscore (_) is the name of the event to which this code will respond. Inside the Sub/End Sub delimiters are the data element definitions and the code written to respond to the "CLICK" event for the mnAboutEBAFORM1 control. This file is created and maintained by Visual Basic.

Module Files (.BAS)

A *module file* is a file containing Visual Basic subroutines (procedures) that are common to the executable. These are programmer-written routines used to perform such common tasks as file I/O, variable manipulation, and calculation and field editing. There are no standard procedures provided in a module file.

Function versus Sub

There are two kinds of procedures a programmer can write in Visual Basic—sub and function. The difference between these two kinds of procedures is purely a matter of semantics. A *sub* procedure does not have a return value. Sub procedures are called by using their procedure names with optional parameters being passed in.

```
Call EditNumeric(vEntryFieldValue, usResponse)
```

where EditNumeric is defined as follows

```
Sub EditNumeric (vEntryFieldValue As Variant, usResponse As Integer)
    If IsNumeric (vEntryFieldValue) Then
        usResponse = 1
    Else
        usResponse = 0
    End If

End Sub
```

In the preceding example, the function EditNumeric will make the variable usResponse a 1 if the entry field is numeric or a 0 if it is not.

A *function* procedure is a procedure that has a return value. The function procedure is called by making a variable equal to its response passing parameters where required.

```
usResponse = EditNumeric2(vEntryFieldValue)
```

Where the Function EditNumeric2 is defined as follows:

```
Function EditNumeric2 (vEntryFieldValue As Variant) As Integer

    If IsNumeric(vEntryFieldValue) Then
            EditNumeric2 = 1
    Else
            EditNumeric2 = 0
    End If

End Function
```

In the above example, the function EditNumeric2 is called with the entry field passed as a parameter. The function will return a response in an integer field. Notice the function code itself. Upon making the determination that the entry field is numeric, the function sets the NAME of the FUNCTION to 1. This is how the return value is set.

General Objects

Both forms and modules contain a "(general)" object. The *general object* is used to declare variables and code procedures that will be accessed globally (Figure 7.8). Global variables are made in the definitions procedure. Any variables defined and procedures coded in the general object of a form are global across that form only. Any variables defined and procedures coded in the general object of a module are global across the project.

Control Files (.VBX)

Visual Basic Standard Edition provides 19 standard controls incorporated into the work environment (Figure 7.9). One of the enhance-

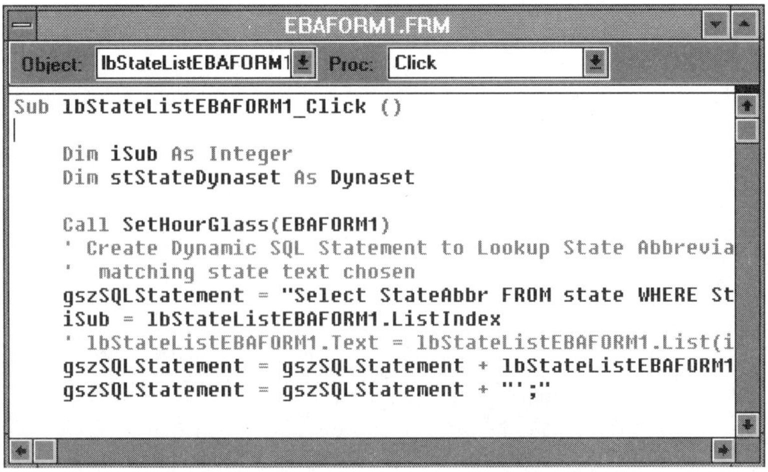

Figure 7.8   The Visual Basic code window.

Figure 7.9   Visual Basic extended controls and their corresponding VBX files.

ments provided with the Professional Edition is the addition of 19 custom controls. These additional controls were written by third-party vendors. The code required to access and use any control is stored in a .VBX file. You will notice that when you open a new project, the tool box contains all 38 controls. You will also notice a new project causes several .VBX files to be loaded into your project automatically. If you remove a .VBX file from your project, you will notice the icons for any controls that .VBX file supports will also disappear from the toolbox. You cannot remove a .VBX file from your project after you have used that control in your application. Be aware that any custom controls you choose to use, whether provided by the professional edition, third-party, vendor or written by you—the .VBX file supporting those controls must be included in your project.

The Components of a Visual Basic Application

An executable in Visual Basic is made up of three basic objects (Figure 7.10): forms (.FRM files), containing event specific and form specific variable definitions and code; modules (.BAS), contain global variable definitions and global sub and function procedures; and control (.VBX) files, containing the object code necessary to support one or many extended controls. A project (.MAK) file is used to keep track of project-level default overrides and information pointing to all .FRM, .BAS, and .VBX files required to build an executable.

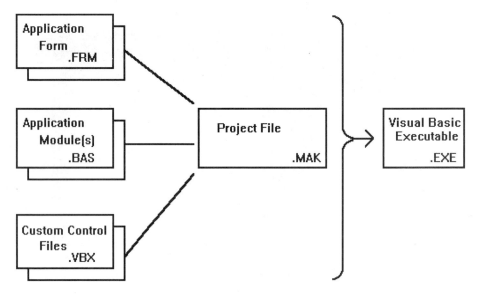

Figure 7.10   The elements of a Visual Basic Executable.

The Visual Basic Workbench

The Visual Basic Workbench is broken into five distinct parts (Figure 7.11): the VB menu bar, tool bar, project window, properties window, and a blank form. Before discussing the specifics of how we used these tools to build our application, let's talk about what each of these tools is and how they're used.

Menu Bar

The Visual Basic menu bar can be moved around the screen, and contains all of the buttons and menus required to perform all administrative tasks (Figure 7.12). Everything from creating to saving, from debugging to running, from workbench attributes to project attributes—the menu bar controls these functions.

There are two active sections on the menu bar. The top section contains pull-down menus to control the file, edit, view, run, debug, options, window, and help selections. Underneath the pull-down menus, there is a line of icons. Each of these icons perform tasks which the programmer is likely to need to access frequently. Each of these tasks would usually require several mouse strokes. For example, to open an existing project, the user has to click on the file menu and click on open project. Instead, the user could just click on the quick-access icon (an open folder with an arrow over it) and accomplish the same task. These quick-access icons can make it much easier to accomplish many of the repetitive tasks you will have to do.

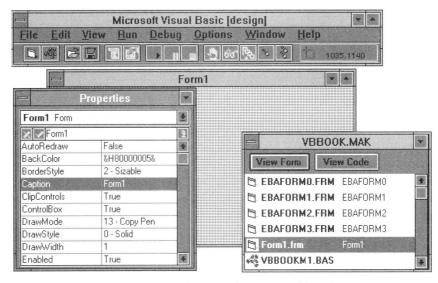

Figure 7.11   The Visual Basic Workbench.

Next to the quick-access icons are the debugging icons. These three icons, which look like keys on a tape recorder, are used to run, pause, and stop your application. The next group of icons is used to set break points, view or variables, show active call structure, and execute either one statement or one procedure during debug.

The maximize button on the toolbar will expand to cover the width of the screen. The minimize button on the tool bar will minimize all of the windows in Visual Basic, including the menu bar.

Tool Box

The *tool box* is a movable window usually placed on the left side of the screen (Figure 7.13). The tool box contains an icon for each control available in your Visual Basic session. The icons shown depend on the extended controls you have available. Professional Edition comes with 18 additional custom controls that the Standard Edition does not have. Furthermore, you can purchase extended controls

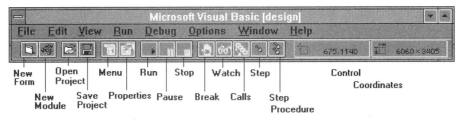

Figure 7.12   The Visual Basic Menu Bar.

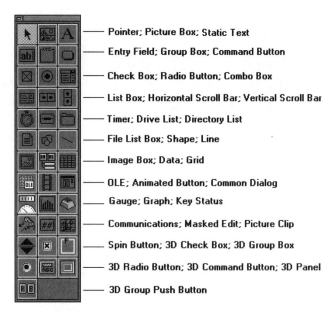

Figure 7.13 The Visual Basic tool box.

from third-party vendors or write them yourself in any programming language that can produce a Windows DLL (a custom control is actually nothing more than a Windows DLL with APIs conforming to the Visual Basic programming model).

Having .VBX files installed on your machine does not make them available to Visual Basic. You must include the .VBX file in your project in order to have access to the icon(s) for those custom controls in your tool box. The arrow icon in the upper left of the tool box is standard. It is used for pointing, marking, and moving controls on the screen. The next 19 controls are part of the standard edition. Any remaining icons are the result of custom controls. Pointing at an icon in the tool box and clicking with the right mouse button turns your mouse pointer into a pointer for that control. You can then move your mouse pointer to the form, and place the control on the form where you would like it. The size and position depend on how you draw the control. Choose a starting position, left click, and drag to enlarge a box. The size of the box dictates the size of the control.

Project Window

The project window usually appears somewhere on the right side of the desktop (Figure 7.14). It can be moved or minimized. The project window contains a list of all the files contained in the currently active project. Most of the files listed here are .VBX files representing custom controls. The other files are the various forms in your project and the module files (if any).

Figure 7.14   The Visual Basic project window.

Note the icon next to the filename. This icon can be useful, for example, to tell whether forms are standard, MDI, or MDI children. To work with a particular form or module, double-click on the object in the project window, and the form or module will come up on the screen. You can also select the form or module with a single click and select view form or code (if you select a module, the view form button is deactivated).

You can have multiple objects (several forms or a form and a module, for example) open on the desktop at once. While it is possible to close a form or module on the desktop, remember—closing it does not save or update its contents, it merely removes it from view. Forms and modules can be saved or updated from the file menu either by saving a particular file or by saving the project (saving the project saves all forms and modules to disk and saves the project file).

Form

When starting a new project, you usually get a blank generic form in the center of your desktop called FORM1 (Figure 7.15). A form is, in itself, just another control. It is a special control in that it holds other controls. However, it still acts like any other control in that it has properties and code. To get a new form, choose the new form or new MDI form option off the file menu. Double-clicking on the white space of a form brings you into the code window for that form. Single-clicking on a form's white space and pressing F4 will make the property window show properties for the form.

Properties Window

The *properties window* shows the available properties for the currently active control (Figure 7.16). The properties shown in this win-

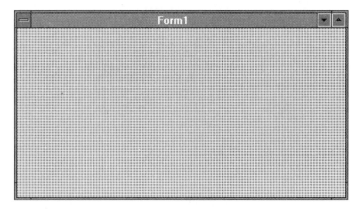

Figure 7.15   The Visual Basic form.

dow will change to show the properties of the control with which you are working. The properties window can be closed, moved, or minimized. To bring the properties window into the foreground, choose properties from the window menu option or press F4 after making a control active (single-clicking on it).

To modify the contents of a specific property, simply click on the property with your mouse. You will notice the property will become the active property listed in the entry field next to the X push button and check push button. To change the assignment of a property, you can enter this entry field and overtype the contents with the new data. For example, to change the caption property of a static text field (label), you can simply overtype the new text in the entry field.

To view or change the properties of another control, choose the control you want to work with from the drop-down listbox located at the top of the properties window. This can be much faster than finding your way back to the form and single-clicking on another control.

In many cases, the options available for a specific property are limited. For example, the autosize property of a static text field can be

Properties	
EBAFORM1 Form	
X ✓ Employee Benefit Application	
AutoRedraw	False
BackColor	&H80000005&
BorderStyle	3 - Fixed Double
Caption	Employee Benefit Ap
ClipControls	True
ControlBox	True
DrawMode	13 - Copy Pen
DrawStyle	0 - Solid
DrawWidth	1
Enabled	True

Figure 7.16   The Visual Basic property window.

either *true* or *false*. By double-clicking on the property, you will notice the property changes from *true* to *false* and back again. This can save some time and keystrokes.

Other Visual Basic Tasks

Menu design. Menus under Visual Basic are treated as special controls. To add menus to a form, you need to go into the menu-design facility. To do this, make sure a form is the active control and use the window pull-down menu to go into menu design (or use CTRL + M). The menu-design facility will allow you to design any menu structure you want for that form. More on this later.

Color palette. One of the strong reasons for going GUI is the use of color in an application. Use of color is not for aesthetics only (Figure 7.17). Color can be used to distinguish between different field attributes, to compare or contrast data, or to convey different levels of severity (the Visual Design guide has four screens on color use alone). If you can't work with the 256 colors (the same 256 colors as the Windows color palette), you can always create your own custom colors.

Environment Options

On the menu bar there is an Options pull-down menu. There you will find two very useful important menu options. The first is environment options (Figure 7.18). Environment options contains the Visual Basic workbench defaults. For example, when you are writing Visual Basic code, you will find the code changes to different colors after you type it. All of these colors mean something, and the color choices can be made here.

More important than colors and aesthetics, there are two items on this pull-down: syntax checking and require variable declaration. *Syntax checking* has to do with whether Visual Basic checks the syntax of every line of code you create as you create it. Obviously, Visual Basic will check the syntax when you try to run your application or make an executable. You may find that having Visual Basic check every line of code you type as you type it will slow you down. For example, you may start typing an IF statement and suddenly forget the name of the variable you were going to query. You start to page up

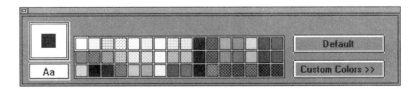

Figure 7.17   The Visual Basic color palette.

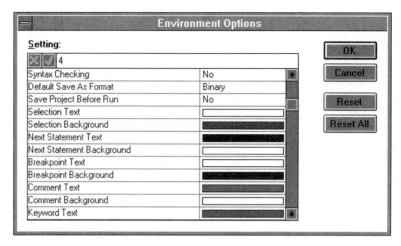

Figure 7.18 Visual Basic environment options.

in the code to find the name of the variable and Visual Basic beeps and gives you an error message box telling you your IF statement is incomplete. If this begins to happen to you often, you may wish to turn line syntax checking off in the editor by modifying this option.

Require variable declaration has to do with whether you are forced to code a DIM statement for every variable you are going to use in a program. If require variable selection is set to no, Visual Basic will assume that if you did not code a DIM statement, it can create the variable with a VARIANT data type for you to save the syntax error. How you set this option is a personal decision. Coming from a background in programming languages with strong type checking, it worries me to have the compiler generate variables with a default variable type. We always have this option set to yes. Consider the setting of this option before you begin to code as it will be difficult to enforce if you decide to change direction midstream.

Project Options

Also under the Options pull-down menu on the menu bar is a project level option (Figure 7.19). The items listed on this menu option effect only the current project.

There are only three attributes to be managed here. The first is *Command-Line Argument.* This option allows you to feed specific command-line arguments into debug executions. The second attribute is one you will have to set. It determines which form in your application will be executed at application startup. As an alternative, you can execute the SubMain procedure, which you can code to do application setup and then determine which form to run at startup. The last attribute, *Help File,* allows you to choose a help file to asso-

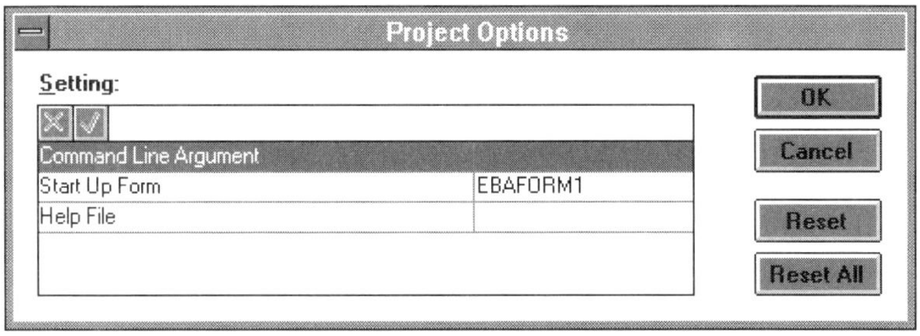

Figure 7.19   Visual Basic project options.

ciate with your application. This would be a help file you created to provide application-specific help.

Coding Standards

Of all the documentation we've read about Visual Basic (or any other programming language for that matter) we've never read any suggestions as to programming style. As you will be looking at large portions of our code, we thought we would take a minute to discuss some ideas on programming style with Visual Basic.

Most seasoned programmers will try to apply some kind of standard to their coding. Some thread of commonality in the way they name variables and procedures, organize code, indent code, and so on. We have no intention of being pedantic and suggesting that you think about all these issues before you begin to code Visual Basic. However, we would like to suggest a few ideas on naming standards for variables within VB code.

It is important to make sure every variable name in VB is unique (as it is in any other language). It is also important, in a somewhat object-oriented approach to programming, that you do what you can to identify what type of variable each is, and where (what module or form) it came from. Along these lines, the naming standard we use is a bastardization of Hungarian Notation, which allows us to better keep track of what our variables are and where they came from.

A variable name always begins with a prefix. The prefix is always in lower case and corresponds to the variables type.

```
Some of the more common variables and controls used in our code are:
Data Variables:       Prefix:
      Integer           i
      Long              l
      Single            s
      Double            d
      Currency          c
      String            sz
```

```
        Variant                  v
        Structure                st

Controls:            Prefix:
        Label                    st
        Frame                    gb
        Check Box                cb
        Combo Box/               lb
        List Box
        Text Box                 ef
        Command Button           pb
        Option Button            rb
```

At the end of each variable name, we put, in upper case, some identifier showing the origin of the variable name. For example, an entry field defined in FORMABC to collect social security numbers, would be named efSocialSecNumFORMABC. Depending upon how verbose you get with the central part of a variable name, this could lead to some long variable names. We think that you will find that being able to determine what a variable is, what type it is, and where it came from will make coding and maintenance of your VB code a much easier task. The standard listed here is not etched in stone. If this standard doesn't work for you, develop your own. More important, we encourage you to consider some type of standard before you begin coding.

Where to Begin?

Well, the stage is set. We know how Visual Basic works and what it can produce. We've examined the tools at our disposal and we have a general idea of what needs to be done. All of our work (unless otherwise specified) will be done within the Visual Basic workbench. Let's get started.

First things first. We know we will only have one executable. One executable means one project. Click on the file pull-down menu and use the save as option to save the default project to a particular subdirectory and specific name. Once the project file is saved, all other files you create (forms and modules) will automatically be saved to the same place. Doing this up front eliminates the worry about where files will be stored, or keeping track of your work later. In our example, we have called this project VBBOOK(.MAK) and saved it to a subdirectory called C:\VBCODE\BOOK.

Creating Forms

Everything in Visual Basic is event driven. The events can be caused by outside influence (DDE or OLE, etc.). However, most events will occur when the user interacts with your forms. As a result, creating a form seems like the next logical step. Our application has four forms.

As this application is an employee financial application, we have called our forms EBAFORM0, EBAFORM1, EBAFORM2, and EBAFORM3. We will not walk through the entire creation of each of these four forms. We will, instead, walk through the creation of the individual control types used on each of the four forms and list the specifics of what to look for in the creation of a control.

Application Forms

For each of the four forms listed, we created the form by choosing the New Form option from the File menu. Notice that each time a form is created, its name is stored in the project window as part of your project. If you create a form and do not intend to use it, make sure you use the remove file option from the file pull down to remove the form from your project. Once a form is created, we went into the properties window by single-clicking on the form. For each form we manipulated the following properties:

Name. The name property on the four forms was changed to EBAFORM0, EBAFORM1, EBAFORM2, and EBAFORM3.

BorderStyle. Usually we use a fixed-single border style. *Fixed single* means a single solid borderline will appear around the window, and the size of the form will be fixed (the user will not be able to drag the border to make the window smaller or larger).

Caption. The *caption* property refers to the text that will be placed in the window title bar. We changed this text to be representative of the information or function the window will be performing, such as EBAFORM0, Employee Benefits Application; Logon; EBAFORM1, Employee Benefits Application; EBAFORM2, Employee Selection; EBAFORM3, Special Transaction.

MaxButton/MinButton. These properties refer to whether the form will have a minimize button and/or a maximize button in the upper right corner. We chose not to allow EBAFORM0, EFAFORM2, or EFAFORM3 to be minimized or maximized. When these forms are brought up, the user must respond or cancel.

Others. Many other properties are maintained by the form painter itself. When we enlarged the size of a form or changed its initial position on the desktop, the ScaleHeight, ScaleWidth, Top, and Width fields, as well as Height and Left are updated by the form painter.

Once a form's properties are set, controls can be placed on the form. Here is a list of the different types of controls we used and how we set up their properties.

Controls

Label—static text. *Static text* (or *labels* as Visual Basic calls them) are the pieces of text placed on the screen to label fields or give instructions. They are read-only to the user and therefore cannot be modified. While technically the text displayed is static, the text property can be modified to change the text displayed during runtime. For this reason, we name all static-text controls just as we would any other. You never know when you might need to programmatically address one, and it makes for better program documentation.

A static-text control is created by pointing to the static-text icon on the toolbar, single-clicking, moving your mouse to the form, then single-clicking, moving your mouse to the form, then single-clicking and holding while dragging the mouse to open a box of the desired length. Once the control is created, enter the properties window to set the controls characteristics.

Name. Each static-text field is given a name. The name starts with an st and ends in the formname in capital letters. The field name in between starts with a capital and is descriptive of what the text is or what entry field it is describing. The static-text field and the entry field often have the same name with the exception of the prefix (st for static text, ef for entry field).

Caption. The caption is the actual text itself.

Word wrap. This property (true or false) controls whether the caption will wrap around if it does not fit on one line. This property is useful if you want a caption to be on two lines (true) or if you want to force it to be on one (false).

AutoSize. The autosize property determines whether a static-text control should automatically resize itself to fit the caption. This property can be particularly useful if you plan on changing the caption programmatically at runtime and don't know the exact size of the caption.

Other. Properties such as height, left, top, and width are maintained by Visual Basic when you place, size, and move the control.

Entry Fields

Entry fields are controls that allow the user to enter data, or allow the programmer to display data. A standard entry field is free-form (no formatting). Visual Basic Professional edition provides a custom control called *Masked Entry Field*. The masked entry field can force a mask (the equivalent of a basic format) on the input data or apply a mask to output data. The controls efSalaryEBAFORM1 (currency format) and efEffectiveDateEBAFORM1 (date formatting) are examples of masked entry fields. This can enhance your application significantly.

One potential problem with entry fields occurs when you attempt to change color. Changing the color of an input entry field (enabled property is *true*) changes the color of both background and text. However, when you make an entry field output only (enabled property is *false*) the color of the text defaults to the color of inactive text set in Windows itself. There is no simple way to change this color within Visual Basic. Your program must either make a Windows API call to change the color within Windows, or you must change the color from Windows yourself. The default color in Windows for inactive text is a very light gray. This color is very difficult to see on an application against virtually any color background. Consider this when you create a read-only entry field.

Another issue when creating entry fields is data justification. While Visual Basic provides the ability to justify data within an entry field, it does not seem to function as you might expect. Right-justifying data in an entry field is tedious and must be done manually. The format command will not do it for you and neither will the alignment property.

An entry field is created in virtually the same way a static text field is created. Choose the entry-field icon from the tool bar, move to the form, click, and drag to open an entry field of the proper size.

We changed the settings of the following properties:

Name. This property is the name of the specific entry field. It starts with ef and ends in the name of the form in capital letters. The middle portion of the name identifies the entry field for the data it represents. If an entry field is multiline, we start the name with mle.

Alignment. You have three choices for alignment: left justify, right justify, and center. Usually, left justify is appropriate.

Enabled. Enabled determines if this is an input/output entry field or an output-only entry field. You can, of course, change a field's enabled property programmatically at runtime.

Multiline. This property determines whether this is a standard entry field or a multiline entry field (MLE). A multiline entry field can have scroll bars (horizontal and vertical) associated with it. The mleCommentsEBAFORM1 control is an example. This control will collect as many lines of comments as the user chooses to enter.

ScrollBars. This property is primarily used on multiline entry fields. Your choices are none, horizontal, vertical, or both.

Text. This property can be used to display initial text in an entry field. It can be modified programmatically during runtime.

PasswordChar. This property can be used to override the character display shown in an entry field. There are several examples of this in our code. The first example is the password entry field on the logon screen. When the user types in a password, all that displays in this entry field is asterisks. This was accomplished by setting the PasswordChar attribute for efPasswordEBAFORM0 to *.

This property can also be modified programmatically. For example, when the user checks the IRA check box, the percentage associated with it should be visible and modifiable. However, when the user unchecks this box, the percentage should become invisible. To accomplish this, manipulate the PasswordChar attribute for the efI-RAEBAFORM1 control. When the check box is clicked, the PasswordChar attribute is set to ". When the check box is unclicked, the PasswordChar attribute is set to " ".

Others. Other properties such as height, left, top, and width are maintained by the form painter.

Combo Boxes and List Boxes

Although Visual Basic considers these two controls to be separate entities, we tend to lump them together in our code (even giving them the same prefix), since they tend to work very similarly and have many of the same methods and properties. Both a list box and a combo box are a list of elements from which the user can choose. A list box contains a list of choices, which the user can scroll through and make choices. A combo box is a combination of a list box and an entry field. This allows users to choose from the provided list or simply type in a nonspecified choice of their own.

Combo boxes come in three styles. A simple combo box is a statically displayed list and an entry field. A drop-down combo box will show only the entry field unless the user requests to see the list by clicking on the button next to the entry field. A drop-down list box is very similar, except that the user is limited to choosing an option from the list box.

One of the nice features of a list box is the ability to have a multiselect list box. *Multiselect* allows the user to make several choices from the available list. Combo boxes cannot be multiselect.

Both combo and list boxes can be sorted, if you so desire. This allows you to programmatically add items to a list or combo box in any order and have that data displayed to the user in sorted order.

Name. We apply the same naming standard to both combo and list boxes. Names start with lb (cb would be confused with check box) and end in the form name.

Style. Related to combo boxes only—this property determines whether this will be a drop-down combo (value 0), simple combo (value 1), or drop-down list (value 2). lbStateListEBAFORM1 is an example of a drop-down combo box. lbEmployeeListEBAFORM2 is a true list box and therefore does not have this property.

Enabled. This property determines whether the user has access to the list/combo box when the form is displayed.

Sorted. If this property is set to true, the list/combo box itself will sort all strings in ascending order in the box, and update the list box index as appropriate. Be careful using this attribute. Remember that sorting the data changes the order. You can no longer match the data in the list box to the original data by index.

Others. Height, left, top, and width are maintained by the form painter.

Group-Box Controls

On the surface, a group box would appear to be used only for aesthetics. However, the group box can also relate the controls inside it to each other. This relationship allows controls to interact with one another without specific code to manage the interaction. When used with radio buttons, for example, the group box around two or more radio buttons is what allows them to maintain a mutually exclusive relationship (i.e., when you click on one radio button, all others are automatically unclicked). The sex group box is a good example of a group box, which allows the male and female radio buttons to be mutually exclusive.

It is important to note that in order to create this relationship, the group box needs to be drawn first and the controls placed on it. If you try to draw the group box after the controls and move the controls onto the group box, they will look correct but the relationship will not be intact.

In cases of more complicated relationships, the purpose of the group box is only to visually group together multiple controls. The state drop-down list box is one example. The group box here only groups the drop-down list box and entry field together. The group box around the funds check boxes and spin buttons is another example.

Name. Group-box control names begin with gb and end in the name of the form.

Caption. The group box control allows for a caption. The caption appears in the upper left and goes across the length of the box. This property is set to a caption appropriate for the group of controls it is encapsulating.

Enabled. This property can be quite useful. Setting enabled to *false* in a group box disables all the controls within the group box.

Others. Height, left, top, and width are maintained by the form painter.

Radio-Button Controls

The question often arises, "When do I use a radio button and when do I use a check box?" While there is no hard-and-fast rule, from a CUA standpoint there is a difference. A radio button is supposed to be used when the choices are mutually exclusive. A check box is supposed to be used when you are being asked to choose one or more options from a list.

When asking the user what sex the employee is, the obvious choice is two radio buttons. By placing the radio buttons inside a group box their relationship as mutually exclusive is maintained by Visual Basic.

Name. Each radio button name starts with rb and ends in the form name.

Caption. This is the text associated with a radio button.

Value. This property determines whether the button has a clicked (true) or unclicked status (false) at startup. This property can be changed programmatically.

Check-Box Controls

Check-box controls are commonly used to select one or more options from a list. Like radio buttons, check boxes are best used within a group box to group the choices into a general category. The use of the group box also allows the check boxes to have a relationship similar to that of radio buttons within a group box.

In our application, we used check boxes to allow the user to choose which funds their investments should be spread across. A user can choose one or more funds. The check-box control is also tied to the corresponding spin-button control next to it. The action of selecting a fund (making a check box *true*) causes the spin button next to the check box to become enabled. Deselecting a fund (making a check box *false*) causes the spin button next to the check box to become disabled.

Name. Each check box name starts with cb and ends in the form name.

Caption. This is the text associated with a check box.

Value. This property determines whether the button has checked status (value 0), unchecked status (value 1), or grayed (value 2) at startup. This property can be changed and queried programmatically.

Spin Buttons

A *spin button* is a new type of visual control. Visually, a spin button is a control that allows the user to choose a value by incrementing or decrementing the value shown by clicking on arrows. In practice, a spin button is nothing more than a control similar to a scroll bar (the arrows without the bar) attached to an entry field.

The spin button can be horizontal or vertical. We used vertical spin buttons to allow the user to choose percentages (salary percentage and fund percentages). With a spin button we can control the increment value and minimum/maximum values.

Name. Each spin-button name starts with sb and ends in the form name.

Delay. This is the delay in milliseconds between registering spin-button clicks. This attribute is important in making sure the spin button does not spin too quickly or slowly.

Spin Orientation. This property determines whether the button has a vertical orientation (value 0) or a horizontal orientation (value 1).

Menus

Menu design for a form is managed through the Menu Design option from the Window menu option (or press control + M). Accessing this will bring up the Menu Design window.

Designing menus in Visual Basic is very simple. Before beginning, you need to know what options to show on your main menu title bar and what options each drop-down menu will have. You should determine what letter will represent each option's hot key and if any of the drop-down menu options will have further submenus. From there, menu design is all academic.

Start by typing in a caption. The caption is the text displayed for that menu item. Placing an ampersand (&) in front of a letter will cause that letter to become the hot key (alt + letter) combination to activate that drop-down menu or menu option. Placing a single dash in the caption field creates a menu separator bar.

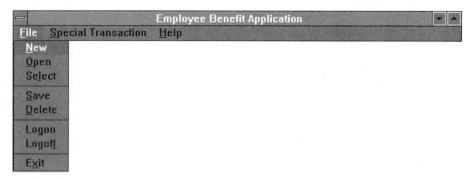

Figure 7.20   The employee benefits application menu.

Next enter a name for the menu item. We usually start menu names with mn and end them with the form name to which they are attached.

A menu item can cause an action or act as a toggle. If you want this menu item to be a toggle, you can choose to have its initial value as toggle on by checking the checked box. This will cause a check mark to appear beside the menu option on display.

You can decide whether the menu option in question is visible and/or enabled at runtime. These values can be changed programmatically as well.

The next, insert, and delete buttons are used to add, insert, and delete menu items. The arrow buttons are used to determine the logical relationships among menu options. A menu item listed all the way to the left (no dashes) will be a high-level menu choice listed on the menu bar. In our application, these are choices such as File, Special Transaction, and Help (Figure 7.20).

Dashes in front of a menu option indicate an indentation or sublevel in the menu structure (Figure 7.21). For example, the New, Open, and Select menu options all exist under the File option.

Checkpoint

This is a good time to take a checkpoint. You've undoubtedly been reading for a while now, and it would be nice to take what you've read and put it into focus. What have we accomplished so far?

We began building our employee benefits application from the ground up. We started by creating the database objects our application required. We began by getting into the Microsoft SQL Server Administrator and using it to create a device. Within the device, we created a database. We also created our own SQL Server ID and assigned that ID to a group. We then assigned appropriate permissions to that group.

With a database in place, we went to the Visual Data application, which comes with Visual Basic. We used Visual Data to create all

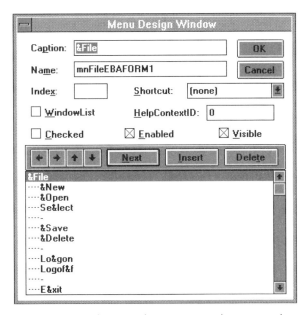

Figure 7.21   The Visual Basic menu design window.

tables and indexes required. We also used Visual Data to populate any static tables (such as the state table) with data.

Once we had determined what data was required and a test bed was available, we could begin to develop a user interface in earnest. A Visual Basic application always begins with a project. The project contains or holds all the objects an application will require. We created a project called VBBOOK.MAK. Within our project we created four forms: an application logon form (EBAFORM0), the main application form (EBAFORM1), the employee selection window (EBAFORM2), and the special transaction window (EBAFORM3). We also created a code module to go with this application (VBBOOKM1.BAS).

Our next step was to put the required controls for our application on each of the skeletal forms in the project. For each form, that form's properties had to be set. Next, any controls to be displayed on that form had to be drawn. Our application was specifically written to make use of Visual Basic standard controls (spin button was the only exception). We discussed static-text controls, entry fields, multiline entry fields, group boxes, radio buttons, check boxes, list boxes, combo boxes, push buttons, spin buttons, and menus. Each of the controls on each form also have properties. We discussed the common properties set for each control.

So, here's our checkpoint. We currently have an application with four complete forms. We are ready to begin tying those forms together into a usable application. In other words, it's time to add code.

Visual Basic Code

Before we jump into the specific code required for our application, we should review a few concepts critical to understanding how Visual Basic works.

Control Properties

Each control in Visual Basic has a set of properties specific to that control. When we created these controls we assigned values to some of these properties at design time. We determined if a control was visible or invisible to the user by setting the visible property. We determined the default text displayed on a control by setting the text property for that control when it was painted.

It is important to note that each of these properties can be queried and modified during runtime. For example, to determine what data a user typed into an entry-field control, you will query and use the text property in your code. For example: szTestText = efStateTextEBAFORM1.Text. This line of code pulls the text property out of the state text entry-field control and puts it in a string variable.

More specifically, you will need to query certain properties to determine the current state of a control. Check boxes and radio buttons are good examples. To determine if a check box is currently checked or unchecked, use the Value property where 0 is checked, 1 is unchecked, and 2 is grayed. Examine the following code:

```
If cbIRAEBAFORM1.Value = 1 Then
    sbIRAEBAFORM1.Enabled = True
    efIRAEBAFORM1.PasswordChar = ""
Else
    sbIRAEBAFORM1.Enabled = False
    efIRAEBAFORM1.PasswordChar = " "
End If
```

This code will check the value of the IRA check box to see if is checked or unchecked. If the box is checked, the IRA spin button will be enabled (the user will be allowed to access it), and whatever data is in the entry field part of the spin button will be made visible to the user. If the box is unchecked, the spin button is disabled and the data is hidden. This is an excellent example of how you can use and modify controls' attributes during runtime to accomplish your job.

Control Methods

Each control and object in Visual Basic comes with some functions or methods that are part of the control itself. These methods allow us to perform basic functions on a control without having to recode the instructions for those functions in each system we create. A perfect example is the set-focus method.

Virtually every control has a set-focus method associated with it. This method will call windows and request the application focus be given to the control in question. For example, efSSNEBAFORM1.Set-Focus. This code will call windows and request the application focus be given to the social-security number entry field on EBAFORM1. The code required to accomplish this task is embedded in the setfocus method attached to that entry field.

Events

Visual Basic is an event-driven programming environment. What does that mean? That means that each control in Visual Basic has a series of events to which it is capable of detecting and responding. An *event* is an occurrence such as clicked (the user has clicked on the control with the mouse). An event can also be a state such as gotfocus (the control just received application focus).

Just because a control is capable of responding to specific events doesn't mean it must. An event is only a hook available to the programmer. If the programmer assigns code to be executed for a specified event, the code will be executed; otherwise, the Visual Basic default action will occur, which is usually nothing. Therefore, it is the programmer's job to determine what events are important and how to respond to their occurrence.

For the purposes of our discussion, let's look at this another way. Let's break down our coding tasks into specific tasks to be accomplished. We need Visual Basic code to perform the following tasks: determine the screen flow of our application, database access, and field edits. We going to approach the coding of this application by accomplishing each of these tasks.

Functions and Subprocedures

While in many cases the use of functions and subprocedures is optional, there are some cases where their use is required to keep your code understandable and maintainable. For example, many of the database-access functions such as Database Open and Create Dynaset (which we will discuss later) will cause an error trap to be activated. If you code a database open in a function, that function can set up a trap to capture an error. That way, the error can be trapped within the function. As a result, the function can return an error flag or return a good flag. You will see an example of this later in the chapter.

Variable Definition

Variables in Visual Basic are defined as follows:

```
iCounter As Integer
```

where iCounter is the name the source code will use, and where we are defining iCounter as an integer.

Variables can be defined as local to an event, or function as globals to a specific window or the entire application (Table 7.1). To define a variable as global, you must go into the general object, declarations procedure of either the form or a module and define the variable there with the keyword *global* before it (Figure 7.22). Remember, a global variables are expensive—use them sparingly.

Establishing Screen Flow

Our first task is to connect our application screens together to establish application flow. The first decision to be made is which form will be displayed when the executable is started. In our case, the main form in our application is EBAFORM1. On the Visual Basic tool bar, on the options menu, there is a project menu pick. Under this option, you will find the start-up form property. Double-clicking on this property will show you a list of forms available in the active project. Choose EBAFORM1. From this point on, whenever you run the application, the EBAFORM1 will be displayed. To test this theory, you can run the application by pressing the run button on the tool bar, choos-

Variable Type	Number of Bytes	Min and Max Values	Define Variables With Suffix	Example Variable Definition
Integer	2 Bytes	−32,768 to 32,767	% Dim iCount%	Dim iCount As Integer
Long	4 Bytes	−2,147,483,648 to 2,147,483,647	& Dim IRecordCnt&	Dim IRecordCnt As Long
Single	4 Bytes	−3.402823E38 to −1.401298E-45 for negatives; 1.401298E-45 to 3.402823E38 positive	! Dim sngPctg!	Dim sngPctg As Single
Double	8 Bytes	−1.797693134862315D308 to −4.94066D-324 for negatives; 4.94066D-324 to 1.797693134862315D308 positive	# Dim dblPctg#	Dim dblPctg As Single
Currency	8 Bytes	−922337203685477.5808 to 922337203685477.5807	@ Dim cPmtAmount@	Dim cPmtAmount As Currency
String	1 byte per character	0 to about 65,535 characters possible	$ Dim szinputLine$	Dim szinputLine As String * 20
Variant	As required	As Required will take on the datatype of whatever data is assigned to it.	None	Dim vFlag As Variant Dim Variable

Table 7.1 Variable definition.

Figure 7.22 Defining Visual Basic global variables.

ing Start from the Run menu, or pressing F5. To stop execution, click on the Stop button on the tool bar.

When the Employee Benefit Application starts up, we want to display the main form, but before we allow users to perform any application tasks, we want them to logon to our application to make sure they have access rights. To accomplish this, we need to put up our logon screen.

To display a form in Visual Basic, use the Show method. The format for the Show method is Form.Show Mode, where form is the name of the form you want to display and mode is either modal(1) or modeless(0). When you display a form modally, it means you are giving users the form, and that users cannot get to any other form in the application until they have responded to the modal form. If a form is displayed in modeless mode, the user can click on another active form or control giving it focus without responding directly to the form just displayed. More important, if a Show command is executed modally, the next line of code after the Show command will not be executed until the user responds to the form shown. If a form is shown in modeless mode, the Show command will display the form and immediately continue executing. This will become an important consideration in your application.

Getting back to the task at hand, we need to get the main application form (EBAFORM1) to show the logon screen (EBAFORM0) at startup time. Because we do not want to allow users to get to our main form until they've logged on, we will show the logon screen modally. The only problem we have to overcome is where to place the Show command. We want the logon screen to be displayed once and only once. The only time we want the logon screen to be displayed is at startup time.

You will remember that everything displayed in a Visual Basic application is a control—including the form itself. The form has properties that can be set and events which can be coded to. Of all the events available for a form, there are three that we primarily code to: load, activate, and resize.

The *load event* occurs when a form is loaded into memory. This usually occurs only once. The *show method* will load a form if is not already loaded and make it visible to the user. The *activate event* occurs when the form becomes the application focus, usually when the form is shown or becomes the focus of the application. This event can occur many times (each time the form receives focus). The *resize event* occurs each time the form is resized. The resize event happens at display time and occurs each time the user attempts to move or resize the form.

In our case, we want to execute a show command for the EBAFORM0 form from the EBAFORM1 form when the EBAFORM1 is first loaded. To accomplish this we need to code the show command in the load event. To bring up the Visual Basic code window, you can double-click on the form to which you wish to add code. Double-clicking on the EBAFORM1 will bring up the code window for the form. (Notice that the object listed is *form* and the procedure or event listed is *load*. To see a list of objects available for this form, use the object's combo box. To see a list of events for the object chosen, use the event combo box).

Within the load event of the EBAFORM1 form, we placed the following code:

```
' Display the Logon Screen
EBAFORM0.Show 1
```

While this code is functional, it may be difficult to maintain later—after all, what does the 1 after the Show command do? An alternative is to define a constant called MODAL and assign it the value of 1. To do this, we need to go into our module (VBBOOKM1.BAS) and define the constant. Double-click on the module in the project window and the code window will come up. The place to define global and constant variables to be used across the application is in the general object, declarations procedure.

The option explicit line forces the compiler to make sure each variable used in a procedure is defined explicitly. Code the following after this line:

```
Global Const MODAL = 1
```

Now we can go back into the EBAFORM1 load event and change the code as follows:

```
EBAFORM0.Show MODAL
```

This will make it easier to understand what we are trying to accomplish.

Before we test our code, we have to figure out how to complete the execution of a form and make it disappear. If we do not close the logon form, the user can never get to the rest of the application. We have two conditions to concern ourselves with: The user has filled out the logon screen and we want to verify the id and password. If the id and password are verified, we should give the user access to the application. The user does not want to logon to the application, but simply wants to cancel out and effectively end the application.

To handle both these conditions, we need to figure out how to close a form (end its display) and how to end the application (exit). To close a form, you have to issue the unload procedure. The format of the Unload procedure is:

```
Unload formname
```

To terminate the application, you have to issue the end command.

In either case, we need to add code to the EBAFORM0 form. If the user clicks on the cancel button, we want to unload the logon form, unload the main application form, and end the application. If the user clicks on the OK button, we want to process the logon and either return the user to the main application screen if the processing is successful, or give them a message saying the logon id and password were incorrect and force them to try again.

The code for the cancel button should be placed in the clicked event. The code should be listed as follows:

```
' Unload the Logon and Main forms and end the App
Unload EBAFORM0
Unload EBAFORM1
End
```

The code for the OK button is obviously more complicated. At the moment, let's avoid concerning ourselves with the code necessary to verify the id and password. Let's just put in the code necessary to close the logon form and return control to the main application form.

```
Unload EBAFORM0
```

With the logon form unloaded, focus will revert to the main application screen.

If you run the application now, you will see the main application form and, immediately after, you will see the logon form. You will also notice that you cannot exit the logon form until you have responded to it by clicking on the OK or cancel buttons. Clicking the cancel button closes both the logon and main application forms and ends the application. Clicking on the OK button closes the logon form and returns control to the main application form. At this point there is no way to exit the main application form short of closing the form (by clicking on the system-menu box and choosing close) or stopping the application by clicking on the stop button off the Visual Basic Toolbar.

To remedy this, we need to put some code in the exit option from the file menu of our application. Click on the file menu on the main application screen and double-click on the exit option. This will give you the code window for the exit menu option. Put the following code there:

```
' Unload the main form and end the Application
Unload EBAFORM1
End
```

This code will allow you to end the application nicely.

With these basics down, we can place appropriate shows and unloads in the application to complete the screen flow. Place a show command under the select option on the file menu to show the selection window (EBAFORM2). Place another on the add option from the special transaction menu to show the special transaction form (EBAFORM3). Both of these forms should be shown modally. In each of these forms, under the clicked event for both the OK and cancel buttons, put an unload to return control to the caller.

At this point, you should be able to run the application and successfully navigate to all the forms.

Database Access

With general screen navigation complete, we can move on to a more substantial topic: database access. We will cover database opens, selects, reads, writes, updates, deletes, and closes. All of these functions will be performed through Microsoft's ODBC (open database connectivity) API. There are two very good reasons for using ODBC as our point of access for database calls: first, unless you purchase third-party software, ODBC is the only way to get to SQL Server. Second, by coding to ODBC APIs, if your database choice changes the parameters on your open database call must change while the rest of the application stays intact.

The best place to begin a discussion of database connectivity is with the open-database call. We have chosen to code an open-database call as a function, independent of any given form. This means we will be coding in the VBBOOKM1.BAS module.

Double-click on this module in the project window and a code window will be displayed. To create a new function or subprocedure click on the new procedure option from the view menu on the Visual Basic Tool bar. A window will be displayed asking for the name of the procedure and whether this procedure is to be a function or subprocedure. You will recall the difference between the two is that a function can have a return value while a subprocedure cannot. In this case, we want to create an OpenEBADatabase function. The code for this function will be as follows:

```
Function OpenEBADatabase (szUserId As String, szPassword As String) As
Integer

    Dim szDBConnect As String

    ' Set Error Trap
    On Error GoTo OpenDBError

    ' Open Employee Benefits Application Under My Id
    szDBConnect = "ODBC;UID=" + szUserId + ";PWD=" + szPassword
    szDBConnect = szDBConnect + "DSN=PRAGMAS2;DATABASE=bk_efadb"
    ' Open
    Set gstDatabase = OpenDatabase("", False, False, szDBConnect)
    iDatabaseOpen = True

    Exit Function

OpenDBError:
    Beep
    MsgBox "Error: Database Open; Message = " + Error$, 48
    OpenEBADatabase = False
    Exit Function

End Function
```

Let's dissect this code carefully, as the open database command is probably the most complicated and important in Visual Basic.

Function Definition

The definition of the function determines the parameters to be passed and the format of the return value. In this case, the OpenEBADatabase function requires two parameters: user id and password. The last part of the function definition is the return value for the function—in this case, an integer.

The first line of this function is a variable definition. We have defined one string: a database connect string required by the Open-Database command. The next line of code sets an error trap. The OpenDatabase command does not return a value telling you whether it worked or not. If the call is unable to open the database with the parameters you pass, it generates an error condition. This trap will capture the error condition and jump to the OpenDBError: label to handle the condition. More on that in a moment.

The next few lines of code set up the database connect variable for processing. The format of the database connect string is dependent upon the type of database to which you are connecting. For SQL Server, the database connect string must have the following information: user Id, password, server name, and database name. With a proper ODBC SQLServer connect string, we can attempt to open the database. The format of the OpenDatabase command is:

```
OpenDatabase(databasename, exclusive, readonly, connectstring)
```

For an SQLServer ODBC database, database name is in the connect string. Therefore, database name in the openDatabase command will be blank. *Exclusive* refers to whether we require exclusive (single-user) access to the database. Usually, this parameter is *false*. *Readonly* determines whether we have read/write or read only access to the database. We require read/write access and, therefore, this parameter is *false* as well.

An OpenDatabase call will set up a database handle. Since we use the database across our application, our database handle is a global object. Global objects must be defined in the VBBOOKM1.BAS module. In the declarations section of the general object, the following line of code will declare our database object:

```
Global gstDatabase As Database
```

After the OpenDatabase command is executed, one of two things will occur: either the database will have opened successfully and the next sequential line of code will be executed, or the open will fail, in which case the error trap will catch the error and jump to the OpenD-BError: label to process the error.

If the open was successful, we want to return a value of *true*. The way you set the return value of a function is by setting the name of the function to a return value. In this case, we set the name of the function to *true* and exit the function with an exit function command.

If the open failed, we branched to the OpenDBError label. From here we will cause the computer to beep to notify the user of the error and put up a message box containing the reason for the error.

The message-box function will be used repeatedly throughout the application. The format for a message-box command is MsgBox message, type, title where *message* is the message to be displayed, *type* determines if there is an icon displayed in the box and whether there are push buttons on the message box (like yes and no or OK), and *title* is the text displayed on the title bar of the message box. A message box is really a modal window. The window must be responded to by the user before continuing.

In this particular case, the Error$ string is a global variable containing the text describing the particular error. This string is managed by ODBC and contains a string provided by SQL Server.

With this function, we are ready to put the application code required in our application to manipulate the database. The open database call set up a global database handle for us to use. Database manipulation from here commonly occurs through a vehicle called the *dynaset*.

A dynaset is like a dynamic dataset that can be created to give the programmer access to data in a specified format. A dynaset is almost

like having a cursor into the data after a select except it is more powerful. A dynaset can be created to extract data from one or many tables.
For example, set gstDynaset = gstDatabase.CreateDynaset("STATE")
creates a dynaset against the state table. This dynaset will allow us to
easily load the state drop-down combo box as well as derive the state
abbreviation from the state text chosen.

A dynaset can also be created as the result of an SQL query. The
code listed below will retrieve the state abbreviation from the state
text chosen in the lbStateListEBAFORM1 list box:

```
' Create Dynamic SQL Statement to Lookup State Abbreviation for
'  matching state text chosen
gszSQLStatement = "Select StateAbbr FROM state WHERE StateText = '"
gszSQLStatement = gszSQLStatement + lbStateListEBAFORM1.Text
gszSQLStatement = gszSQLStatement + "';"

Set stStateDynaset = gstDatabase.CreateDynaset(gszSQLStatement)
If Not stStateDynaset.EOF Then
   efStateTextEBAFORM1.Text = stStateDynaset("StateAbbr")
End If
stStateDynaset.Close
```

The resulting dynaset is almost like a flat file made up of the
resulting data. The current row can be manipulated. You can also go
to the next and previous rows. The dynaset also has seek, and several
find methods, which are useful for dynaset row positioning.

There are methods to tell whether this is the first row in the
dynaset or that you have reached the end of the dynaset. Dynasets
can also be created from dynasets to allow for additional filtering or
sorting.

Data can be added to a table (or tables) using a dynaset. To add a
row, use the AddNew method followed by an Update method:

```
stFundDynaset.AddNew

stFundDynaset("SocSecNum") = CLng(efSSNEBAFORM1.Text)
stFundDynaset("Type") = szType
stFundDynaset("EffectiveDate") = Format$(efEffectiveDateEBAFORM1.Text,
          "mm/dd/yy")

Select Case szType
    Case "I"
     stFundDynaset("FundPer") = CSng(efIRAEBAFORM1.Text)
    Case "K"
     stFundDynaset("FundPer") = CSng(efKeoghEBAFORM1.Text)
    Case "S"
     stFundDynaset("FundPer") = CSng(efStockOptEBAFORM1.Text)
End Select

stFundDynaset.Update
```

A row can be updated from a dynaset just as easily. In fact, you will see only a minor difference in code between an add and an update. The major difference in an update is the correct row to update in the dynaset must be found first. The row is prepared for update using the edit method and modified using the update method:

```
stFundDynaset.Edit

stFundDynaset("SocSecNum") = CLng(efSSNEBAFORM1.Text)
stFundDynaset("Type") = szType
stFundDynaset("EffectiveDate") = Format$(efEffectiveDateEBAFORM1.Text,
        "mm/dd/yy")

Select Case szType
    Case "I"
     stFundDynaset("FundPer") = CSng(efIRAEBAFORM1.Text)
    Case "K"
     stFundDynaset("FundPer") = CSng(efKeoghEBAFORM1.Text)
    Case "S"
     stFundDynaset("FundPer") = CSng(efStockOptEBAFORM1.Text)
End Select

stFundDynaset.Update
```

Deleting data can be handled in one of two ways. There is a delete method available to delete a single row. Simply use one of the find methods or the seek method to find the row you want to remove and use the delete method to remove it.

However, in our application, when we delete an employee, we may need to remove several rows from the fund and comment tables. As a result, for the tables that have a many-to-one relationship with the employee table, we often used dynamic SQL execution to process these deletes. For example:

```
On Error GoTo FundTblErrDel

' Setup For Delete From Fund Table
gszSQLStatement = "DELETE FROM fund WHERE (" +
        efSocSecNumEBAFORM1.Text + " = fund.SocSecNum);"

' Execute Dynamic SQL Against Fund Table
gstDatabase.Execute gszSQLStatement

FundTblErrDel:
 gszTitle = "Fund Table Delete Error"
 gszMsgText = "ERROR: Fund Delete; Message = " + Error$
 giMsgRes = MsgBox(gszMsgText, MB_STOP, gszTitle)
```

Delete functions also make a good case for bundling your database access into transactions. In the case of an employee delete, we do not want to actually delete any rows for any of the tables until all of the rows for that employee can be successfully removed. To accomplish this, Visual Basic allows us to group database-access functions under a transaction, which will not be committed until all database access is complete. For example:

```
' Begin Transaction
gstDatabase.BeginTrans

' Delete Employee Row Function
iResult = EmployeeTableDel(CStr(glSocSecNum))

' Delete Fund Data or Quit
If (iResult = True) Then
   iResult = FundTableDel(CStr(glSocSecNum))
Else
   efStatusLineEBAFORM1.Text = "Transaction Failed - Ready"
   gstDatabase.Rollback
   Exit Sub
End If

' Delete Comment Data or Quit
If (iResult = True) Then
   iResult = CommentTableDel(CStr(glSocSecNum))
Else
   gstDatabase.Rollback
   Exit Sub
End If

gstDatabase.CommitTrans
```

To make our code easier to understand and maintain, we coded all of our database access as subprocedures or functions. There is an open database function, a close database function, and many subprocedures to add, update, and delete a row from each of our application tables. From here, we coded higher-level functions, which could be called to add, update, and delete data in a related group. For example, we have functions that can add data to all application tables when the user indicates the employee data entered on EBAFORM1 should be saved. With these functions and subprocedures coded, all we had to do was put the appropriate calls to these procedures in the proper control events to give our application database access. Several examples follow:

```
Sub mnOpenEBAFORM1_Click ()
    Dim iResult        As Integer
    Dim szMsgText      As String

    If (Len(efSSNEBAFORM1.Text) = 9) Then
       glSocSecNum = CLng(efSSNEBAFORM1.Text)
    Else
       glSocSecNum = 0
    End If
```

```
      If (glSocSecNum > 0) Then
         Call SetHourGlass(EBAFORM1)
         Call PerformEBAInq
         Call ResetMouse(EBAFORM1)
      Else
         gszTitle = "Get Employee Row"
         gszMsgText = "ERROR: Open Function Requires You to Have Entered A
Valid Social Security Number"
         giMsgRes = MsgBox(gszMsgText, MB_ICONEXCLAMATION, gszTitle)
      End If

End Sub
```

This code will edit the social-security number field, get all required rows off our application tables, and populate the window controls with that data when the user clicks on the Open menu option from the File menu.

```
Sub mnSaveEBAFORM1_Click ()
    Call SetHourGlass(EBAFORM1)
    Call PerformEBATran
    Call ResetMouse(EBAFORM1)

End Sub
```

This code will call the PerformEBATran function to create a transaction, update each of our application tables, and commit the results if there are no errors.

At this point, we have an application that can navigate between forms, and retrieve, save, and delete application data from application tables. We're almost done. All we have to do now is install the cleanup code. We'll need to perform appropriate data validation and edits.

Data Validation

Coding the data validation, edits, and the spit and polish that make an application real are the time-consuming parts of a Visual Basic application. Much of the work is accomplished using VB functions such as LEN to test the length of a data-entry field, and data-conversion functions to convert text to numbers and so on. Functions such as IsDate, IsEmpty, and IsNumeric are useful to test data fields to see if they are valid.

The rest of the application code handles special navigation. For example, we looked at some code earlier that activated and deactivated the IRA spin-button control depending upon the value of the IRA check box. This type of code consists mostly of manipulating a control's properties to get focus when appropriate, become active or inactive from the user perspective when appropriate, and to share or accept data with other controls when appropriate.

To complete your application, you must walk through each panel of your application and ask yourself the question, "What do I expect the application to do here?" You may want some fields accessible to the user and some not. You may want messages to be displayed when the user tries to do certain things. Most of this sort of code involves looking at each control and trying to determine if that control should be responding to any specific events. For example, if an entry field should only allow the user to enter numbers (as opposed to alphanumerics), you can code the following in the change event:

```
If Not IsNumeric(efSSNEBAFORM1.Text) Then
    beep
End If
```

This sort of code will do some of your editing up front lessening the chance of a user error.

You may also want to add a few bells and whistles, which make your application more professional looking. For example, code can be added to database functions that changes the icon associated with the user's mouse from an arrow to an hourglass during database access and back to an arrow once the access is complete. This notifies the user the application is working and not hung up.

Another important feature of an application is context-sensitive help. Microsoft provides the help compiler, which allows you to create detailed application help in any word processor and, using the specifications provided in the help compiler, tie that help to your application. It is attention to detail here that can make the difference between a mediocre and a superior application.

Reports

Our application requires a history report be created from the special-transactions table for a user. When we first wrote this system, we created this report manually by writing all the code necessary to collect the records from the special transaction table, sort it properly, print the report, and produce a subtotal. As our report was relatively simple, there was not a great deal of code to write. As we got to know Visual Basic 3.0 better, we discovered the power of a utility VB provides called *Crystal Reports.*

Crystal Reports is a report painter for Visual Basic that interfaces directly with a VB database (Figure 7.23). Creating complicated reports with Crystal Reports that are complete with headings, footings, data from multiple tables, control breaks, subtotals, and grand totals is easy and requires no coding.

Visual Basic also comes with a Crystal Reports graphical control. This allows you to tie a report created in Crystal Reports to a form.

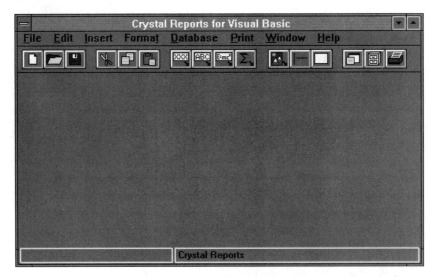

Figure 7.23 Crystal Reports.

The control allows you to produce reports in your windows for user viewing. In a different scenario, you can have a print-report button on your window, which will go to Crystal Reports to print the report. In this case, the Crystal Reports control should be invisible on the screen. The user does not even need to know that it exists.

Creating an Executable and Distribution

With our application coded and tested, it's time to build an executable. Executable creation in Visual Basic is a simple task. Under the file menu there is a "Make EXE File . . ." option. Choosing the make option will bring up a make window (Figure 7.24). The path and name of the .EXE file to be created will default to the path the

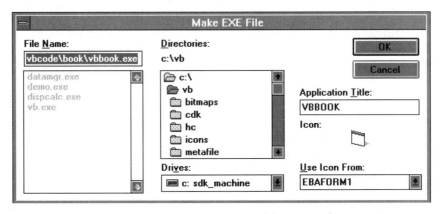

Figure 7.24 Creating an executable in Visual Basic.

application files reside in and the name of the main form in the application. You can change this to another location or name if you require.

You can also choose a specific icon to be associated with the executable. Usually, you choose the icon associated with the main form of your application to be the application icon and Visual Basic defaults to this choice. You can, of course, change this.

Once you are satisfied, simply press the OK button. Visual Basic will create an EXE and return. It's that simple.

Application Distribution

Distributing that EXE in the past has been significantly more complicated. Determining what files need to be shipped with the EXE (.VBX files, VB DLLs, and so on) was more a matter of trial and error than choice. However, Visual Basic 3.0 comes with a utility called *Application Setup Wizard* which changes all that (Figure 7.25).

Application Setup Wizard will use your project file (.MAK) to pull together all the different files required for distribution. ASW will create a set of master-distribution diskettes for your application and generate a SETUP1.EXE file which will run under Windows and install your application. ASW makes the distribution of your Visual Basic Application a snap.

Other Features of Visual Basic

Our application is relatively simple in scope and presentation. Corporate and professional applications require a higher level of sophis-

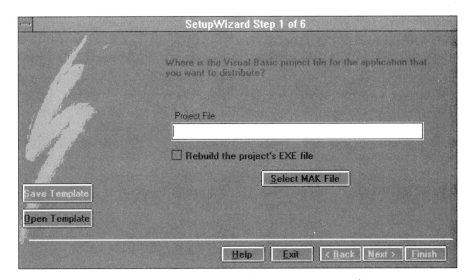

Figure 7.25   The Visual Basic Setup Wizard.

tication. Visual Basic provides for this in two ways: VB features such as MDIs, DLL, OLE, and DDE communications; and an open API interface, which allows third-party vendors to code add-on products to fill any holes Microsoft may have left.

There are features of Visual Basic that can make an application look and feel more professional. The most significant is the use of an MDI (Multiple Document Interface) form in your application. An MDI form provides a background or desktop for your application. An MDI usually presents application pull-down menus and often has a corresponding graphical toolbar associated with it. This allows the user to press icon buttons to access the various functions in your application, adding a professional look and feel.

Visual Basic can interface with a DLL (dynamic link library) to perform more complicated application functions. Complicated computation functions may be coded in C, compiled into DLL format, and called from Visual Basic. Visual Basic 3.0 documentation also contains the specifications required to write your own custom graphical controls in C and create .VBX files for use in application development and distribution.

The ability to access DLL functions from your code allows you direct access to the Microsoft Windows APIs. This gives you access to low-level Windows functionality. This open access gives you the ability to create applications with unlimited levels of sophistication.

It is this open interface which has allowed several vendors to enter into the Visual Basic add-on business. Many companies are producing three-dimensional graphical controls, improved data-access controls, and shell environments that allow the Visual Basic programmer to create more interesting, sophisticated applications, and work more efficiently with Visual Basic.

Using the intercommunication facilities managed by Microsoft Windows (object linking and embedding or OLE, and dynamic data exchange, or DDE) allows your executable to communicate with other Windows executables. You can share objects with other popular Windows products such as Microsoft Word and Excel, as well as write your own executables that communicate with one another.

One popular implementation of DDE is to write an executable to manage communication with another platform (like the corporate mainframe). This executable will run in the background while our main application collects user data or processes queries. When the main application requires data from another platform, it makes a request via DDE to our communication executable, which processes the request and sends the data or confirmation back when it is complete. In the meantime, our main executable is free to continue with any other user tasks.

What Does It All Mean?

You still think Basic means *basic?* If you got nothing else from this chapter, it should have been Microsoft's Visual Basic is a powerful tool.

Data processing managers in companies across the country have begun to see some major changes in the way they do business. Strategic corporate direction is calling for a decrease in costs and a shrinking of personnel while the demand for more and better information continues to rise. It is a challenging environment in which to work.

We have to find better ways to do what we do. Our applications must be flashy and intelligent but cost effective. When developing those applications, we need to develop them quickly and we have to be able to support them afterward.

All of these goals have led to the success of application-development tools like Visual Basic. Client/server applications are, without a doubt, the standard of the future. However, while the concept of Client/server technology introduces some very deep bits-and-bytes issues, developers such as Microsoft have found it unnecessary to require the client/server application developer to be an advanced technology expert.

Visual Basic takes the pain out of C/S development. It's simple and it's quick. Put more succinctly, it's basic. And yet VB does not limit your creativity. The application developed in this book served its purpose—it gave you a taste of what you can accomplish with Visual Basic. But remember, one of VB's primary features is its open interface. There are literally hundreds of vendors who have developed or are developing extended controls and middleware to either enhance the Visual Basic development environment or allow your VB application to work with their products.

So what does it all mean? Consider your current corporate applications. Think about your direction and what your future goals are. Dream your wildest dream. Visual, audio, database, communications—it's all available. And you can tie it all together with Basic.

8

Client/Server GUI Development Using SQLWindows

A good place to start would be to ask, "What exactly is SQLWindows?" After reading this chapter we hope you have a better idea of the product. In a nutshell, SQLWindows is a development tool used with client/server GUI (graphical user interface) applications. SQLWindows comes equipped with a state of the art DBMS (database management system) called SQLBase, which has been a leading DBMS in the marketplace for a number of years. SQLWindows can connect to numerous other DBMSs on minicomputers or mainframes. The SQL-Windows toolset comes equipped with a variety of application development tools like project management, database administration, report writing, and GUI application development. The SQLWindows development environment includes basic graphical objects like data fields, list boxes, radio buttons, push buttons, menus, and others. SQL-Windows' special features include DDE (dynamic data exchange), OLE (object linking and embedding), MDI (multiple-document interface), and drag-and-drop features. SQLWindows lets the developer program using object-oriented style. This allows code to be reusable in other programs and increases new program reliability.

We had been working with the SQLWindows 3.1 for some time and were eager to try out version 4.0, which was shipped in April 1993. The Gupta Corporation sent us the beta version of 4.0. There is a big difference between the two versions. New with version 4.0 is TeamWindows, used to manage team projects, and SQLWindows templates, a data repository for TeamWindows; it also includes Quest 2.0, which gives the developer quick-and-easy access to databases, tables, views, and indexes. Version 4.0 also includes a new object called the Quest window. The Quest window object makes database table manipulation in an application a breeze. This chapter will discuss briefly

TeamWindows and the data repository while concentrating mostly on the SQLWindows client/server application development tool.

First, let's cover some historical highlights of the Gupta corporation. It was started in 1984 by Umang Gupta, then Vice President of Oracle's Microcomputer Division, and Bruce Scott, coauthor of the original Oracle database engine. By 1986, Gupta introduced the world's first SQL database designed specifically for networked PCs, SQLBase Server for DOS. In 1988, SQLWindows 1.0 was shipped as the first Windows-based client/server application system. That year, SQLBase Server for OS/2 was also shipped, as was SQLNetwork, which enabled PC users to access DB2 data on the mainframe. The year 1990 was a big one for Gupta. In May of that year, SQLWindows 1.3, which supports Windows 3.0, was announced and in June, Gupta announced connectivity to Oracle on any platform (SQLNetwork for ORACLE). Later that year, SQLWindows 2.0 was released with many new features including ReportWindows, a graphical report writer. The year 1991 was no sleeper for Gupta, either. First, SQLWindows 3.0 shipped with many major upgrades, and SQLWindows runtimes were made available for distribution royalty free. In June 1991 Gupta announced the release of Quest, which gives developers and users direct access to their corporate databases. On the SQLNetwork side, in 1990 Gupta released connectivity to Btrieve, Microsoft/Sybase SQL Server, OS/2 Extended Edition Database Manager; and announced SQLGateway for DRDA, which gave SQLWindows and Quest users access to all IBM SAAdatabases, including OS/2 EE Database Manager, AS/400, DB2, and SQL/DS. In 1992, Gupta announced support for ODBC, IDAPI, and SQLHost Application services, which provided a specialized API for programmers to develop applications accessing non-DB2 mainframe data, such as VSAM and IMS legacy data, and dumb-terminal applications. Gupta also shipped SQLBase 5.0 NLM, setting a new performance standard for PC-LAN Databases. SQLBase NLM was benchmarked at 102 transactions per second, making PC networks viable platforms for downsizing mission-critical applications. In 1993, Gupta announced SQLWindows 4.0, Quest 2.0, and TeamWindows, introducing the concept of collaborative programming for PC application development. There were many other milestones reached by the Gupta corporation. Anyone on Gupta's mailing list knows that there is something new and big happening all the time. There are training partnerships, software partnerships, and more being formalized constantly.

Installation

Hardware and Software Requirements

The software used was SQLWindows 4.0 Corporate Edition, installed on a 386 PC, 25 mhz, eight megabytes of RAM, and Windows 3.1.

Hardware requires an IBM-compatible PC capable of running the following software:

—DOS 3.1 or later

—Microsoft Windows 3.1 or later

—SQLWindows runs in standard or enhanced mode and will not operate in real mode

If you're writing DLLs for SQLWindows you will need:

—Microsoft C compiler (version 5.1 or later)

—Microsoft Windows Software Development Kit

　or

—Borland C++ (version 2.0 or later)

The PC must have at least 2.5 megabytes of memory for completed applications, and at least four megabytes of memory for development. The SQLWindow manuals recommend at least four megabytes for completed applications and at least eight megabytes for development. The PC must have at least six megabytes of disk space for the minimum installation of SQLWindows and the SQLBase. You will need at least 12 megabytes for a complete installation of all components. The database engine for this chapter is a local version of SQLBase.

Installing Software

Installation of SQLWindows is found on diskette one and is called SWSETUP.EXE. It allows you to install all the components at the same time, one at a time, or any combination thereof. If you choose to install SQLWindows using Options, a dialog box appears that lets you select the components to install, and allows you to change the default directories.

To install Quest, insert the first Quest disk and run qstsetup. You will then get a setup menu. The setup menu lets you install using the defaults, or install Quest using options. Options include the drive and directory to install Quest, and you can install a single user local version of SQLBase.

At the completion of installation (assuming all the components were installed), the PC client will have SQLWindows 4.0 Group created with several icons in the group. These represent the development environment available to the PC developer. The following tools are available with the Corporate Edition.

SQLWindows. This is the graphical client/server development tool for the Windows development programmer. First there is the tool palette, which is used for adding graphical items to a form. The graphical items include data fields, multiline text fields, listboxes, combo boxes, table windows, Quest windows, drop-down listboxes, radio buttons, check boxes, menus, table windows, and other graphical items. Custom graphical objects can be used as well. As the form is being painted, predefined template code is added to the outline defining the attributes of each item (color, size, font, etc.). Attributes for the graphical objects can be modified by selecting objects customizer or changing the code in the outline. The next step is to go into the outliner to add application logic to the application template using SQLWindows application language—called SAL (SQLWindows Application Language). Once coding has been completed, compiling, testing, and debugging can begin.

ReportWindows. This is Gupta's graphical report writer. Report-Windows is used to design report templates that can be used to report on data from different sources, like flat files and databases. The report template can be used to specify headings, footings, formatting, graphics, and totals.

TeamWindows. This is brand new with release SQLWindows 4.0, and is Gupta's answer to the multiprogrammer environment. Team-Windows has a multitude of tools used in the development life cycle. The tools in TeamWindows manage projects, set up project security levels, manage template libraries, and maintain application source code with features like a module check in/check out feature, program modification logging, versioning, and error logging. If you have worked on a project team, you know how important this can be. TeamWindows comes with a series of standard control reports that can be used for project-management reporting and can be modified to meet other project-reporting needs. TeamWindows allows the team to have different levels of security depending on each team member's role: the levels are administrator, project manager, developer, and tester. The administrator has the highest security level, and the tester has the most limited access. Team members also have a promotion level used to control movement of modules to three promotion levels supplied by TeamWindows: development, test/shared, and production. Development can check modules in and out for development. Test/shared can promote modules to test status. Production can promote modules to production status. Team members can be given other authorities, which include Template Engineer, with the ability to create and modify templates; Database Administrator, which can modify the database in the Data Dictionary Manager; Test Sign Off, which is used for signing off modules that are being tested, and Log All Errors; whereby the user captures database errors that are written to a log file.

TeamWindows comes with a feature for creating and managing templates or screen classes that can be used when creating new applications. Templates are very much like typical SQLWindows applications, with some template code unique to templates. The templates are stored in template libraries. The SQLWindows product comes with a set of several common templates that can be used for developing applications. Development teams can create their own application templates of common window functions or code. Generic templates can speed up the application process by employing commonly used code or functions for developing windows and giving the applications a consistent look and feel.

EditWindows. EditWindows is the resource editor for SQLWindows applications. With EditWindows you can modify the runtime version of an application without making any changes to the source code. EditWindows can tailor an application for different groups; for example, hiding certain fields from the users that can be displayed by the development team, change tab order, hide data columns, and relabel column titles, to name but a few.

SQLWindows Sampler. This icon is used for examining several program samples supplied by Gupta. On opening the icon you will see the window displayed below (Figure 8.1). The left listbox displays the titles of the different applications in the samples, and as you highlight the different titles the second listbox shows the appropriate description that corresponds to the application title. The data-entry box displays the DOS filename of the selected application. The push buttons allow the developer to either run the sample

Figure 8.1   SQLWindows sampler.

program or go into the SQLWindows development to view and/or edit the sample application program.

Data Dictionary Manager. The Data Dictionary Manager is a component of the TeamWindows data repository. This data dictionary stores information about the structure of your application databases. This information is imported directly from the system catalog, and contains the names of the tables and columns, primary and foreign key relationships, information about data types, column default values, display formats, and validation criteria. The dictionary tracks changes to this information and stores it in a log file. The data dictionary also manages user-access levels.

Configure Repository. Used to install or upgrade the database used by TeamWindows. It's also used to update details about the repository path or company name.

SQLTalk. SQLTalk/Windows is a Windows-based user interface for Gupta Technologies' SQLBase and other database engines. It is mainly used by data administrators, developers, and end users that need to work with multiple databases. SQLTalk is intended for ad hoc querying, session controls like connecting/disconnecting to database engine, environment settings, isolation levels, table privileges, add/modify users, creating/editing/executing SQL script, and more. The SQLBase database engine can be installed locally for a single user or on a NetBios-compatible LAN for access by multiple users. SQLTalk requires that SQLBase or gateway software be installed on a 286/386 machine running DOS or OS/2. SQLTalk requires two megabytes of memory for use with a locally installed SQLBase. SQLTalk requires a 286/386 machine and 640k for use when SQLTalk is installed locally and SQLBase installed on a remote server. SQLTalk requires DOS and Microsoft Windows version 2.0 or higher on the machine on which it is installed.

SQLBase Server. This is an icon to start or stop the locally installed SQLBase Server engine.

Release notes. Release notes cover last-minute changes and other topics not covered in either the SQLWindows online documentation or the printed documentation.

Database

Database Connectivity

SQLWindows can access data in local and remote SQLBase databases. It can also access data in DB2, Database Manager, Oracle, Sybase, SQL

Server, NetWare SQL, Teradata, HP Allbase/SQL, IBM AS/400, and many more. To connect to these other databases you will need Gupta's SQLNetwork products. Gupta's SQLNetwork products give users access to enterprise-wide SQL databases, minicomputers, and mainframes with the same graphical interface. SQLWindows connects to SQLBase single-user SQLBase database servers by executing DBWINDOW.EXE installed on the same computer. To communicate with the SQLBase database server running on a LAN server you must install a router on the client's PC where the application is running. SQLBase software can run in multiple-network environments. Gupta Technologies' DOS and OS/2 software can run with any software package that supports a standard NetBIOS interface. NetBIOS interfaces are available with many network software packages including IBM's Token Ring or PC Network and PC LAN Program, 3Com's Lan Manager and 3+, Novell's Netware, Banyan's VINES, and Starlan.

Database Administration

Database administration tasks for Gupta's product can be done in two ways. First is SQLTalk/Windows, which is a Windows-based interface to SQLBase. SQLTalk comes in two flavors—SQLTalk/Character, a DOS-based SQLTalk; and SQLTalk/Windows, a point-and-click version. The product we will be referring to is SQLTalk Windows 2.0. According to the manuals, SQLTalk may also be used as a front end to other database engines like DB2 with the use of SQLGateway from Gupta. The second way to do database administration is to use Quest 2.0, which is also Windows-based and can be used with SQLBase and several other database engines. SQLTalk has more functionality, including table-security functions, user-access levels, and synonym maintenance. For our purposes, we used Quest to perform our database-administration tasks. The different activities in Quest include creation and modification of databases, tables, views, and indexes. Quest has a facility for executing SQL from DOS files, developing reports, and an easy way of editing data in database files.

Quest is a graphical database manager. It comes bundled with Gupta's SQLWindows and performs many of the same functions as SQLTalk, but is point-and-click driven where SQLTalk is text driven and requires the user to be SQL knowledgeable. Quest allows Windows access to SQL databases in an organization, whether they be LAN-based, minicomputer, or mainframe, without the user having any knowledge of SQL. Quest is very easy to use as a data-administration tool, allowing the user to create/drop databases, create/modify/delete tables, indexes, views, as well as having a reporting feature. You can use Quest to edit table columns and add user data. It is also great for adding and editing test data. Quest is also accessible by other Windows applications that support DDE (dynamic data exchange) and

OLE (objectlinking and embedding). These applications include Microsoft Excel, Lotus 1-2-3 for Windows, Ami Pro, Microsoft Word, Borland Object Vision, and Microsoft Visual Basic, to name a few. Quest is used for all levels of database activity. At the opening of the Quest icon you get a menu bar, activity bar, and Quest work space. Quest's work environment includes a dynamic menu bar, which changes to reflect the options of the current activity (Figure 8.2). Quest's activities include database/table administration, query management, importing and exporting data, and a reporting feature.

Another important feature of Quest is its ability to interface with a number of SQL-based databases including SQLBase, DB2, OS/2 Extended Edition Database Manager, SQL Server, Informix, AS/400, and Oracle. Quest can move data to and from a number of applications using the Windows Clipboard. Quest supports Windows DDE and OLE facilities. It can also access CSV files (comma-separated variable files), DBF (dBase III), Lotus, and Excel files.

Database Creation/Modification Using Quest

Quest maintains its own catalog of databases. It allows the developer to create a new database or select one from the current DBMS. The databases defined to Quest are displayed in the drop-down listbox on the Quest toolbar. To start a database activity, select the Utilities menu from the menu bar in the Quest window, select the Database option, and choose an activity: add, remove, configure, or create. Add allows the developer to select a database to add to the Quest catalog, remove deletes the database from the Quest catalog; configure modifies database parameters like database password, defer connection on start up, prompt for user password on first connection, enable catalog

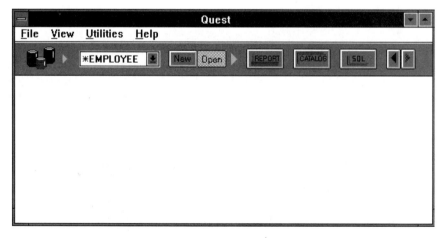

Figure 8.2   Quest work space.

caching, and parameters for table and index creation; and create will create a new database.

Tables, Views, and Indexes Using Quest

Table activities start with selecting the database from the drop-down listbox on the Quest toolbar. The next step is to click the Table pushbutton on the toolbar, causing the Create Table window to open. The Create table activity allows the developer to create tables from a file, clipboard, catalog activity, or by entering a unique table name in the Table Name entry box, a label in the Label entry box, any comments about the table, and clicking the OK button (Figure 8.3).

Creating Indexes Using Quest

Indexes can be created or modified by selecting the Catalog pushbutton on the Quest toolbar, and then selecting the Catalog menu selection. The developer then selects the activity: browse, create, modify, or delete. Choosing the Browse menu selection displays a list of indexes in the catalog on the current database (Figure 8.4).

The Create menu selection opens a cascading menu where the developer can select Index, causing the Create New Index window to open (Figure 8.5).

Select the table from the For Table dropdown listbox, and fill in the name of the index in the Index Name box. From the Columns selection list select or deselect the columns to be used in the index. The two pushbuttons at the bottom right of the Index On listbox are used for selecting ascending or descending on the specific columns of the index. The check box labeled Unique should be checked if the index

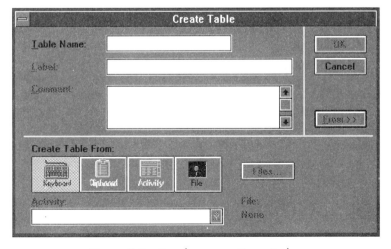

Figure 8.3   Database creation window.

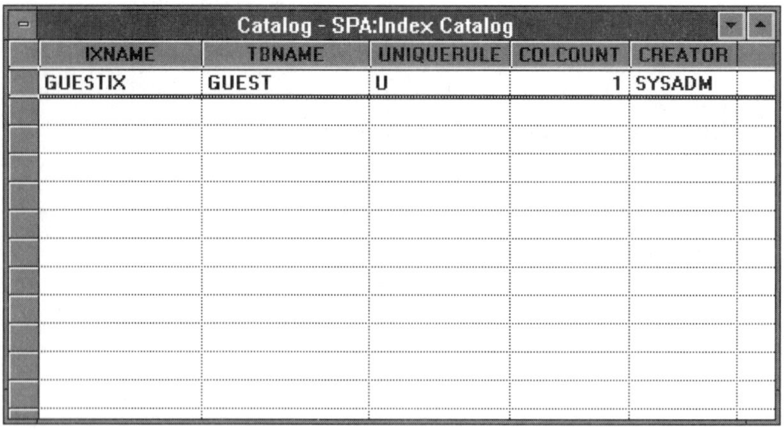

Catalog - SPA:Index Catalog				
IXNAME	TBNAME	UNIQUERULE	COLCOUNT	CREATOR
GUESTIX	GUEST	U	1	SYSADM

Figure 8.4   Index Catalog.

will be unique for all rows in the table or unchecked if nonunique index can exist. Click the OK pushbutton and the index will created.

To begin the modify index process, choose the Modify menu selection, select Index from the cascading menu, and the same window and parameters as the Create New Index Window will open with a different title and will display indexes currently on the tables.

To delete an index, select the Delete menu selection, select Index from the cascading menu, and the Delete Index window will open (Figure 8.6).

Select the table from the drop-down listbox in the upper left corner, and the current index(es) will display in the listbox below. Select the index or indexes to delete and click the OK pushbutton.

Views

Views can be created or modified by selecting the Catalog pushbutton on the Quest toolbar, then selecting the catalog menu selection. The

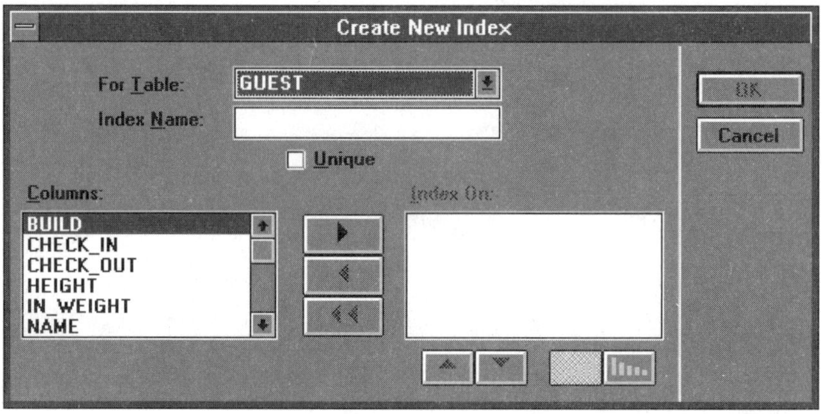

Figure 8.5   Create New Index window.

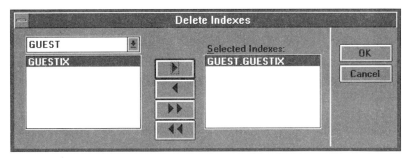

Figure 8.6   Delete Index window.

developer then selects the activity: browse, create, modify or delete. Choosing the Browse menu selection displays a list of views in the catalog on the current database (Figure 8.7).

Create and Modify View use the same window. Select the saved query from the DOS file, and the directory will store the query.

To delete a view, select Delete from the Catalog menu, then select View from the cascading menu and the Delete View window will open (Figure 8.8).

Highlight the view(s) to delete, then select the OK button.

Populating the Database

To populate a table, select the Table pushbutton and a listbox with all the tables in the current database are displayed. Select the table you wish to edit, then click the OK pushbutton.

To insert a new row, select the Table menu, and the table data will display in a tabular form. Select the New Row menu selection. The display inserts a new row in the display (Figure 8.9). Enter the data as needed. To update a row, click on the column to update and type in the new value. To display the table data in a free form format select As Fields selection under the View menu (Figure 8.10).

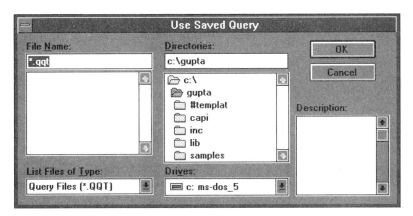

Figure 8.7   Browse Views window.

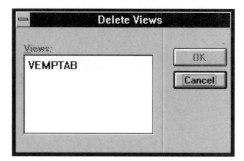

Figure 8.8 Delete View window.

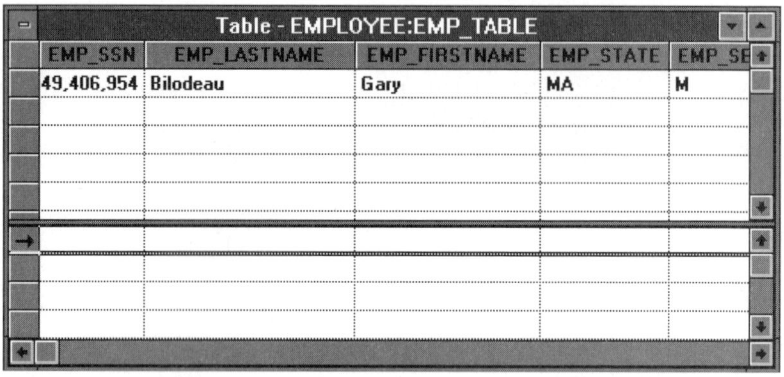

EMP_SSN	EMP_LASTNAME	EMP_FIRSTNAME	EMP_STATE	EMP_SE
49,406,954	Bilodeau	Gary	MA	M

Table - EMPLOYEE:EMP_TABLE

Figure 8.9 Adding rows to a table using column edit style.

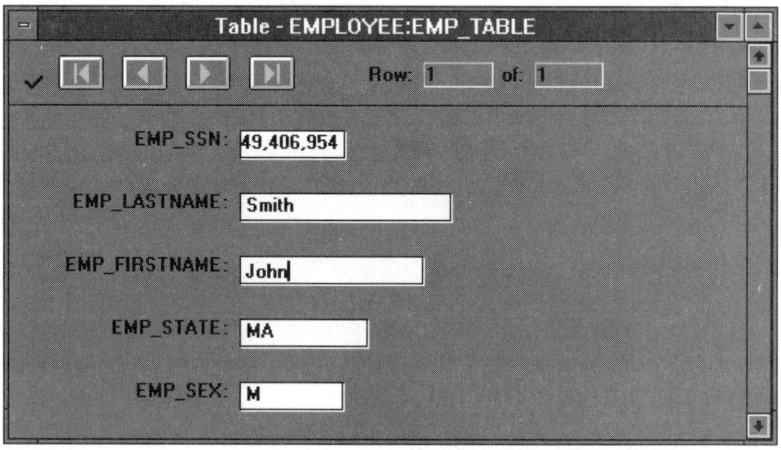

Table - EMPLOYEE:EMP_TABLE

Row: 1   of: 1

EMP_SSN: 49,406,954

EMP_LASTNAME: Smith

EMP_FIRSTNAME: John

EMP_STATE: MA

EMP_SEX: M

Figure 8.10 Adding rows to a table using free form entry style.

To save the changes, choose the Apply Edits selection in the Table menu. To cancel the edits, select the Discard Edits menu.

SQLTalk

A second method by which to accomplish database activities is to use the SQLTalk facility. SQLTalk is a text-driven facility. Tables, views, indexes, and data entry are accomplished by executing SQL script in the Input Window. The result displays in the Output Window (Figure 8.11). SQLTalk is mainly used for database-administration activities. These include setting user access authority, creating or dropping synonyms, and editing and manipulating SQL script.

Upon opening the SQLTalk icon, the window will display an input window, output window, and a menu bar. The input window is used for editing and executing SQL commands or scripts; the output window is used to display the script or command results. The menu bar contains several high-level selections for using SQLTalk. The first selection is the File menu selection for performing DOS file functions like open, close, and save, and is used for editing, modifying, or deleting script stored in DOS files. The second menu selection is the Edit selection, which is used for performing copy, cut, paste, clear input window, and/or clearing the output window. The next selection is the menu item Session, which is used for connecting/disconnecting to the database and setting environment options and query and script management, like aborting the current query/script, suspending script, continuing script, and script-navigation functions. The menu selection Utilities is used for activities like Copy, which copies the entire data

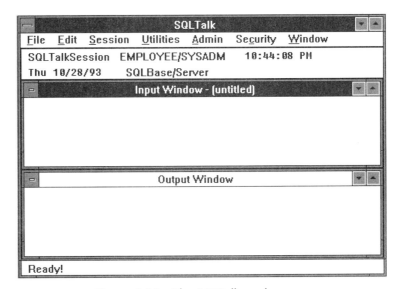

Figure 8.11   The SQLTalk work space.

from a table or view to another table or view, Extract copies the result of a query to a table or view, Execute runs a SQL statement previously compiled and stored in the database, Precompile compiles and stores the SQL statement in the database, and Remove deletes the previously compiled SQL statement. The next two selections are Import, which loads tables and/or data from an external file into the current database, and Export which unloads or copies some or all of a database to an external file. This can be used for backups or data transfer. The last two selections under the Utilities menu are local catalog functions. One is for updating the local catalog, the other for clearing the local catalog from the server. The Administration menu selection contains selections like start/stop/apply journal for managing journaling. *Journaling* logs all SQL statements that modify a database. *Start* opens a log file that logs all the SQL statements that modify the database. *Stop* discontinues the journaling. *Apply* runs the log file against the database. This is used to recreate a damaged database. First the administrator would restore the database using the last backup and then apply the log file to bring the database up to date. The Backup and Restore selections have not been implemented at this time. The next two selections are database functions to install a database, which creates a new one or reinitializes an existing one and Deinstall, which takes a remote database offline and removes the database from the list of available databases. The last menu bar selection is Admin, used for security administration. The systems administrator (SYSADM id) can add or modify users' authority levels. These authority levels are database level, not table level. The different authority levels include connect, resource, and DBA. Connect gives the user the ability to connect to the database and perform any table privileges that have been assigned. Resource allows users to create/drop their own tables, and to grant, modify, and revoke privileges on these tables. DBA authority is the level of authority just below SYSADM. DBA has authority to assign privileges on all tables in a database. The difference between a DBA and SYSADM is that a DBA cannot modify passwords or authority levels of other users. The next selection under Admin is Table Privileges, used to assign or revoke table privileges. Last under the Admin selections is create and drop synonyms. This enables a user to refer to a table without having to specify the prefix or name of the table's owner or creator.

The SQLWindows Development Environment

To start, the developer selects the SQLWindows icon, which opens the SQLWindows development facility (Figure 8.12).

There are three major components to the development facility: the outliner window, a blank form window (frmMain), and the tool palette.

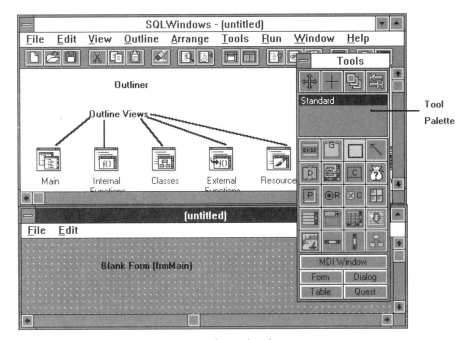

Figure 8.12   SQLWindows development environment.

The tool palette is used for adding graphic objects to the current application. Listed in Figure 8.13 are the object control-buttons on the tool palette.

The outliner has menus to control the environment, and outline views, which are represented by the icons in the Outliner window. These icons let the developer view selected parts of the code outline like internal functions, named menus, main, and classes. The main icon displays the entire outline. The blank form is a starting point for the developer to paint the application window. The graphical objects are placed on the blank form using the tool palette. The tool palette has other drawing tools like the object duplicator, object selector, and window grabber, which are used to manipulate objects currently on the window. Window objects can be added or modified by coding them in the code outline.

Outliner Menu Options

The Outliner window has several menu selections used for controlling and/or modifying the application. The developer may also display a tool bar, which has some of the more common menu selections.

File Menu

- New—Creates a new SQLWindows application.
- Open—Opens a dialog box where the SQLWindow application

Window Grabber - Selects one or more objects. Select Multiple objects by holding the shift key then select.

Object Selector - Selects multiple objects. Use to move objects to a new location or cut, clear, copy, or paste objects

Object Duplicator - Duplicates select object or objects

Background Text

Group Box

Frame

Line

Data Field

Multiline Field

Custom Controls

Pushbutton

Radio Button

Check Box

Option Button

List Box

Combo Box

Child Table Window

Quest Window

Picture

Horizontal Scroll Bar

Vertical Scroll Bar

Create MDI Window

Create Form Window

Create Dialog Box

Create Top-Level Table Window

Create Quest Window

Figure 8.13   Objects on the tool palette.

may be selected. The drive, directory, and application suffix may be modified to select applications from other than the default locations.

- Save—Saves the current application to disk. If the application is unnamed, the developer is prompted for an application name.
- Save As—Saves the current application under a new name. You may save it under an existing application, and SQLWindows will prompt the user to verify replacing an existing application. The Save As option lets you select how you would like to save the application: the choices are normal, compiled, text, and indented text. Normal saves it in an internal format that loads quickly and saves quickly at design time. Compiled saves the code in compiled format. Text saves the application in text format that can be opened with a text editor. Indented text is the same as text, except the sections and subsections are saved with tabs for the different levels.

Libraries—Opens a Cascading Menu that Manages Included Objects

- Edit Item—Starts a new instance of SQLWindows where you can edit the library of the selected item.
- Show Item Information—Displays information about the selected include item.
- Refresh—Reincludes all included objects.
- Merge—Merges all included objects into the current application.
- Make Executable—Creates an executable (.EXE file) from the current application, and assigns the application an icon.
- Make Runtime—Creates a .RUN file from the current application. The Make Runtime selection is used for backwards compatibility, use the Make Executable to create an executables for the current version of SQLWindows.
- Print Outline—Prints the current outline. You may print the entire outline or the currently highlighted section.
- Print Setup—Selects standard Windows printing options.
- Preferences—Customizes the SQLWindows development environment. The options here include the filename of the new application, default application file extension, slow animate speed in seconds, library file paths, and outline text attributes like fonts and colors.
- Exit—Exits the SQLWindows development environment.

Edit Menu

- Undo—Reverses the last editing or formating option.
- Cut—Removes code that is highlighted in the outline and puts it in the clipboard.

- Copy—Copies highlighted code to the clipboard.
- Paste—Copies the clipboard contents to the current mouse location.
- Paste Link—Pastes the OLE object in the clipboard in the picture that has the focus, and links that object to the source application where it was created.
- Paste Special—Selects the format of the clipboard data before pasting. Common formats are Paintbrush Picture Objects and BMPs.
- Paste From—Opens a dialog box to select a file containing an image to paste into the picture that has focus.
- Clear—Deletes selected items without saving them in the clipboard.
- Grid—Aligns items to a grid on the window form.
- Show Grid—Displays grid pattern on the window form.
- Align to Grid—Aligns selected items to the closest grid lines.
- Find—Finds text in the application outline.
- Repeat Last Find—Repeats the last find without opening the Find dialogue box.
- Change—Replaces specific text in the outline.
- Links—Displays the current OLE links in the application.
- Object—Starts the application that created the OLE object.
- Insert Object—Inserts an object into a picture from an OLE application.

View Menu

- Toolbar—Toggle for displaying the outline windows toolbar below the outline menu.
- Status Bar—Toggle for displaying a status bar at the bottom of the Outline window. The status bar displays information like num lock, scroll lock, current menu pick, or toolbar pick.
- Outline Options—Opens the Outline Options dialog box. This dialog box displays code that is applicable to the current position in the outline.
- Library Browser—Opens a dialog box that lets you view libraries, objects in the libraries, and displays the object's last modification date and time.
- Tool Palette—Toggle to display or hide the tool palette.
- Show Window—Opens a dialog box that lists hidden top-level windows. Select the window to display.
- Hide Window—Opens a dialog box that lists hidden top-level windows. Select the window to hide.

- Temporary Positioning—Changes the position of the window without changing the position in the outline. The next time the application is opened, the window displays in the old position.

Outline Menu

- Insert Line—Inserts a blank line in the outline at the same level as the current selected item.
- Comment Items—Makes selected outline code items comments. Commented code is prefixed by an exclamation point (!).
- Uncomment Items—Removes comments' prefix (!) from selected lines of code.
- Expand One Level—Expands selected items one level.
- Collapse—Compresses items so that only the parent items are visible.
- Expand All Levels—Expands all levels of selected items.
- Collapse Outline—Collapses outline so that only top-level items are visible.
- Move Left—Moves selected code one indent level to the left.
- Move Right—Moves selected code one indent level to the right.
- Move Up—Moves selected code above the previous code.
- Move Down—Moves selected code below the next code.

Arrange Menu

- Bring to Front—Brings objects that are under other objects to the top for editing.
- Send To Back—Sends object on the top layer to the back.
- Tab Order—Opens a dialog box to set the tab order for the objects in the window.
- Align—Aligns two or more selected objects. The first object is used to align the rest of the objects.
- Even Spacing—Spaces selected objects evenly horizontally and/or vertically.
- Equal Sizing—Makes selected objects the same size, including width, height, or both.

Tools Menu

- Class—Opens a cascading menu to create a new class object, create a class from another class object, or edit a class object.
- Windows—Displays a cascading menu to select a top-level window or MDI window to add to the application.

- Draw—Opens a cascading menu to select a tool (Window Grabber, Object Selector, Object Duplicator), or select a child object.

Run Menu

- User Mode—Compiles the application and puts the application in run mode. Click on user mode again to put the application back in design mode.
- Compile—Compiles the application. If checked, the application is already compiled.
- Break—Opens a cascading menu for managing breakpoints. Breakpoints allow the developer to suspend execution at specific points in the application.
- Animate—Displays the code as it executes line by line.
- Slow Animate—Same as Animate, except at a slower speed.
- No Animate—Stops the Animate or Slow Animate options.

Window Menu

- No Auto Tiling—Outline view windows do not tile automatically as you open and close views.
- Auto Tile Horizontally—Tiles the outline view horizontally as you open and close the views.
- Auto Tile Vertically—Tiles the outline view vertically as you open and close the views.
- Cascade—Displays the outline views layered or cascaded.
- Arrange Icons—Arranges outliner view icons at the bottom of the outline.
- Close All—Closes all views except the main outline view.

Help Menu

- Index—Displays the help facility index.
- Functions—Displays help for system functions, internal functions and external functions.
- Messages—Displays help for messages.
- About SQLWindows—Displays the version number of SQL-Windows.

Outline Code Window

The outline-window area contains the source code for the window's application. Every line in the outline is called an *outline item*. The diamond to the left of the code indicates whether there is more code associated with the outline item. A filled black diamond indicates that there is more code associated with the outline item. This is referred to as a *parent item* or section; the subordinate code is called the *child item* or subsection. An empty diamond indicates there are no more levels of code or child items. The design window is where you can graphically construct your application. The tool palette lets you drag and drop window objects onto the design window.

SQLWindows starts the application with a default application called NEWAPP.APP, which starts with the basics of an SQLWindows application. This skeleton application is the starting point for application development, or you can create an application skeleton specific to the application as the starting point. For example, in a development application there may be common windows that can be used as a starting point instead of starting from scratch. You can modify the application that is used for brand-new applications in the Preferences selection under the File menu.

As objects are drawn on the form, skeleton code is generated with default object attributes that define the object (color, font, field size, etc.). These attributes can be modified by selecting the window grabber from the tool palette and double-clicking on the object or clicking on the object with the right mouse button. The customizer list will appear on the screen, modify the attributes for the object, and exit. The attributes vary depending on the object type selected.

The developer can add and edit objects, actions, and procedures. When the outline is first brought up several outline items appear on the outline window (Figure 8.14).

Application Description is the top-most item and describes your application. Design Time Settings display the settings that control the appearance, location, and size of the outline window, outline options,

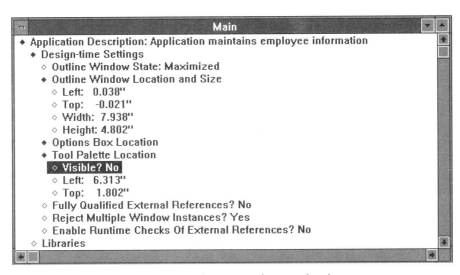

Figure 8.14   Application outline top-level items.

dialog box, and the tool palette. You can expand the design time settings by double-clicking on the solid diamond to the left of the outline item. The libraries section is used to specify included libraries. A *library* is a collection of SQLWindow objects. Libraries allow developers to share components with one other. The type of objects in libraries are top-level windows, MDI windows, internal functions, external function definitions, class definitions, global variables, and constants. A library may contain items from other libraries. Include Objects can be library internal functions and their global variables; libraries of dialog boxes, their constants and global variables; and external function declarations for user defined DLLs. Global Declarations define any external or internal functions, variables, constants, or application actions used in your application. Global Declarations have several subsections (Figure 8.15).

The first subsection of Global Declarations is the Window Defaults. The developer can set up default settings for all window objects. Double-clicking on the solid diamond expands a list of attributes to which you can assign defaults. Double-clicking on the icon next to the window or clicking the right mouse button opens a customizer where the defaults can be modified. The developer may modify the defaults by changing the code. The defaults are such items as Display Style, Font Name, Font Size, Font Enhancement, Text Color, and Background Color. The subsection Formats contains input masks and output formats for numeric and date/time values. The developer can add new formats or modify existing ones.

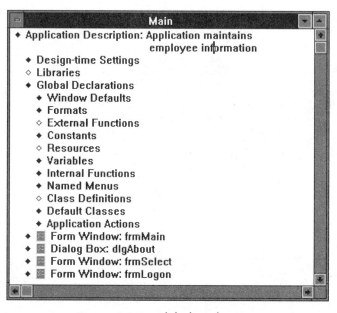

Figure 8.15   Global Declarations.

The next subsections are External Functions, Constants, Resources, and Variables (Figure 8.16).

The External Functions section is used for declaring DLLs (dynamic link libraries). See Figure 8.17 for an example of declaring a DLL in an SQLWindows application.

The *Library Name* specifies the name of the DLL. The item function is the name of the function that lives in the DLL. The parameters for the function are description, export ordinal, returns, and parameters. Description is text that describes the function. *Export ordinal* is the number that identifies the function. This number is declared when creating the DLL's .DefFile. *Returns* defines the data type returned by the function. *Parameters* are the data types of the parameters passed to the function.

The *Constants* subsection defines global system and user constants. System constants are sets of predefined constants supplied by SQLWindows. Some examples include Booleans like *true* and *false,* and messages like SAM_Click, SAM_Create, and so on. *User Constants* are defined by the developer. The *Resources* subsection is used for naming icons, cursors, and bitmap resource files. The *Variables* subsection is used for defining variables that will be global to the application. The format is data type, variable name. Global variables remain active as long as the application remains active and should be used sparingly to minimize the use of window's resources. The Internal Function subsection defines functions that are global to the application (Figure 8.18).

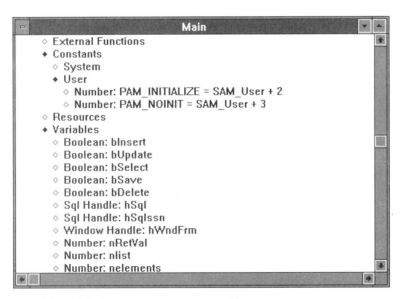

Figure 8.16   Global Declarations—External Functions, Constants, Resources, and Variables.

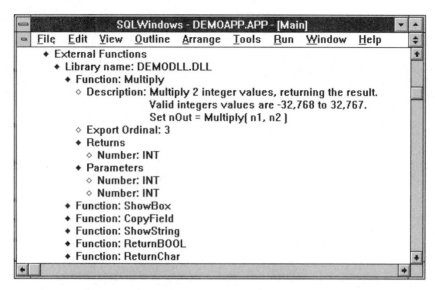

Figure 8.17   Declaring a DLL example from the sample programs.

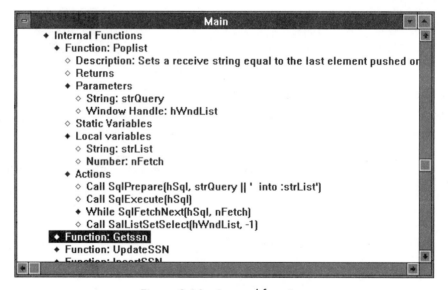

Figure 8.18   Internal function.

The first item is *Function Name*, which is the name you would refer to when calling the function. The *Description* is text describing the function. *Returns* is used for declaring the variable(s) name and the data type the function will return. The Returns can be left blank if the function returns no values. The *Parameters* item is variables that are passed to the function. The data type must match the data type of the variable being passed. *Static variables* are variables that retain their values between calls to the function. *Local variables* are variables local only to the function. *Actions* are SQLWindows code, and functions that define the function.

The subsection *Named Menus* are pop-up menus that the windows in the application share. The Named Menus in this application are supplied by default when the application is started by using the NEWAPP.APP shell. Named Menus can be used to create menus dynamically. To use a named menu in an application, specify its name in the menu definition (Figure 8.19).

The next subsection, Class Definitions, contains templates for classes. *Default classes* are class definitions used in the application (Figure 8.20).

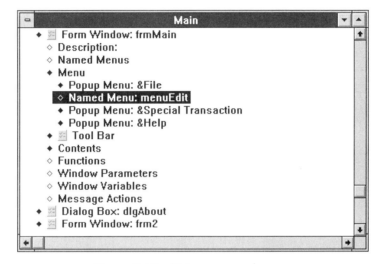

Figure 8.19   Using a named menu.

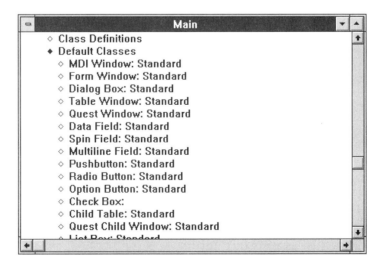

Figure 8.20   Default classes.

The subsection *Application Actions* performs application-level processing. For example, it handles events like application startup and closing the application. The next sections are definitions of top-level forms. The top-level forms are form windows, table windows, dialog boxes, and MDI windows. Top-level forms have several subsections: *Description* is text to describe the form, *Named Menus* are used to define Named menus used in the form, *Menu* is used to define the menus used in the application, *Tool bar* is used to define toolbars for the form, and *Contents* defines the child graphical objects the make up the form. Child graphical objects are represented in the outline with a customizer icon prefix (Figure 8.21).

Double-clicking on the customizer icon or clicking on the cutomizer icon with the right mouse button opens the customizer for that object. Customizers are available for the form, toolbar, and child graphical objects.

The last group of subsections for the form are: *Functions,* used for defining window functions; *Window Variables,* variables defined only to the form; and *Message Actions,* used for form-level events like form create or destroy.

Creating the SQLWindows Application

The SQLWindows application can be developed in a couple of ways. The first is developing in the SQLWindows development environment. The second way is by using SQLWindows templates. There are several templates installed with the Gupta product, or you may wish to develop your own templates. The templates are easy to use and can cut development time tremendously. The Gupta manuals include a very good tutorial on developing an application using some of their templates. After going through the tutorial, we were able to create a

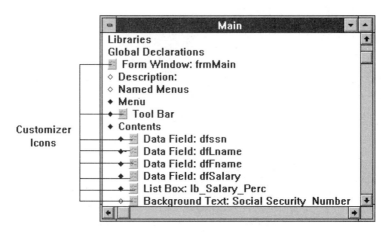

Figure 8.21   Customizer icons.

window with a master/detail update in about an hour—that same application would have taken much longer from scratch. Coding with templates may not give you the complete application, but it sure offers a good start. The discussion that follows will cover the SQL-Windows development environment.

Creating the application using the SQLWindows development environment involves several steps:

1. Paint the window.
2. Set the fields attributes and properties.
3. Code the script to respond to specific events.
4. Code the script to control the application.
5. Debug and test the code.

Paint the Window

The best way to add child objects to the window is by clicking on the Window Grabber control button on the tool palette, then clicking on the blank form. The object is then placed on the form at the same time the skeleton code for the objects is added to the outline.

The object can be move to another position on the window by clicking and dragging the object to the new location. To size the object, click on the object, then click on the object's handles (Figure 8.22), and drag the handle to the create the desired size. Complete the window by adding the rest of the objects to the window. Size and position objects as needed. To duplicate objects on the window, select the Object Duplicator control button on the tool palette, then select the object to duplicate on the form, drag the Object Duplicator cursor to the desired location, and release the left mouse button. This duplicates the object and the object's code. Another way to duplicate an object is copy and paste in the code outline.

Each object on the screen has a set of properties or attributes that can be set at design time. To display the properties of an object, you can double-click on that object or click on the right mouse button and

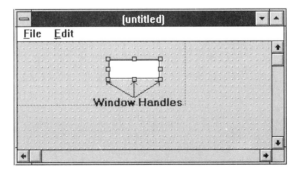

Figure 8.22   Child object on a form.

the customizer for the object will open (Figure 8.23). The customizer is specific to the object. For example, the customizer for a data field is different then that for a listbox. Options on the customizer can open another selection box, data entry field, or a toggle to turn an option on or off. Some of the basic options of the customizer are the object's name, color, text color and font, location and size, and whether the item is visible or invisible.

To add code using the customizer, choose the edit actions selection—this will place outliner at the spot where the developer codes the functions and events that apply to the selected object.

Navigating the code outline can be done by double-clicking on the iconized outline selection in the outliner window you want to edit. If the section is not displayed, select the Window menu, then select New Outline View, and the New View window will open (Figure 8.24). Select the outline section(s) to view.

The Outline Options dialog box is a powerful coding tool (Figure 8.25). This tool displays the possible events, code, functions, objects, and variables that are available at the current line of code in the outline.

The Outline Options dialog box is opened by selecting Outline Options . . . in the View Menu selection. The Outline Options dialog box is divided into two sections. The left side refers to code that can be added to the same level as the current line of code. For example, if the current line of code is an event, the Add Same Level listbox will list all the possible events. On the right side, the Add Next Level listbox will list things like if statements, do untils, and all the SAL functions that are a level below or child items to SQLWindow events. The

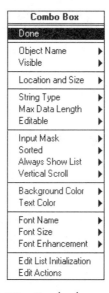

Figure 8.23   Combo box customizer.

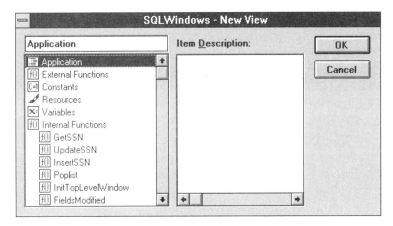

Figure 8.24   New outline view window.

listbox selections can be selected and the code will be entered onto the outline. Functions are placed in the outline in a skeleton form with placeholders for the parameters. The variables can be pasted in from the Outline Options box.

Once the application has been coded, the debugging and testing can begin. In real life the developer would probably be testing as certain parts of the application were completed. All the options to test the application can be found in the Run menu. The *User Mode option* is a toggle that flips the application back and forth between execution mode and development mode. Animate, Slow Animate, No Animate, or Break are different options used in execution mode. *Animate* dis-

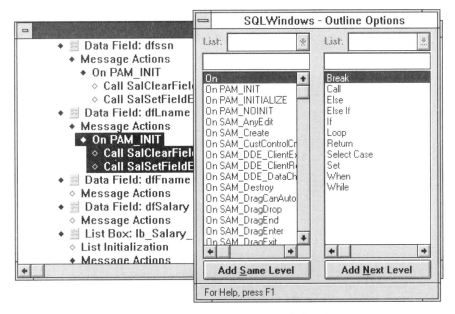

Figure 8.25   Outline Options dialog box.

plays the line of code that currently is being executed and *Slow Animate* displays the line of code being executed at a slower speed. The *No Animate* option suppresses the display of the code. *Break* is used to set breakpoints at specific lines of code. If there is a breakpoint in the code, at execution time the program will stop at the line of code before it's executed. At a breakpoint the Debug window opens (Figure 8.26).

The buttons on the right side allow the developer to continue the application, step over the breakpoint code, step through the code line by line, halt execution of the application, or close the debug window. The developer can display contents of variables by typing them in the Eval window, and the result will be displayed. Other activities are selecting Watch Messages, Variables, or Stack. Select the Watch Messages push button and the Watch Msgs window will open (Figure 8.27).

As SQLWindows messages or window messages are sent they are displayed in the watch window.

Select the Watch Variables push button and the Watch Variables window will open (Figure 8.28). The Select Variables pushbutton opens a list with all the variables available to that window. The developer can then select the variables to watch.

Select the Watch Stack push button and the Watch Stack window will open (Figure 8.29). The Watch Stack displays the stack as the application is executing.

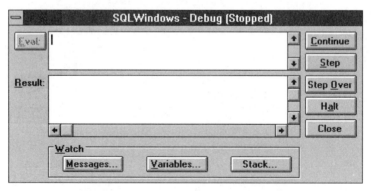

Figure 8.26   SQLWindows debug window.

Message	Window	wParam	lParam	
WM_ENABLE	4950	0001	00000000	
407	4f38	0000	00000000	
WM_CTLCOLOR	4950	0b96	00024f38	
4004	4fd4	0000	00000000	
WM_ENABLE	4950	0000	00000000	

SQLWindows Debug - Watch Msgs

☐ SAM_Msgs Only

Figure 8.27   Watch messages window.

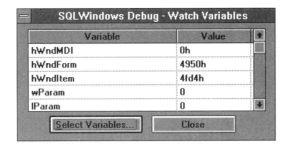

Figure 8.28   Watch variables window.

Figure 8.29   Watch stack window.

Once the application is fully tested, it can be generated into an executable and installed on the application user's machine. See the section on creating the executable for details.

Developing the Employee Update Window

There are several ways to add graphical objects to an application in the SQLWindows development environment. Child windows and graphical objects can be added using the tool palette. Top-level windows can be added using the Tools menu. Top-level windows can be form windows, table windows, Quest windows, or dialog boxes. To add background objects like text, group boxes, lines, and frames use the tool palette drawing tools. Adding code to the code outline can add any one of the objects discussed here.

The application being created using SQLWindows is explained in detail in Chapter 5. Basically, it's an employee information application that captures employee social-security number, name, address, salary information, and investment information. The purpose here is to show actual application development using Gupta's SQLWindows.

The following pages will go into detail in developing the application. We will start with painting the top-level form(s), modifying the form attributes, adding the child graphical objects, modifying the child objects attributes, and finally showing some coding examples. Start up the SQLWindows environment by double-clicking on the SQLWindows icon. The outliner, tool palette, and a blank form are displayed and ready for us to begin.

Top-Level Objects

Top-level objects have several attributes in common. They all have a border and a title bar. Optionally, they can have a toolbar and/or status bar. Top-level objects, except for dialog boxes, have the following:

- Are the only objects that can have menus.
- Can have minimized or maximized pushbuttons.
- Can be created automatically when the application starts.
- Have an initial state of maximized, minimized, or normal.
- Can be resizable at runtime.

A specialized form of a top-level window is the MDI window. The MDI sheets inside the MDI can be form windows or table windows. The MDI sheets do not have menus. The MDI sheet or child object uses the MDI top-level windows menu.

To modify the attributes of a top-level object with the customizer, double-click on whitespace on the form or click the right mouse button on the form (Figure 8.30).

Using the top-level form window's customizer we modified the following attributes: the *Object Name* is the name of the window. The *Object Title* is the text that displays in the title bar. Other attributes of importance are Accessories Enabled, Accessories, and Automatically Create. *Accessories Enabled* allows the Accessories option to be

Figure 8.30   The form window customizer.

enabled. *Accessories* is used for adding a toolbar and/or a status bar to a form window. If the *Automatically Create* selection is toggled to yes, the form window will be created at application start up (an application logon window), otherwise the window will be created by executing the SalCreateWindow function. Once the form window's attributes have been set we can add the child objects onto the form.

Child Objects

Child objects were added using the tool palette tools and objects. In modifying the attributes we used the object's customizer. Double-click on the child object or click on the child object with the right mouse button and the object's customizer will open.

The first objects that were added to the form were the data fields. These fields include social-security number, employee first and last name, employee salary, amount to invest, and effective date.

Several attributes need to be modified using the customizer (Figure 8.31). To modify the attribute for social-security number, click on the Object Name selection and type in dfssn. All data fields should be prefixed with df. The next attribute is the Input Mask, which will format the social-security number in the proper format. Select Input Mask, then type in 999-99-9999 and the social-security number will be formatted as the user is typing it in. The dashes between the numbers will appear automatically. You will notice in the application outline that this format is added to the Format subsection of Global Declarations. For employee's first and last name, just assign the object a valid name. The names assigned are dfLname for last name and dfFname for first name. For amount to invest, assign the object a valid

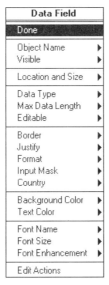

Figure 8.31   The Data field customizer.

name, dfAmtToInv, change the Data Type to a numeric data type, and Format to one of the standard numeric formats. This field is not editable as it is calculated from the salary and salary percentage fields, so the Editable attribute was set to *no.* To employee salary, we assigned the Object's Name dfSalary; because it's a money field we selected Data Type numeric and assigned it a numeric Input Mask. To effective date we assigned the object's name dfEffdt, to Data Type we assigned a data type of date/time, and assigned effective date a format of MM-DD-YY.

The next task is to add text to the data fields. Select the background text push button from the tool palette and label the data fields.

For the background text customizer attributes select Object Title and type in the text (social-security number, last name, first name, etc.) (Figure 8.32). In this application the background color is set to red and the text color is white.

The next object type is the multiline field used for entering comments about the employee.

The customizer attributes changed here were Object Name to mlComment. The standard prefix is ml. Set Word Wrap to yes so that text automatically word wraps as the user is typing, and set Vertical Scroll to yes to put a vertical scroll bar on the multiline text field (Figure 8.33).

Another object type we have is a listbox—in this application we have several listboxes, one for the salary percentage selection, and three for percentages of investment depending on the plan.

Change the Object Name attribute to reflect valid SQLWindows names (Figure 8.34). The standard prefix for a listbox is lb. The salary percentage listbox was named lbSal_Perc, and the investment listboxes were named lbIra, lbKeogh, lbStockOpt. In this application the listboxes were single selections, so the Multiple Selection attribute is set to *no,* which is the default. The only other attribute change for this application was that Vertical Scroll was set to *yes,* so that a vertical scroll bar would appear if needed.

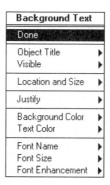

Figure 8.32   Background text customizer.

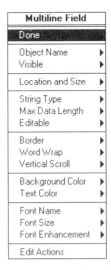

Figure 8.33   The multiline data field customizer.

A combo-box object was used for state selection. In real life it probably would have been a listbox, but we made it a combo box for the purpose of illustration. A *combo box* is a combination of a listbox and data field. This allows the user the possibility of selecting from the listbox or typing in data in the data-field portion.

As always, change the Object Name from the default to a meaningful name like cmbState. The standard prefix for a combo box is cmb. The other attributes modified were Editable, Sorted, Always Show List, and Vertical Scroll. Editable was set to *no,* which means the data field portion of the combo box would not allow data to entered into it. Sorted was set to *yes* to sort the state abbreviations in sorted order. Always Show List was set to *yes,* so that the listbox por-

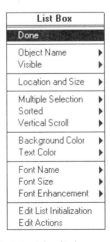

Figure 8.34   The listbox customizer.

tion is always visible. Vertical Scroll was set to *yes* to allow scrolling through the listbox portion (Figure 8.35).

The radio-button object type was used to indicate employee sex. The sex selection was also enclosed by a group box to visually group selections.

The customizer attributes modified were Object Name and Object Title. Object names were rbMale and rbFemale (Figure 8.36). Radio button's standard prefix is rb. The object title is the text associated with the radio button (male, female).

The group box's customizer Object Title was modified to sex, to label the group box (Figure 8.37). A pushbutton was used in the application. It was placed on the Employee Select window and is used to close the window. See Figure 8.38 for pushbutton attributes on the customizer.

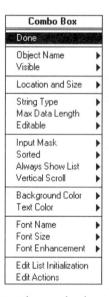

Figure 8.35   The combo-box customizer.

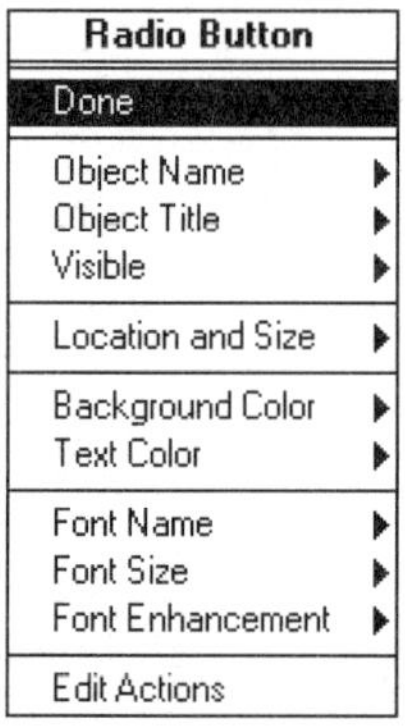

Figure 8.36   The radio-button customizer.

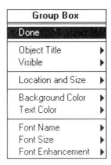

Figure 8.37   The group-box customizer.

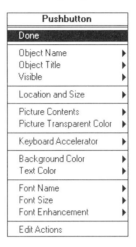

Figure 8.38   The push-button customizer.

The attributes modified for the push button were Object Name and Object Title. Object name was named pbClose and Object Title was changed to Close. The standard prefix for a pushbutton is pb. Other attributes of note are Picture Contents and Keyboard Accelerator. Picture Contents allows the developer to use a bitmap picture on a pushbutton. Keyboard Accelerator allows the developer to use a keyboard key to select the pushbutton (F1, F2, etc.).

The last object type in our application is the Quest child window. The Quest child window is a specialized object type for SQL-Windows.

The attribute modified is Object Name. The Object Name was modified to tblMaster. The standard prefix for a Quest window is tbl. The Auto Execute attribute specifies whether to automatically execute the Quest window at application startup or to let the application control its execution. Discardable and Max Rows in Memory are attributes relating to using a Quest window for update. Discardable says that when the maximum number of rows in memory limit has been reached, start discarding old rows. The Max Rows in Memory is used to specify the number of rows before SQLWindows starts discarding the rows (Figure 8.39).

At this point the form has been created, so the step left to do, which is of course the longest step, is to code the events and script for each of the controls.

Coding the Application

SQLWindows, like many other Windows applications, is event driven. The events like mouse click, application startup, mouse double-click, keyboard commands, and so on activate sending of messages. SQL-Windows applications have their own set of messages prefixed by SAM (SQLWindows application messages). SQLWindows uses three kinds of messages: SQLWindows application messages, window messages, and application-defined messages. Window messages are prefixed by WM. SQLWindows sends messages to all objects, except for lines, frames, background text, and group boxes.

Application Code

In this section we're going to present the code that was involved in developing the application. The code examples will be SQL coding features, database connections, functions, menu code, and code related to the specific controls or objects and events. SQLWindows software comes with manuals of standard functions. SQLWindow functions are prefixed by Sal and Sql. The *Sal function* categories are data manipulation, file, application communication, data formatting and validation, window management functions, reporting, printing, and others. *Sql functions* access and manipulate database data.

The first process is a logon window to the application (Figure 8.40). The logon window attempts to connect to the database using the logon and password supplied in the data fields on the logon window. If the connection is unsuccessful, display an error message and halt the application.

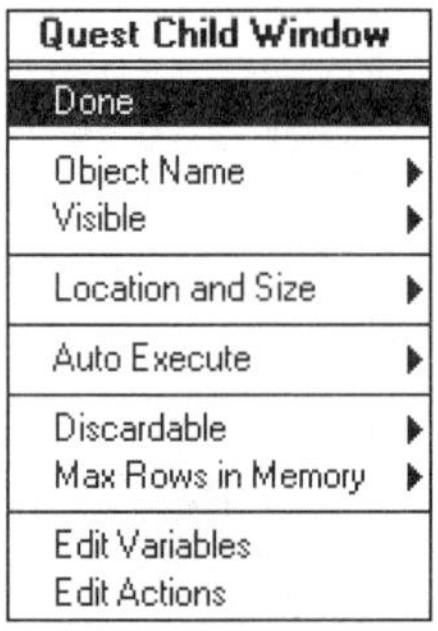

Figure 8.39   The Quest child-object customizer.

Employee Logon
Logon Id
Password
OK
Cancel

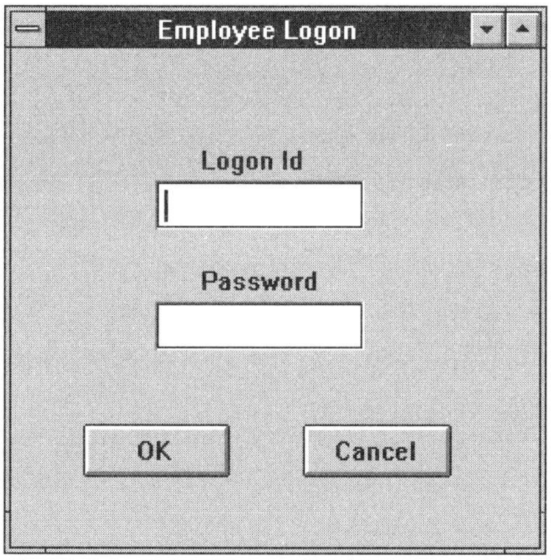

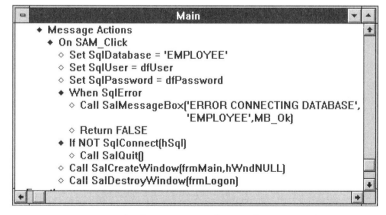

Figure 8.40 The logon window.

Assuming we are connecting to a SQLBase dbms, here's the parameters that must be filled in to satisfy the connection. If we had used another dbms, the parameters would have been different. The user fills in the id and password data fields, and clicks the OK pushbutton; the OK pushbutton code connects to SQLBase database (Figure 8.41).

The SQLWindows Message that is generated is SAM_Click. In our application the database is employee and the id (dfUser) and password (dfPassword) are from the window data fields. If the connection is unsuccessful the code When SQLError is executed, and displays the messagebox with an error message—the user is then not allowed to connect to the database and the application halts. If the connection is successful, the window opens the employee-update

Main
◆ Message Actions
◆ On SAM_Click
◇ Set SqlDatabase = 'EMPLOYEE'
◇ Set SqlUser = dfUser
◇ Set SqlPassword = dfPassword
◆ When SqlError
◇ Call SalMessageBox('ERROR CONNECTING DATABASE',
'EMPLOYEE',MB_Ok)
◇ Return FALSE
◆ If NOT SqlConnect(hSql)
◇ Call SalQuit()
◇ Call SalCreateWindow(frmMain,hWndNULL)
◇ Call SalDestroyWindow(frmLogon)

Figure 8.41 Code that connects the application to the DBMS.

window (Figure 8.42), which is done with SalCreateWindow command, and closes the Logon window with the SalDestroyWindow command.

This window controls displaying, updating, deleting, and saving employee information. The window uses menu items to control these activities.

The menu bar has three selections named File, Special Transactions, and Help. *File* has several menu selections used for manipulating employee data. *Special Transactions* is used for adding special investment transactions and reporting on employee transaction history. *Help* can be used for application help. In this case, we also have an *About* selection that displays a dialog box with the developer's name.

The file menu selections are New, Open, Save, Delete, and Exit. *New* clears the fields in the entry boxes so that a new employee may be added (Figure 8.43). *Open* retrieves data based on the social-security number from an employee list in a Quest window. Clicking on a row in this window populates the employee-update window with that employee's specific data. *Save* saves revised or added employee information. *Delete* deletes all the related information for that employee. *Exit* is used for closing the application.

The line Menu Item & New is the text that is displayed in the menu. The & creates a mnemonic for the menu. The menu settings Enabled When and Checked When are blank so that the menu selection defaults to always enabled and never checked. The code exe-

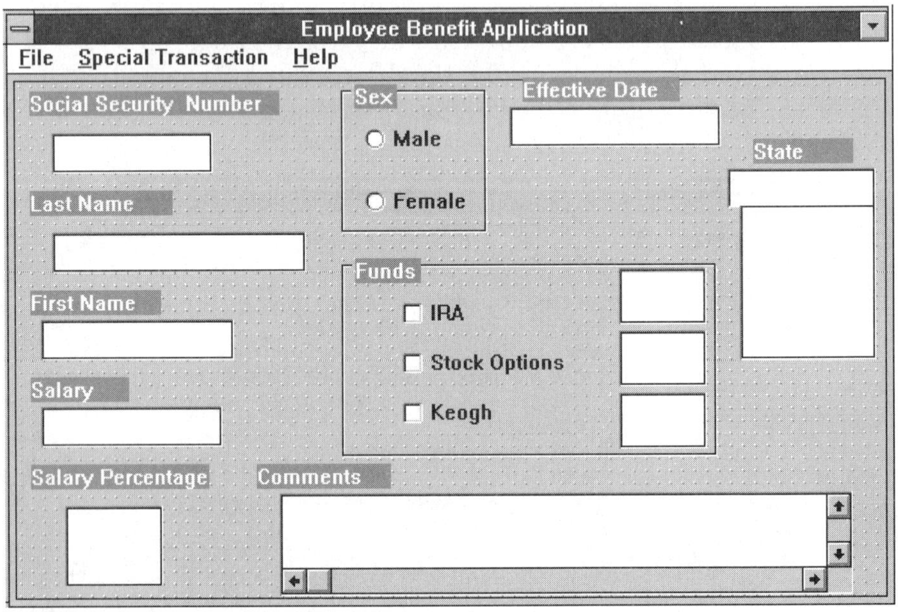

Figure 8.42   Employee-update window.

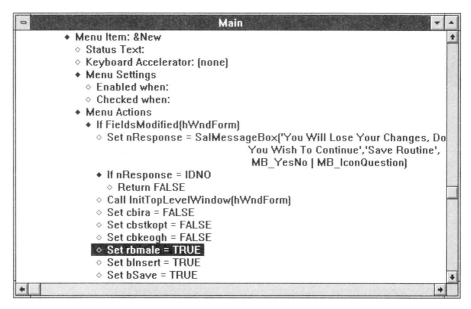

Figure 8.43   Code for the new menu selection.

cuted is in Menu Actions section. The Add menu first calls a function FieldsModified. This function loops through the data fields, and multiline data-field objects on the window and checks to see if any of the fields have been modified. If they have been modifed display a message prompting the user to continue, the changes will be lost if the user continues. This is done to make sure the current changes on the window have been saved before clearing out the fields to allow the addition of a new employee. The function continues by a call to another internal function called InitTopLevelWindow, which loops through all the child objects—if the type is a data field or multiline data field, set the field to spaces and set the edit flag to *false*.

The FieldsModified (Figure 8.44) and InitTopLevelWindow (Figure 8.45) are internal functions in some of the sample applications supplied by SQLWindows and were pasted into this application. There are several other internal functions in the sample applications that you may want to use for your applications. If you notice the way these two functions are written, they can be copied into any SQLWindows application and be used without modifying the code.

The parameter passed to this function is the window handle of the window where we wish to check for modified fields and is identified in the parameters section. The return of this function is *true* or *false: true* means a field has been modified and *false* that no fields have been modified. The function SalGetFirstChild gets the first child object on the window and then falls into a loop, if it has found a valid child object (hWndNull signals no child objects are left and the loop

Figure 8.44   FieldsModified internal function.

has completed). The loop starts by executing the SalGetType function, which returns the type of the child object (data field, listbox, text, etc.). If it's a data field or multiline data field, then execute function SalQueryFieldEdit, which checks the edit flag for the object. The edit flag is set to *true* when the field has been modified. If the loop finds a field that has been modified, it returns *true* from the function and the function terminates.

The parameter passed to this function is the window handle of the window where we wish to check for modified fields and is iden-

Figure 8.45   InitTopLevelWindow internal function.

tified in the parameters section. The function SalGetFirstChild gets the first child object on the window and then falls into a loop if it finds a valid child object (hWndNull signals no child objects are left and the loop has been completed). The function SalClearField clears the data field and SalSetFieldEdit sets the edit flag to *false.* An alternative method and a more object-oriented approach to do this would be define a user message called PAM_Init. In the function InitTopLevelWindow, execute the function SalSendMsgToChildren(hWndTopLevel,PAM_Init,0,0), which sends a message PAM_Init to all child objects. Then, put code in the child objects to respond to the PAM_Init event. Some examples follow:

Code for datafield dfSSN:

```
On PAM_INIT
    Call SalClearField(dfSSN)
    Call SalSetFieldEdit(dfSSN,FALSE)
```

Code for listbox lb_Salary_perc:

```
On PAM_INIT
    Call SalListSetSelect(lb_Salary_Perc,0)
```

The SalListSetSelect function highlights the entry in the listbox. In this example we are setting the listbox to the first entry in the list box.

At the Open menu selection, the Menu settings Enabled When item is blank, so that menu item is always enabled. The Checked When item is blank, so the Open menu selection never displays a check next to the menu selection (Figure 8.46).

The Menu Actions item executes the function SalCreateWindow. This function opens the window frmSelect, a form window with a Quest window child object used for selecting employees (Figure 8.47).

The Quest window lists all the employees, sorted by last name and first name. Double-clicking on a row in the Quest window calls

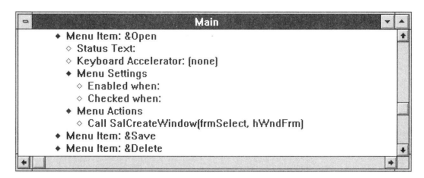

Figure 8.46   The open menu selection code.

Figure 8.47   Form window frmSelect.

the internal function GetSSN, and passes the first column of the Quest window (tblMaster#1), which is the social-security number as a parameter to the function GetSSN. The function GetSSN populates the employee-information form based on the social-security number. The Quest window does not display social-security number, as the assumption is that the user will be using the employee's name as the key. The other message this Quest window responds to is SAM_Create. When the event SAM_Create occurs (when the form is opened) it populates the Quest window using the function SalQuestTblPopulate(tblMaster) (Figure 8.48).

The internal function GetSSN executes several SQL selects based on the social-security number to retrieve data, and then populates the employee-update window (Figure 8.49 and 8.50).

This code is the first part of GetSSN function. We define our parameter as strSSN, and several local variables will then be used for our processing.

The first code item in Figure 8.50 is SalWaitCursor(True), which sets the cursor to the hour-glass cursor when this function is executed. This lets the user know that the application is performing a task and that the user should wait until notified or the cursor returns to the arrow cursor. The next several lines of code involve executing SQL. The SQLPrepare command compiles the SQL statement. It checks the syntax of the SQL statement, checks the system catalog, and identifies the bind variables (into variables). Some of the into variables are the actual object names like dfSSN, dfLname, and dfFname, because they do not need to be formatted programatically. The

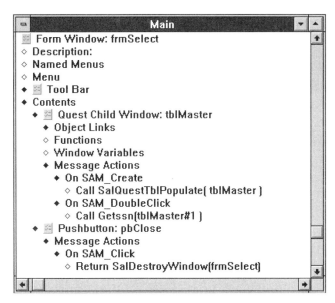

Figure 8.48   Outline items for frmSelect.

row id was selected to prevent the lost update which is only needed in a multiuser environment. The first parameter of the SQLPrepare command is hSQL and is the SQL handle associated with the SQL command. The next item, SQLExecute, executes the SQL statement prepared in the previous SQLPrepare statement. The parameter to SQLExecute is the SQL handle (hSQL). The SQLFetchNext retrieves a

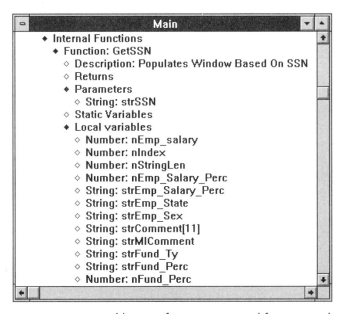

Figure 8.49   Partial listing of GetSSN internal function code.

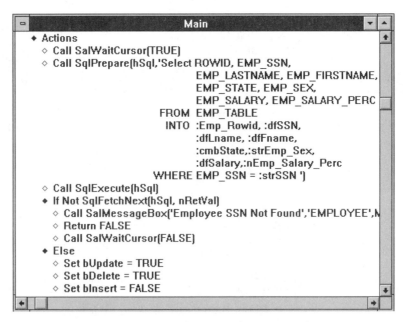

Figure 8.50   GetSSN code, continued.

row from the result set. There is another command for scrolling backwards in a result set called SQLFetchPrevious. If the SQLFecthNext is not successful or the end of the result set display an error message, reset the cursor to the arrow cursor with the SalWaitCursor(False), indicating the process has completed. If there is data in the result set, continue first by setting some global variables that will be used for disabling and enabling menu options (bSave, bDelete).

Code that follows formats the data for display on the employee Information window.

This section of code in Figure 8.51, which is a continuation of the GetSSN function, sets the sex radio buttons based on the variable strEmp_Sex used as an into variable in the SQL select. Setting a radio button to *true* sets the button on, *false* sets the radio button off.

This application has several listboxes. The code that follows is the code that highlights the salary percentage of the current employee, based on the employee selected (Figure 8.52).

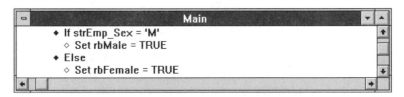

Figure 8.51   GetSSN code, continued.

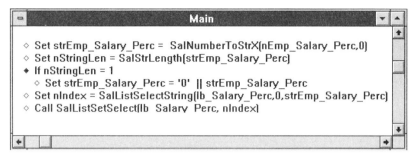

Figure 8.52   GetSSN code, continued.

The values in salary percent listbox are string characters. The first line converts the into numeric bind variable nEmp_Salary_Perc to the string strEmp_Salary_Perc. The command SalStrLength calculates the length of the string strEmp_Salary_perc. If the string length is 1, then concantenate the string with a leading zero. The reason for this is that the listbox percentages are 02, 04, 06, etc and the salary percentage number convert to a string would be 2, 4, 6, and so on. We would not get a match without the leading zero. The next line, Sal-ListSelectString, searches the listbox lb_Salary_Perc for a match on strEmp_Salary_Perc, starting at the first entry, and returns the index of the listbox entry with the match. The last line, SalListSetSelect, highlights the selected listbox entry based on the index number.

Some other miscellaneous code examples we will show are populating a listbox, first with an array and second with an SQL statement.

The first example will populate using an array. The application populates the salary percentage listbox with an array (Figure 8.53).

Upon opening a window, the message generated is the SAM_Create message. This event occurs for every object that can receive messages, which includes the form, data fields, listboxes, and combo boxes but not objects like lines, pictures, and group boxes. To populate this listbox we set up a loop with the While command. It loops

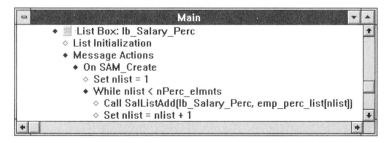

Figure 8.53   Populating a listbox with an array.

until the llistbox reaches the end of the array which is in the variable nPerc_elmnts. The SalListAdd function adds the entries into the listbox.

The next example populates the listbox portion of the state combo box (Figure 8.54). This listbox is populated using the data from an SQL select.

Populating a listbox or a combo box with an SQL select is fairly simple. The command SalListPopulate command handles the loop—all you have to do is supply the select statement.

Coding Summary

We could go on for pages and pages about the different aspects of coding an SQLWindows application. Instead what we tried to do was give you some samples of code used in the application. One thing you will notice about SQLWindows is that developers have the flexibility of coding an application using object-oriented techniques if they choose to do so, but it is not required. What we have noticed is that using object-oriented techniques and learning a new product are sometimes difficult to bring together. As the developers gain experience with the product, applying object-oriented techniques will get easier and the real payback for application development will start to happen.

Creating the Executable

To install an SQLWindows application on a user's computer, the following components must be installed:

1. The program executable or .EXE file.
2. The SQLWindows runtime product. The SQLWindows runtime product contains files that are need by the application and registers the application with the Gupta Corporation.
3. The runtime is supplied with a DLL called SQLAPIW.DLL, which allows the application to run, but without a connection to the

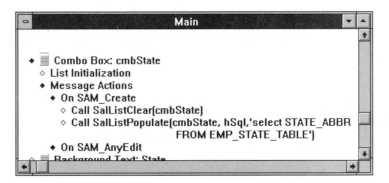

Figure 8.54 Populating a combo box with an SQL select.

database. There are other products that supply the user with a copy of SQLAPIW.DLL that give the user access to the database. The options are:

a.   Gupta's local SQLBase database server. The files are DBWIN-DOW.EXE or DBWSERVR.EXE.

b.   A Gupta SQLRouter, which gives the application access to a remote SQLBase Server or SQLNetwork gateway. The SQL-Network gateway gives the application access to many SQL based databases.

c.   A database interface from a vendor other than Gupta.

Creating an executable is the final product of application development. It creates an .EXE file that is then loaded onto the customer's computer, allowing the customer the ability to run the application. The .EXE is a compiled version of the application. SQLWindows provides an easy way to create the executable. First, open the SQL-Windows development environment by double-clicking on the SQL-Windows icon. Second, open the application that you want to deliver to the user, then select the Make Executable in the File menu. This opens the make executable window (Figure 8.55). Note that the Make Runtime menu selection is for downward compatibility, use the Make Executable instead.

Select or enter the name of the .EXE you will create in the file-name entry box. Set the directory and drive to the location to create the .EXE. You can use the drives and directory to locate an .EXE already created. Make sure the EditWindows enabled checkbox is checked if you are going to use EditWindows to tailor the application

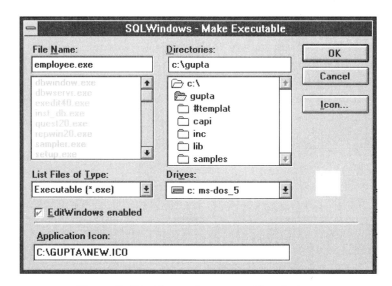

Figure 8.55   The make executable window.

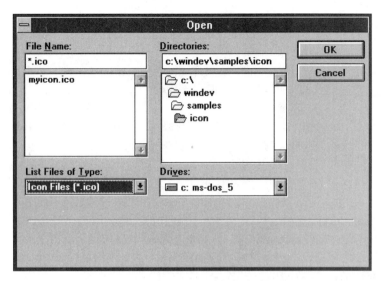

Figure 8.56   The icon select dialog box.

before distribution. To select an icon, click the Icon push button and the Open Icon window will open (Figure 8.56).

Select the icon from the drive and directory where the icon is located. The selection will display in the Application Icon entry box on the Make Executable window. Select the Ok push button and create the .EXE.

SQLWindows Summary

SQLWindows has just about everything a developer might need for client/server application development. The software has several tools that simplify development of GUI client/server: applications like the Tool Palette, Outliner Options, Customizer, application templates, and TeamWindows project management functions. SQLWindows offers connectivity to multiple DBMSs, whether they be on the local computer, are LAN based, or on a mainframe. The learning curve for the software is moderate, but a little time invested it offers a slick client/server development tool.

9

C/S-OO-GUI Development Using PARTS Workbench

Digitalk PARTS (parts assembly and reuse tool set) Workbench is a toolset technology that enables rapid application construction from prefabricated software parts. PARTS Workbench is language-neutral to the user. No programming languages are required to develop applications with this product. The PARTS interface provides the development platform, shielding the developer from the complexity of the operating system.

The PARTS Workbench runs under OS/2, Microsoft Windows 3.1, and Windows NT. PARTS is based on Smalltalk/V object technology, a high-level language that has enabled programmers to create applications by manipulating graphics, list panes, menus, text windows, dialog boxes, and other graphical controls of the platform.

The PARTS Workbench application-development environment enables point-and-click, graphical assembly, and interconnection of parts on a desktop window. It is delivered with over 60 ready-to-use visual and nonvisual application parts. The visual parts conform to IBM's latest common user access (CUA) design standards including notebook, value set, container, horizontal, and vertical sliders. Other parts include drop-down lists, menus, text panes, check boxes, combo boxes, push buttons, multiple-choice lists, picture fields, static groups, windows, and many others. Nonvisual parts provide the data access, computation, and other services for the application. These include a Btrieve database file accessor, several data structure parts, DDE client and DDE server connections, DLL accessor, disk accessor, file accessor, printer access, file system interface, and external-program launch pad.

The developer works out of a PARTS Catalog of objects called *parts.* Each part has a common interface, so catalog parts or newly created ones can be assembled more rapidly into finished applications.

New parts can be created visually with the PARTS Workbench, or modified with the built-in scripting language, PARTStalk. You can also create parts with Smalltalk/V, C, C++, and other development languages, making it possible to leverage your investment in existing technologies.

Parts are as easily integrated and interchanged. They can be dragged and dropped among folders, catalogs, and applications. No special protocols or DBMS systems are needed to integrate or access components.

In PARTS, any DLL—for example, an existing DLL created in C—can be exchanged and reused with the standard coding, compiling, and linking process. Code from existing applications like C and COBOL can be integrated using a wrapping process.

Requirements

PARTS Workbench requires a computer running any 386 or 486 processor. At least eight megabytes of RAM is recommended with at least 12 megabytes of free hard disk space for file storage.

OS/2 Installation

Note: If any version of Smalltalk/V is installed on the same machine, be sure that you install all PARTS files and DLLs into their own directories or folders.

1. Insert disk 1 in drive A:.
2. Bring up an icon view of drive A:. (You can do this by double-clicking on the OS/2 system icon on the desktop. This displays the drive folder; double click on it to see the drive A: icon.
3. Double-click with the left mouse button on the drive A: icon. A window appears displaying the contents of disk 1.
4. Locate the file INSTALL.EXE. Double-click on this and the dialog box shown in Figure 9.1 will appear, asking you to name the main directory to which to install PARTS.
5. Either accept the default directory provided (PARTS), or enter a custom pathname of your own. If the directory you specify doesn't exist, it will be created.
6. A second dialog box then appears, asking the name of the subdirectory in which to install the PARTS DLL (dynamic link library) files. The default is to install the DLLs into the same directory as the main program, but some users like to place the files into a separate directory. Either accept the default subdirectory provided (\PARTS) or enter a directory name of your own.

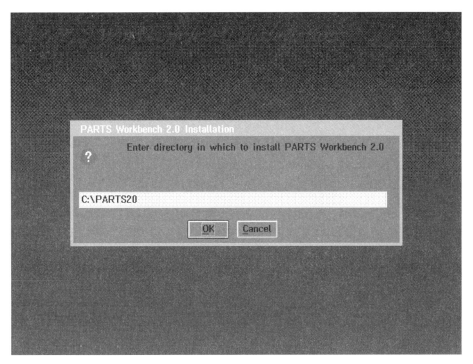

Figure 9.1   PARTS install screen.

7. The Install program will decompress the files from the disks, each in turn, place them in the directories you select, and bring up a window with the PARTS file icons.

A complete listing of all the files provided with the current version of PARTS Workbench and notes about any enhancements are contained in an ASCII text file named README.TXT. You can read this file on disk 1 before installation, or afterward in the \PARTS directory.

The directory you specify for DLLs (step 6) should be in your OS/2 system's LIBPATH. For this to work, either the PARTS directory must be on your system's LIBPATH or more generically a period, '.' must be in the LIBPATH. (This means the system looks in the current directory first when looking for DLLs.) Your system may already have this set up properly, since any OS/2 program with DLLs requires it. You can check this by looking at the file C:\CONFIG.SYS. This file has a statement like the following:

```
LIBPATH=C:\OS2\DLL;C:\;D:\NETWORK;
```

If you installed your DLLs to the same directory as the rest of your PARTS files, enter a period, semicolon (.;) as the first characters, as follows:

```
LIBPATH=.;C:\OS2\ dll;C:\D:\NETWORK;
```

Note that the above LIBPATH statement has '.' at the beginning of the directory list. If you installed the DLLs in a subdirectory of your main directory, you need to modify the statement as follows:

```
LIBPATH=C:\OS2\DLL;C:\;D:\NETWORK;C:\PARTSDLL
```

assuming you put the PARTS DLL files in C:\PARTSDLL. Whenever you modify your CONFIG.SYS file, you must reboot your computer before those changes will take effect.

Starting PARTS Workbench

Start your installed PARTS environment as you would start any of your other OS/2 applications. Installation automatically brings up a folder called PARTS and a window containing the PARTS file icon, labeled PARTWORK.EXE. Double-click on the main icon to access the PARTS Workbench interface.

   If you have any trouble, check that your CONFIG.SYS file reflects the correct LIBPATH choice as discussed, and that your files are all installed correctly, as described in the README.TXT file.

Tutorial

The online tutorial provides an excellent hands-on introduction to the PARTS system. This is useful if you are already familiar with the OS/2 interface, because it gives you practice learning PARTS implementation of the CUA '91 mouse protocol for manipulation and selection of objects.

   If you are new to OS/2, you can especially benefit, because the tutorial helps you exercise the OS/2 interface, which then helps you work more easily with the PARTS interface.

   To start the tutorial:

1. Move the mouse pointer or cursor over the PARTS Workbench icon and click the left button once. This makes the Workbench the current window, ready for further instructions.
2. Place the mouse pointer over Help on the menu bar, and click the left button once. This is called *choosing* Help.
3. Move the mouse pointer down the Help menu that displays, and position the pointer over the menu-item tutorial, so that it highlights. Then let go of the left button and the tutorial program will execute.

You have several tutorial lessons from which to choose. Each one builds a running application moving from simple to more complex, using and modifying parts found in the Catalog menu. Several sample programs built entirely with PARTS Workbench are available for you to load and explore. Find them listed in the README.TXT file. Feel free to load them, inspect them to see how they are constructed, and to reuse them in application building.

Exiting the PARTS Workbench

Choose File/Close from the menu bar in the Workbench window, or press Alt-F4 in the Workbench window, or double-click on the system menu icon at the upper left corner of the Workbench window.

If unsaved changes have been made to an application, you will be asked if you want to save the application to a file before exiting. You must close each Workbench window separately if you have opened more than one, since they are unrelated.

PARTS Workbench Overview

We are now ready to take a brief look at the menus and environments for the PARTS Workbench and PARTS Catalog. If you are already an OS/2 user, you will be familiar with the terminology we will cover in this part of the chapter. There are, however, specifics that apply separately to the Workbench and catalog work areas (Figure 9.2):

- Workbench window—where you edit a previously existing PARTS application or create a new one.

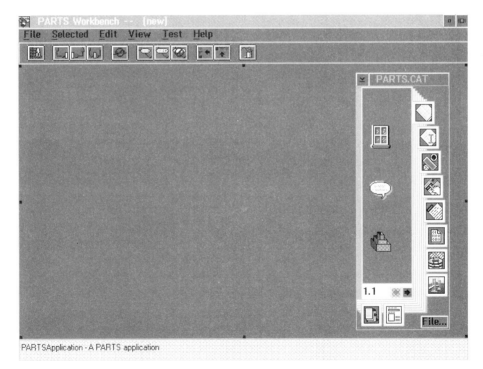

Figure 9.2   PARTS Catalog and Workbench.

- Catalog window—The main source of parts for your PARTS application.
- Title bar—Provides the title bar icon, the name of the PARTS application, and the minimize and maximize icons.
- Menu bar—The source of pull-down menus in OS/2 windows.
- Toolbar—A palette of buttons that provides shortcuts for commands.
- Cursor—Your pointer on the screen—changes in its appearance indicate a variety of activities being performed.
- Title-bar icon—Clicking this pulls down the standard OS/2 title bar or system menu. Double-clicking on it with the left button closes the window.
- Information area—The area at the bottom of the Workbench window that displays hints or information about the object to which the cursor points.

The Catalog Window

The *catalog* is a tool for organizing your parts. When you open the Workbench, the default catalog window also appears unless another catalog is already displayed. You may open as many different catalogs as you like. All opened catalogs float on top of the active workbench.

PARTS Pages

A PARTS *catalog* is an OS/2 Notebook control with pages indexed by tabs. When you click on a major or minor tab, the notebook flips open to that page. Major tabs are on the right side of the page and correspond to categories of parts. Minor tabs at the bottom indicate that there are more pages in that category. If you move the mouse over a page background, the information area will display a short description of the parts in that page. The page–forward and page–backward arrows at the lower-right corner of each page step through pages in sequential order. Page numbers are displayed at the lower left corner of each page.

Customizing Your Catalog

The default catalog is stored in the file parts\system\parts.cat, but modifying your catalog is easy and you are encouraged to customize one or more catalogs to meet your needs. Catalog files are traditionally stored with a .cat extension, but this convention is not mandatory.

The catalog's File menu, invoked by the File push button in its lower right corner, provides the mechanism for customizing your catalog. It allows you to open a separate catalog window, add or delete pages, set major and minor tabs, manipulate a part and its placement on a particular page, edit the page hint, and save the catalog to a file. The catalog's File menu is also invoked by clicking the right mouse button in the catalog.

The Workbench Window

Once you've located a part in the catalog, drag it into the workbench, drop it, and connect it to other parts (Figure 9.3). Workbench menus and the Workbench toolbar provide operations to manage your application, view it in different ways, select and manipulate its links and parts, and execute it.

Workbench Menus

The File, Selected, Edit, View, Test, and Help menus are always visible in the menu bar at the top of the Workbench. In addition, the title-bar icon in the upper-left corner of the window is always available.

The Workbench's File menu allows you to specify global PARTS preference settings, create a new PARTS application or view one saved previously in a separate Workbench, obtain a textual description of the current application, save an application in various formats to a file, and close the Workbench.

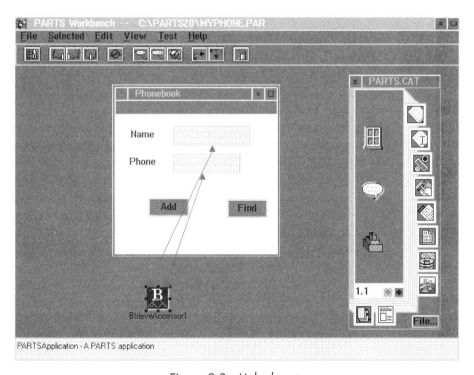

Figure 9.3   Linked parts.

The *Selected* menu provides operations that affect the selected part or parts only, such as changing its properties or displaying links attached to it.

The *Edit* menu allows you to manipulate parts, such as cutting, copying, pasting, aligning, and resizing parts. It also provides undo and redo commands as well as facilities for importing other applications.

The *View* menu controls the display of hints, links, labels, and grids—settings which are set on a per application basis. It contains toggle selections that determine whether hints in the information area are shown or whether link labels are displayed with links by default. You can also open a new catalog through this menu.

The *Test* menu allows you to test (launch) an application, open the debugger on it, and control the setting of breakpoints in the application.

The *Help* menu provides access to the help facilities, including an online tutorial and information about each of the system parts and how to use them.

The context-sensitive Link pop-up menu manipulates aspects of a particular link, such as its visibility, labels, control points, and breakpoints. It also allows you to change its origin, destination, event, and message.

The Workbench Toolbar

The toolbar (Figure 9.4) contains the following buttons for quick access to frequently used commands from the Edit, Selected, View, and Test menus.

A   Launch: Execute an application test

B   Show incoming links: Display all links with destinations in the selected parts group.

C   Show outgoing links: Display all links originating at a selected part.

D   Show links: Display all links connected to the selected part(s).

E   Hide all links: Hide all links connected to the selected part(s).

F   Show labels: Display all labels on the shown links so that event and message names are visible.

G   Expand labels: Expands all labels on the shown links so that event and message names are visible.

H   Hide labels: Hide all labels.

Figure 9.4 Workbench toolbar.

I   Align parts left: Visually align selected parts vertically.

J   Align parts top: Visually align selected parts horizontally.

K   Delete selected parts: Remove part(s) from the Workbench.

Visual and Nonvisual Parts

Parts such as buttons and menus that have visible counterparts in the runtime application window, are called *visual parts. Nonvisual* parts are those that serve as variables to hold data, access a system resource such as a file or timer, or perform some utility such as a conversion. Although these nonvisual parts have icons and are used in the workbench, they are not seen at runtime.

Child Parts

Some parts contain other parts, such as panes inside a window or menu items in a menu. The upper level part is referred to as the *parent part,* and its immediate lower-level part is referred to as its *child part.* Most parts that can serve as parents are commonly referred to as panes, since most parent parts deal with the construction of windows. The application part, which is your entire application in progress, is an exception to this rule.

When the Workbench first opens, the application part is represented by the workspace background, which is gray by default. It serves as the top-level parent for all other parts. It is also a holder for comments and other information about your application as a whole. Place nonvisual parts on the Workbench background—they are direct children of the application.

To make a child part, drop one part on another, as when you place a button in a dialog window. When the parent and child parts are both visual parts, they remain visible in the runtime application and are always seen together.

Many operations affect the children as well as the parent. For example, if you move a window, its children move with it. If you copy or delete a window, you copy or delete its children as well.

The following illustration shows an application with several different kinds of parts. The *speaker* is a nonvisual part that makes sound on request. The window part labeled *Untitled* represents the runtime window. It has a menu label in its menu bar. When the menu option is activated, it displays the menu to the left of the window. The window also contains a button and a group pane. The group button appears to hold two radio buttons, but the group pane and the two buttons are actually siblings (Figure 9.5).

Figure 9.6 shows the hierarchical parent and child relationships among these parts: The application is the parent of a speaker (a nonvisual part), a window part, and a menu pane that contains menu

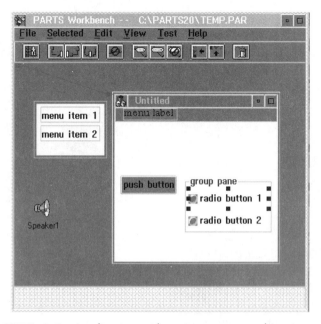

Figure 9.5   Application with various parts combinations.

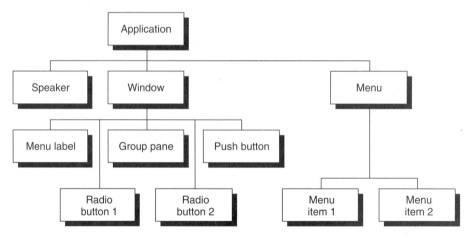

Figure 9.6   Hierarchical relationship among parts.

items. The window is the parent of a menu label, group pane, a push button, and two radio buttons.

Adding Parts to Your Application

Place a part in the Workbench by choosing and dragging it from the catalog:

1.   Position the cursor over a part on a catalog page and press the right mouse button.

2. While holding the mouse button down, drag the part icon to the workbench and release the button to drop it.

If you change your mind, press Esc to cancel the dragging operation. (Esc dismisses menus and dialogs, and cancels operations such as dragging.)

Although most parts are copied from the PARTS Catalog, there are several exceptions to this rule:

- As mentioned previously, the application part appears in the workbench as the background.
- The OS/2 Desktop is also a source for parts—drag these directly off the desktop and drop them onto your workbench as you would from a catalog.
- You can also obtain parts from other application files.

Parts Basics

Parts communicate through events and messages. An *event* is triggered whenever the end user manipulates a visual part, or when some other action occurs, such as a timer going off. Each event has a name. A part can generate a number of different events to respond to different input events, such as clicking with the right mouse button as opposed to the left mouse button. A part can also provide additional information in the form of event values.

In addition to events generated by the part itself in response to an external stimulus, each part also responds to messages that change its properties, retrieve information, or carry out an action. For example, a push button responds to messages to enable or disable itself, and to messages to get or set the text on the button label, one of the properties of a push button.

Links connect events to messages. When an event connected to a link is triggered, the message at the other end of the link is executed. The message execution can, in turn, trigger other events, and trigger other links, which will execute still more messages.

There is more to a message than just a name for an operation. First, every message has a result. A special kind of link, called a *result link,* can be connected to a message result. Whenever the first message finishes execution, the result link is fired and the next message is executed. Thus, many messages can be chained together and triggered by a single event.

Second, a message can have arguments. An *argument* to a message is the same as an argument to a procedure in a procedural programming language—it is a value supplied to customize the message.

Every value and message result has a data type associated with it such as integer, string or Boolean. In most cases, values are of the same type as that expected for an argument, or they are automatically converted to the proper type.

Visual Parts

More than 30 visual parts are supplied with the PARTS system. *Top-level parts* are panes or parts that contain other parts. These are found on the first page of the catalog (Figure 9.7).

The common top-level parts include windows, dialog windows and prefabricated dialogs.

Window

A *window* is a rectangular pane that can be resized or minimized. In order to be displayed on screen, an application must have at least one window or dialog box. A window contains other visual parts in your program. As shown in Figure 9.7, the window-open message is automatically linked to the application-open event when the window is added to your application.

Window properties can be accessed by double-clicking on the window (Figure 9.8). The properties allow you to customize the appearance of the window by changing the title, setting the initial size, button, functionality in the title bar, type of border, and so on.

Dialog Window

The *dialog window* is a rectangular window that performs a single function in your application, such as notifying the user of an error

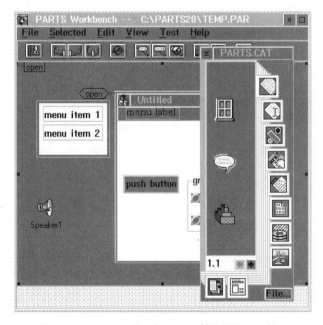

Figure 9.7   Top-level page of PARTS catalog.

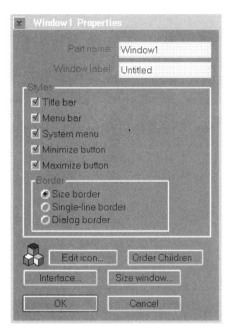

Figure 9.8   Window properties.

condition or obtaining parameters for an operation. In addition to being able to create your own dialogs, the catalog contains several prefabricated dialogs for the most common uses. They appear on the third top-level page of the catalog. Included dialogs are:

- User information
- Confirmation
- Confirm with cancel (Figure 9.9)
- Prompter for a line of text
- File for a list of files

Other visual parts include buttons, menus, drop down lists, spin buttons, multiple-choice lists, field labels, fields, and so on. We will cover these parts in more detail in the sample application.

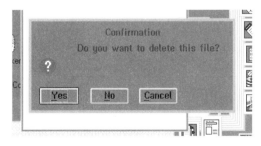

Figure 9.9   Confirm with cancel prefabricated dialog.

Nonvisual Parts

A class of parts called *accessor parts* are provided in the catalog on the File, Device, Interface, and Language pages that let you access a Btrieve database, the services of the operating system, and services from other applications. These parts, in the following list, are shown on the Workbench (Figure 9.10):

- Btrieve accessor
- File accessor
- Disk accessor
- Clipboard accessor
- Launch pad
- Printer
- Speaker
- Timer
- DLL accessor
- C structure
- DDE client
- DDE server

This section will briefly introduce you to these access or parts. For more detailed information about each of them, see the relevant sections in the *PARTS Workbench Reference Manual.* Look also in the

Figure 9.10   Nonvisual accessor parts.

samples subdirectory of your PARTS installation directory for completed applications using these parts.

The Btrieve accessor. The *Btrieve accessor,* found on the file page of the catalog, lets you create a new Btrieve database and access either a new or existing database from your application. Btrieve is a key-based database. Operations are supported for searching by key value, and adding, deleting, and updating records.

A correspondence between visual parts in our application and database fields can be automatically established. You can define the database layout by specifying the visual parts that contain the information, or, given a database layout, you can create visual parts automatically that correspond to the database fields. An overview of the main points in using the Btrieve accessor is given in the Sample Application section of this chapter.

Accessing the file system. Two parts are supplied to access the file system. The file accessor performs operations on a single file. The disk accessor navigates through directories in the file system. These file system access parts are located on the file page of the catalog.

The file accessor. The *file accessor* lets you read, modify, and query the status of files in the file system. Files can be copied, renamed, and deleted. You can access information about the file's size and time of last modification. In addition to the message provided to access this information, the file accessor provides events such as noSuchFileException, which is triggered when a specified file can't be found.

The disk accessor. The *disk accessor* lets you access files and directories on the disk. You can query whether a directory exists; create or delete a directory; get the drive, path, or name of a directory; and obtain a list of files and subdirectories in a directory.

Accessing Other System Services

The parts on the Device and Interface pages of the catalog let your application access other system services and devices.

The clipboard accessor. The *clipboard accessor* lets your application save strings or bitmaps to the system clipboard for use by other applications, or to retrieve strings or bitmaps placed on the clipboard.

The launch pad. The *launch pad* lets your application execute any OS/2 command from your application.

The printer. The *printer* lets your application send formatted printer strings or bitmaps to either the default system printer or a printer you name.

The speaker. The *speaker* gives you access to the system sound device so that your application can beep to call attention to an error or provide more sophisticated audible effects. In addition to these preprogrammed responses, you can program the frequency and duration of the speaker with messages.

The timer. The *timer* lets you access the current date and time, or you can use it as an interval timer to cause an event to trigger at specified intervals. You can change the timer interval in the property dialog.

Connecting to Dynamic Link Libraries

Dynamic link libraries provide many services to OS/2 applications. Your PARTS application can take advantage of the services supplied in the standard OS/2 dynamic link libraries, or you can access programs written in other languages that are contained in a DLL file. Dynamic linking gives your application access to functions that are not part of the application. By making new parts that interface with dynamic link libraries for existing programs, you reuse existing programs written in other languages in a variety of PARTS applications.

The DLL accessor. The *DLL accessor* part, found in the Interface page of the catalog, lets you access individual procedures in a single DLL library. You specify the properties of the DLL procedure, including the number and types of arguments and the return type using the DLL accessor property dialog. You can use several DLL accessors in your application to access several different DLL files.

C structure. The *C structure* part, found on the language page of the catalog, is used in conjunction with the DLL Accessor to access DLL procedures written in the C programming language that require arguments of the C struct data type. This data type has named fields, which can differ in type. Specify the layout of the fields in the C structure with the property dialog.

Using Dynamic Data Exchange

The *DDE client* and *DDE server* parts are also provided on the interface page of the catalog. These parts give your application access to either the client side or server side of a dynamic data exchange conversation.

A DDE conversation is a two-way exchange of information between two OS/2 applications, such as a word processor and a spreadsheet. In order to establish a conversation, the applications must know each other's names, must be running, and must share information about the topics about which information can be exchanged.

For more information about establishing DDE links between applications, see the *OS/2 Programmer's Guide*. The DDE client section of *The PARTS Workbench Reference* also contains an annotated example of a PARTS application which uses both a DDE client part and a DDE server part to exchange information.

The DDE client. The *DDE client* part lets your application act as a client in a DDE conversation.

The DDE server. The *DDE server* part lets your application act as the server in a DDE conversation.

Programming Variables

Other nonvisual parts necessary for programming logic include the ability to:

- Declare and access constants and variables.
- Execute messages conditionally.
- Perform relational and arithmetic operations.
- Convert between data types.

The parts used to control these operations are shown in Figure 9.11 and are briefly described in the following sections.

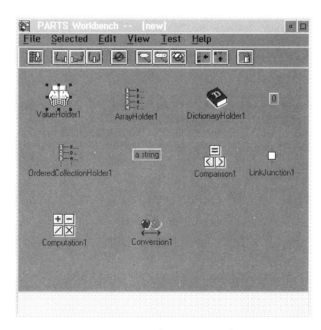

Figure 9.11   Other nonvisual parts.

Value-holder part. A *value-holder* holds a data value, acting like a variable in a traditional programming language. The messages value and setValue retrieve and set the value. When the value changes, the changed event is triggered. Both events and messages produce values that you may need to store for later access.

When a link fires, the event value is available only to links in the same link chain. After the last message in the link chain finishes executing, the event value is no longer accessible. Similarly, message results are available at the time a message execution finishes, but they disappear unless they are explicitly stored or are used as argument values for messages later in the chain. To save an event value or message result for later reference, you need a part that has a message that causes the part to store the value of the message argument, and another message that retrieves the stored value. In conventional programming languages, variables perform these functions.

In PARTS, the value-holder part and its specializations serve the purpose. The setValue message sets the contents of the value holder to be the argument value. The value message retrieves the contents. The changed event triggers whenever a value is stored into the value holder, even if the new value is the same as the previously stored value.

Listed here are five specialized value holders used as constants or variables:

- Array holder
- Dictionary holder
- Number holder
- Ordered collection holder
- String holder

Comparison part. The *comparison part* compares two arguments and triggers either *true* or *false* based on the result.

Link-junction part. The *link-junction* part has two roles: It conditionally triggers either the triggered or triggerFailed event based on properties of the argument, and it is a relay point for links. One message can trigger several links, or several messages can trigger one link.

Computation part. The *computation* part performs arithmetic operations such as addition and multiplication on two numeric values.

Conversion part. The *conversion* part converts values between different types, such as from integer to string.

Many of the parts discussed will be used in the sample application.

Links

Links represent data and communication paths in your application. You create links between parts to program your application—they are the glue for connecting parts with events and messages. When the source part triggers the event associated with a link, the link fires, sending a message to the part at the link destination. There are three kinds of links. An *event link* connects an event to a message. It connects an event from one part to a message belonging to the same or another part. Triggering the event executes the attached message.

In Figure 9.12, an event link causes message1 to execute when event A is triggered:

A *result link* lets several messages be driven from a single event or argument link. Figure 9.13 shows a result link that causes a second message to be executed when the first one finishes.

An *argument link* obtains a value required for a message argument. In Figure 9.14, message3 requires a single argument. Before this message can execute, it must fire an argument link to obtain the argument value, in this case, the result of executing message4.

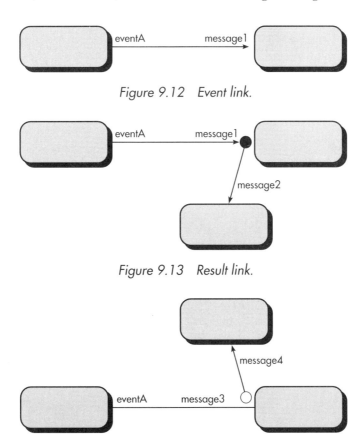

Figure 9.12   Event link.

Figure 9.13   Result link.

Figure 9.14   Argument link.

Event Links

Event links connect an event to a message with a box or event connection at the event end (the *origin*) and an arrowhead or message connection at the message end (the *destination*). Event links indicate control flow between the event and the message. When the event is triggered by the source part, the link is fired to send the message to the destination part.

A single event can trigger links to more than one message, and the same message can be sent from more than one event link, originating possibly at different parts.

Creating an Event Link

One way to create an event link is with the standard left-drag combination, pressing the left button on the origin part and releasing it on the destination part. Event links can also be created using the Workbench Selected menu:

1. Select the part that is to be the origin (source) part.
2. Choose Selected/Create link.
3. A Create Link dialog is displayed with a list of destination parts (Figure 9.15).
4. Select one of the destination parts to display the list of messages available for that part (Figure 9.16).
5. Select a destination message.
6. Press OK to complete the link.

Result Links

When a message executes, it produces a *result value.* A *result link* connects the message result of one link to another message. You cre-

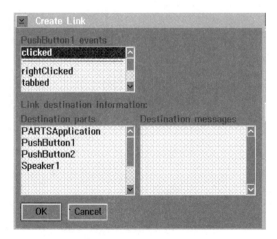

Figure 9.15   Create event link—A

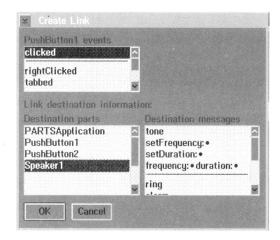

Figure 9.16   Create event link—B.

ate a result link for one of two reasons: to fire a sequence of messages as a result of triggering a single event or to use the result of a message as an argument value for the next message.

Creating a Result Link

1. Press the left mouse button over the message connecting the arrowhead of the link you want to continue.
2. Drag the cursor to the new destination part and release it to display the Result Link window (Figure 9.17).
3. Choose the message from the Create Result Link dialog.

Argument Links

If a message requires arguments, it must first obtain a value for each of its arguments before it can execute. These values are supplied by *argument links.* An argument link originates at the connection representing the argument it is to fill, and points to the source for the value. The direction of the argument link indicates control flow similar to an event link because the progenitor of the argument link ini-

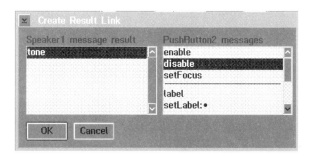

Figure 9.17   Create Result Link.

tiates the request. Unlike an event link, the result of this request is returned to the requester. Thus, data flows in the opposite direction to the control flow.

Creating an Argument Link

1. Display argument connections
2. Press the left mouse button over an argument connection that you want to fill or redefine to display the Argument Link window (Figure 9.18).
3. Drag the cursor to a destination object and release.
4. Select the message to complete the argument link.

Creating the Sample Business Application

Overview

In the sections that follow, we will discuss the assembly of the sample application using PARTS Workbench. For simplicity, and to help you gain an overall understanding of working with prefabricated parts, we will be building a single part that corresponds to the requirements of the application. Realize, however, that any component or subcomponent that we build could be saved as a separate part for use in this or other applications. Additionally, any major components, such as the four windows that drive the application, could be later saved and added to a parts catalog. We will briefly cover the process of cataloging newly created parts after we build the sample application.

As mentioned earlier, the application uses four windows. The main window is pictured in Figure 9.19. With the exception of four lines of code that were repeated six times for a total of 24 lines of code, the entire application can be developed via mouse point-and-

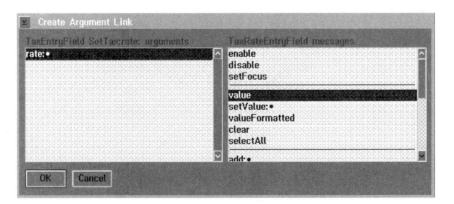

Figure 9.18   Create Argument Link.

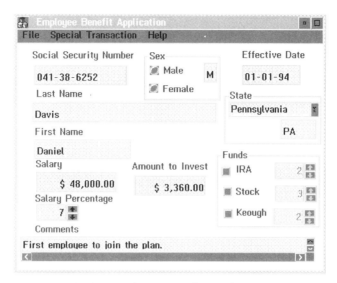

Figure 9.19   Employee Benefit Application screen.

click operations using prefabricated parts straight from the catalog and linking them.

Note also two items are not supported exactly as described in Chapter 5 of this book. The File menu on the Employee Benefit Application screen is slightly different and the scroll list on the Employee Selection screen is not used. This was done to avoid additional specialized coding and to make full use of the PARTS prefabricated technology.

It should also be noted that some basics are intentionally omitted from the application, such as variable initialization and hooking in the Logon screen for id verification, in the interest of covering more critical development options.

Application-Development Techniques

Whether developing a series of independent windows or a group of windows that are bundled together for an application, the first step in using PARTS is to design these top-level parts and group them as needed. Our approach will be to first create the windows (top-level parts) with their subparts, and establish all required links between the parts as a second step. We'll follow the natural flow of the application for both the part layout and linking steps. The Logon window is followed by the Employee Benefit Application window. The Special Transaction and Employee Selection windows are subwindows of the Employee Benefit window.

The text that follows does not direct you to perform saves or test the application at certain points. You may want to do both as often as you would in your natural development environment.

Logon Window

If you have already started PARTS Workbench, you are ready to create the Logon window (Figure 9.20). Using your mouse, place the cursor over the Window part on the Window page of the PARTS Catalog. Depress, and hold down your right mouse button and drag a copy of the window onto the Workbench (Figure 9.21).

When you release the right mouse button, the window will appear on the Workbench. The window can be resized by dragging the borders to their desired position. The window can be repositioned on the Workbench by dragging it to a desirable location. In both cases, the right mouse button is used.

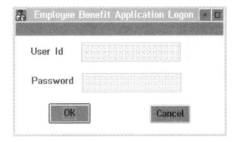

Figure 9.20   Employee Benefit Application Logon window.

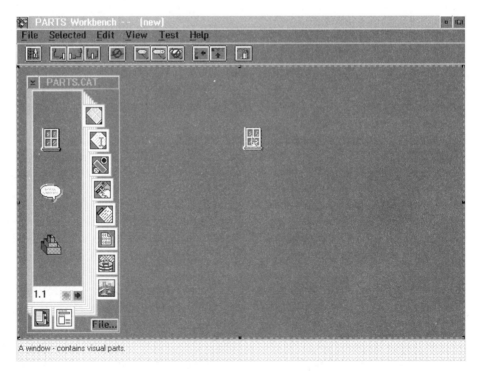

Figure 9.21   Dragging a part onto the workbench.

When a part that has been placed on the Workbench or placed within another part it can be highlighted with a single click of the left mouse button for manipulation with the right mouse button. The result of this manipulation is shown in Figure 9.22 and Figure 9.23.

The next step in window creation is to change the window label. A double click on the current window title, *Untitled,* opens the window properties dialog. Here, retype the label and select OK (Figure 9.24).

Using the same drag-and-drop technique that you used for the window, drag and drop the following parts from the Parts Catalog onto the newly created window. To save time, drop them in the approximate locations shown in Figure 9.20:

- Two push buttons from the button page
- Two alphabetic entry fields from the formatted field page
- Two static text items from the text page

Using the left mouse button, double-click on each static text item and each push button and change the label text for each on their respective dialog screens. The process is the same as changing label text for a window.

The entry fields will also have to resized. A single left mouse button click will highlight the part and, as with window resizing, the

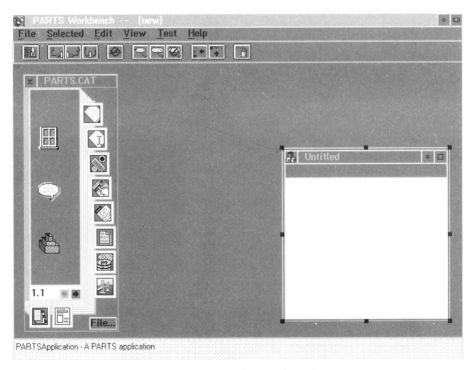

Figure 9.22   A dropped window.

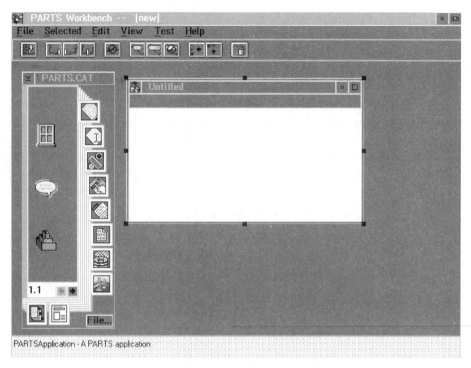

Figure 9.23 A sized and positioned window.

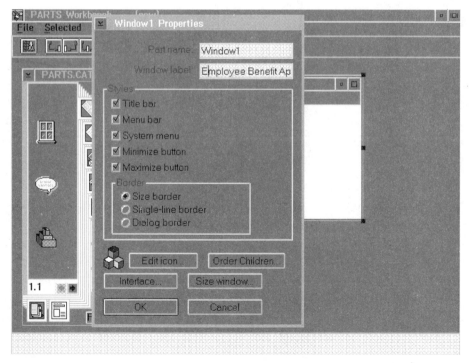

Figure 9.24 Window properties.

right button is used to resize the field by dragging. The right mouse button is also used to reposition any subparts. You'll want to shift these around to look like Figure 9.20 (Figure 9.25).

Realize at this point that a double left button click on the entry fields would bring up the dialog for their properties. This would enable modifying the part names to correspond with field names in our application. However, in this case as with others in our sample application, we will accept the default part names.

This is an excellent time to become familiar with PARTS mouse techniques. Unlike other software, the right mouse button is very functional under PARTS Workbench. Here's a brief review:

- Right mouse button—depressed
  - Drag-and-drop parts from the Catalog
  - Size parts
  - Move parts
- Left mouse button—single-click
  - Highlight a part
  - Establish links between parts
- Left mouse button—double-click
  - Open the properties dialog box for the selected part

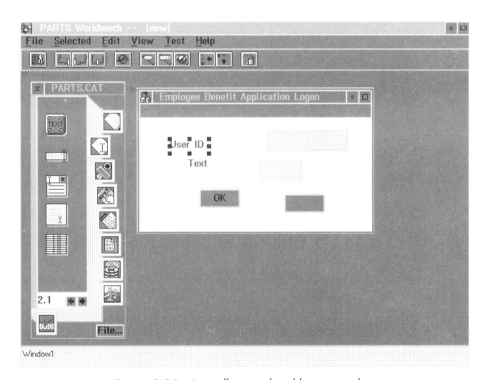

Figure 9.25   Partially completed logon window.

At this point, we suggest that you save your new parts application. From the Workbench file menu, choose Save as, supply a file name and it will be saved with a .PAR file extension. To reaccess this file at a later time, you will choose the Open option from the Workbench file menu and select your file from the list of available PARTS applications. When you reopen the file, you'll find that a second Workbench session is opened to accommodate new development of other application requirements without closing one to open another.

Employee Benefit Application Window

The finished Employee Benefit Application window is shown in Figure 9.20—you may want to refer to it during this discussion. First, drag and drop another window onto the same Workbench that contains the Logon window, making sure to drop it in an open area of the Workbench. Do not drop it in the Logon window. This window will have to be made larger to accommodate all the parts required and should be relabeled to its proper title.

Unlike our first window, this one requires menu-bar options. Drag and drop three menu-text parts from the menu page of the PARTS Catalog directly onto the menu bar in your newly created window. Change the labels to match the requirements of the application (Figure 9.26).

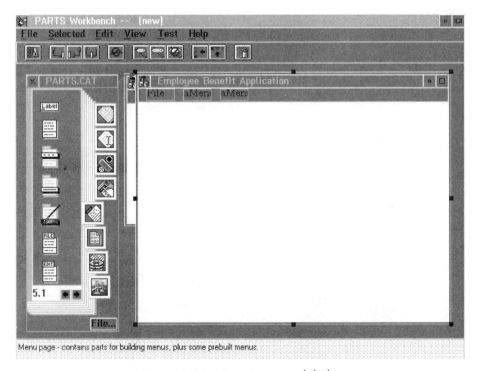

Figure 9.26   Creating menu labels.

Referring to Figure 9.19, you should be able to identify the parts listed below that are required for this window.

- Three group panes—sex, state, funds
- Two radio buttons—male, female
- Three check boxes—IRA, stock, Keogh
- Four spin buttons—salary percentage, IRA, stock, Keogh
- One drop-down list box—state literal
- One text pane—comments
- Five alphabetic fields
- Two currency fields
- One date field
- 13 static text fields

Carefully review Figure 9.27, comparing it to the finished product in Figure 9.19. Figure 9.27 is partially complete, showing the parts positioned and resized, but with the raw parts labels and parts names.

We should point out a few PARTS Workbench-specific design techniques that were used to save coding at this point.

First, note that the comments are not stored separately. A text pane can be placed directly into a Btrieve file as a variable-length field. Second, the actual Sex field is being displayed onscreen. With-

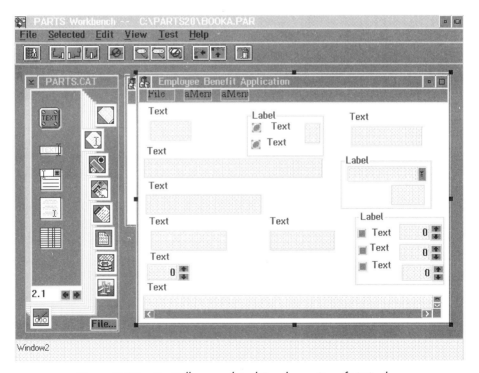

Figure 9.27   Partially completed Employee Benefit Window.

out this display, a message would have to written for the radio buttons to indicate which should be turned on when a record is retrieved.

Remaining Windows

The Special Transaction window and Employee Selection window should be created next. The finished windows are shown in Figures 9.28 and 9.29. Remember that even though these windows are driven by the employee-benefit window, they should be created in open areas of the workbench.

Here again we have strayed from the original design because of our Btrieve file storage system. Rather than coding the requirements to load the Btrieve records into a list box for employee selection, we are providing button access to position and page through the file.

Creating the Data File

Creating the files to store the records from our application is the next logical step in PARTS development. The process is enabled by point-and-click options available on the Btrieve accessor part. Other data items, called *value holders,* will be required for this application as well. Think of these as counters and accumulators. Additionally, with PARTS the need for value holders sometimes arises when you are cre-

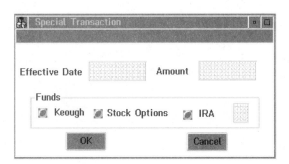

Figure 9.28   Special Transaction Window.

Figure 9.29   Employee Selection Window.

ating links. As with traditional programming, we will add these variables as needed. To create the data file, go to the file page of the PARTS Catalog and drop the Btrieve accessor part onto an empty area of the Workbench (Figure 9.30).

The Btrieve accessor offers many powerful options for file creation and record management. The record layout created with the accessor is known as a database with which you logically associate a PC filename to store records. You can define fields in the database from visual parts that you have placed on screen and, conversely, define a field in the accessor and create the visual part on screen from the definition. With this power comes a limitation. You are free to modify the database structure before the PC file has been opened. Once opened, however, you cannot modify the database. Suggested, therefore, is careful planning of your file structures before actually opening the file to create test records. Since the accessor will allow you to associate a preexisting default file with a new database definition, you might consider outside file maintenance.

The Btrieve properties dialog allows you to create new fields, pick fields from screen with the mouse, or pick the field names from a list of active visual parts. Select Pick fields with mouse (Figure 9.31). The properties dialog moves to the background and the cursor appears (Figure 9.32).

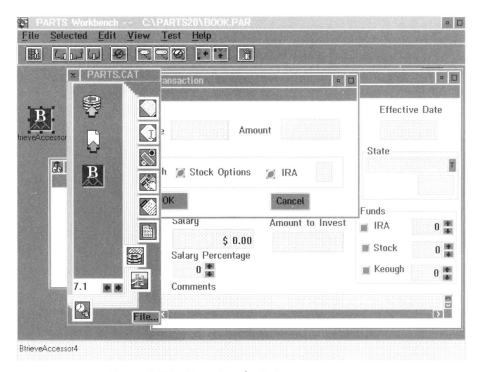

Figure 9.30   Dropping the Btrieve accessor part.

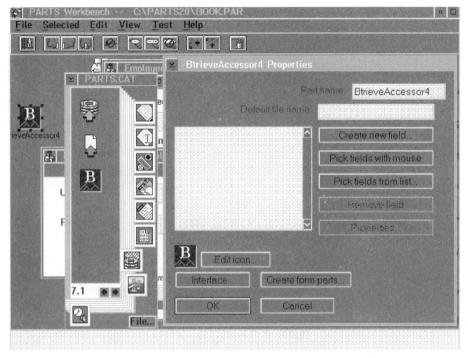

Figure 9.31   Btrieve accessor properties dialog.

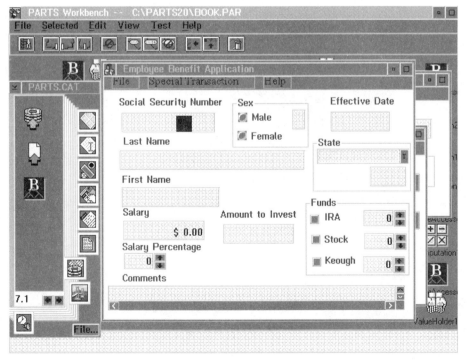

Figure 9.32   Picking fields with the mouse.

The mouse will appear as a black square onscreen. Click on the fields of choice. For our application, you should exclude the state drop-down list and only include the state abbreviation. The drop-down box literals will be stored in a separate file later. You will also find that spin buttons can not be stored in accessor databases. When you have finished adding all required fields from the employee benefit screen, double click the mouse outside the Workbench. You will then be back in the properties dialog. Each field that you clicked on now appears in the field list.

Each field listed also has properties associated with it. Since we need to set an index, double-click on the entry field that represents social-security number, our key field (Figure 9.33).

This screen allows you to modify the field name and change the field type. For our application you will set the field length to 9, or to 11 if you want to include the dashes, click on IS Key, and click on Unique key values.

An inspection of all other fields would be logical since PARTS will set default field lengths. You may not want a first name file capable of holding 64 bytes. You should also note at this point that multiple unique keys can be set in a file. The first key defined will be used as the primary reference key unless you choose to change it while your application is running.

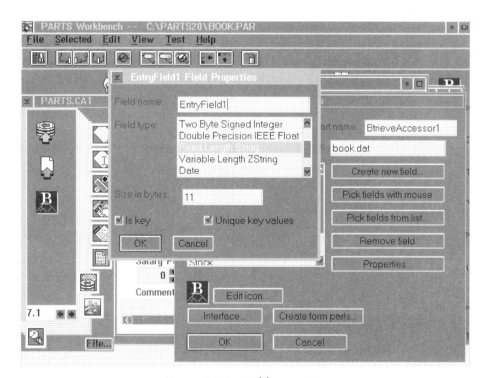

Figure 9.33   Field properties.

Next, using the Create new field option, add four additional Two Byte Signed Integer fields to store the data from the spin buttons. During this process, you will also note that the Btrieve accessor automatically established links for the fields you picked with the mouse. The links are the gateways for passing data between the file and screen. The spin buttons will, however, require manual linking, as we will discuss later.

Before closing the accessor properties window, be sure to supply a PC file name (BOOK.DAT) in the Default file name field. To complete the file creation process, drop a second accessor on the workbench and create a STATE.DAT file with fields for the state literal and state abbreviation. This file will be used to do lookups, and could easily be used by other applications for the same purpose. You will also have to build a mini-PARTS application or populate the table with another data-file editor.

A third accessor will be required to handle the special transactions data (SPECIAL.DAT). Be sure to add (create) an SSNUM field that will later be picked up from the active employee-benefit record when the application is executing.

Menus

Both pop-up and pull-down menus are supported in the PARTS Catalog. Earlier, when we designed the Employee Benefit Application window, we dropped three menu-text items from the menu page of the catalog onto the menu bar of the window. Our next step in menu creation is to drop three menus from the menu page onto an open area of the Workbench.

To create the menu options, drop text menu items from the same catalog page onto the menu parts. Once dropped, double-click on each item to change the properties' labels to match your application needs.

Also supported on the menu page is a menu-item separator part to segregate items in the menus. Drop these into the menu parts at required points.

Figure 9.34 shows the catalog menu page, the finished menu part and the resulting drop-down menu when file is clicked during program execution.

Initializing Selection Items

The last step in developing our application, before establishing links, is to set the values in our selection-item parts. Our Employee Benefit Application window has four spin buttons and one drop-down list. Double-click on the first spin button to access its properties dialog. From the properties dialog, select Edit contents. The Edit contents screen supports ranges of numeric values or lists of items. In our spin-

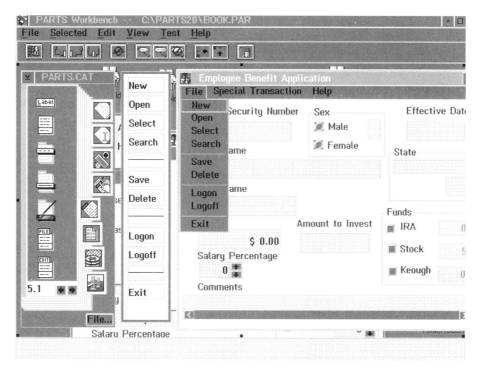

Figure 9.34   Building menu parts.

button examples, we would supply the range of acceptable values for salary percentages and fund percentages, and populate the state dropdown list with literal values. Figure 9.35 shows a spin button properties dialog with the Edit contents dialog selected. Numeric range is selected with minimum and maximum values filled in.

Linking Parts

To get a feel for the links required for our application, take a look at Figure 9.36. This is a display of all links, but realize that many are obscured in background windows and some of them are overlapped three and four levels deep!

Links can be established between any two parts dropped on the Workbench. Some are created automatically for you. For instance, when you dropped your first window onto the Workbench, a link was drawn from the Workbench to the window.

Links are manually established by placing the mouse over the part that is to initiate an action (event). Depress the left mouse button and connect it with a line to the part that is to receive the instruction (message) to perform the action. Figure 9.37 illustrates a simple link with the link labels being displayed.

Clicking on the Cancel push button is a user action or in object-oriented terms the *event*. Note that the label displays the action click.

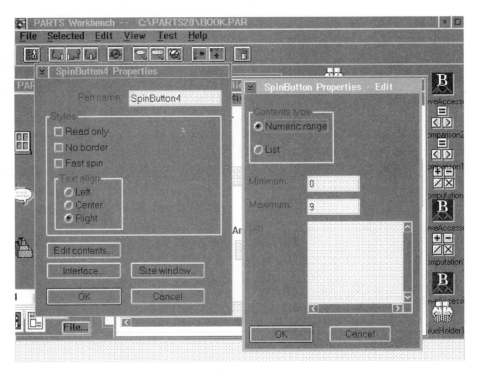

Figure 9.35 Initializing selection-item values.

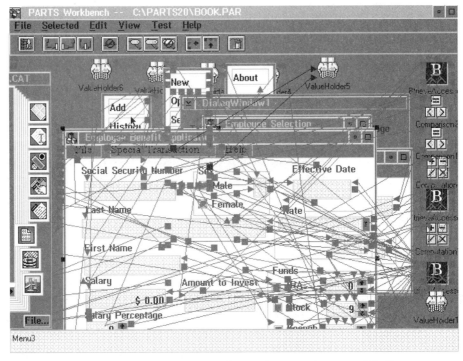

Figure 9.36 Employee Benefit Application showing all links.

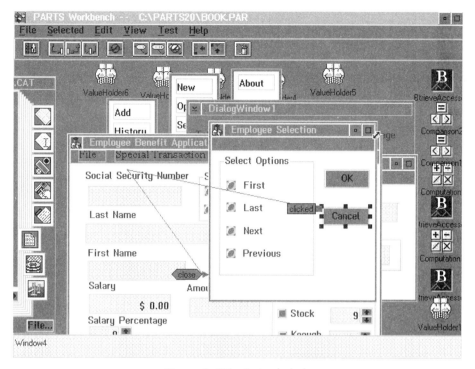

Figure 9.37   A single link.

The message, *close,* is directed to the Employee Selection window. When the application executes, any event can open the window, but clicking on Cancel will close it.

Figure 9.38 shows multiple messages being sent by one click of a menu item. Each link in this illustration links the clicked event to a destination part with the required message for that part.

Link Components

Once a link has been established by connecting two workbench parts, two items of information must be supplied: the event and the message (Figure 9.39). The event is represented by a square at the origin of the arrow and the message as an arrowhead at the destination of the arrow.

When parts are connected by a link, a create link dialog is displayed as soon as the mouse button is released (Figure 9.40). The dialog requires you to select an event and a message from lists of predefined events and messages applicable to the parts being connected.

Our earlier link example discussed a push button used to close a window when it is clicked. Figure 9.40 shows the dialog used to set up the link for runtime. Note that in Figure 9.40 the connected parts are named. Below each, the supported events are listed for a push button and supported messages that a window can receive. Highlight

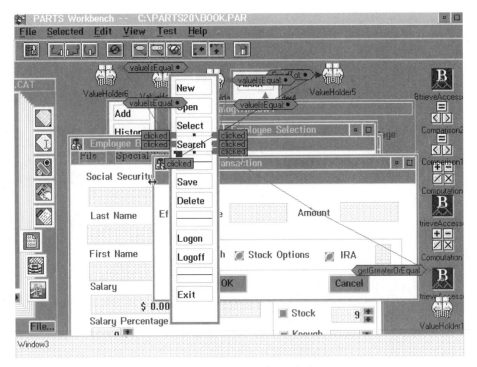

Figure 9.38   A multiple link.

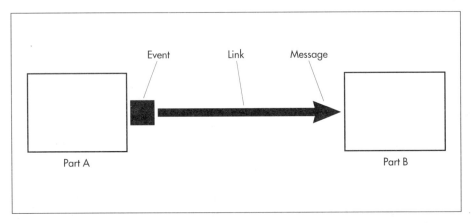

Figure 9.39   Link components.

clicked and close establishes the proper link to close the window
when the push button is clicked. You may want to refer to Figure 9.37
to see the Workbench representation of this link when it is selected.
Keep in mind that Figure 9.37 is displayed with the show labels
option toggled on in the Workbench menu.

Links can also be modified at any time during program construction. You can change the event, message, origin, or destination with a

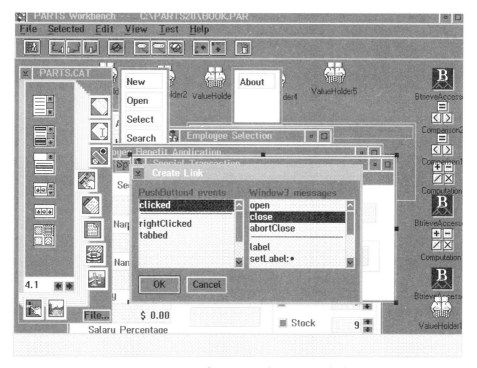

Figure 9.40   Link event and message dialog.

right mouse click on either the link message arrowhead or link event origin box. A pop-up menu will be displayed (Figure 9.41).

Types of Links and Messages

Different parts have different events and messages associated with them, depending on their use. For instance, a push-button part has a clicked event to associate it with an action or message. If you are working with a field part, however, you want a different user action to drive a message. The most common event for a field part is changed. When the field value is changed by the user, you probably want to change a value in a file. The changed event would be linked to a Btrieve accessor to update the field contents.

Conversely, if you retrieve the next record in a file, you will want to fire a link from the Btrieve accessor to the field to change the screen display (Figure 9.42). Note that the labels are displayed showing the events in the rectangles and the messages in the hexagons.

Link Firing Order

When a part such as a push button drives multiple actions, the firing order of the links can be critical. Looking once again to our special-transaction window, the OK button is being used to write the special-

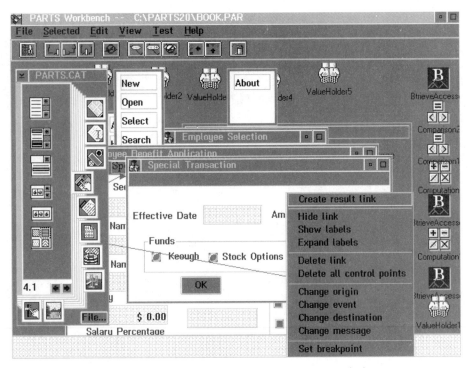

Figure 9.41   Change link event and message dialog.

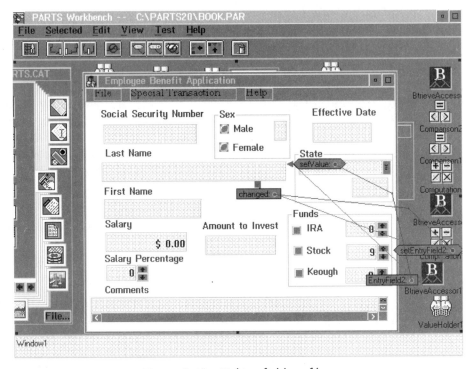

Figure 9.42   Linking fields to files.

transaction record. In addition to the fields in the window, the OK pushbutton is writing the SSNUM field from the record in the original file that populated the Employee Benefit window field values (Figure 9.43). Clearly, link firing order is critical in this case. The field must be updated before the record is written. Links are sequenced, by default, in the order in which you created them. The sequence can, however, be modified at a later time. With the left mouse, highlight the part that needs to be sequenced. Choose Selected from the Workbench menu. From the Selected menu (Figure 9.44) choose Sequence links. The dialog shown in Figure 9.45 will be displayed. The right mouse button can then be used to drag and drop the items into their appropriate sequence.

Custom Messages

There are times when the prefabricated messages available for a part are not sufficient. For instance, in our sample application, radio-button clicks are used to update the Sex field onscreen. A click of the Male button must update the field with an M and a Female click, an F. In other words, a clicked event must set a field to a specific value. To accomplish this, a special script, written in PARTS Script Language, must be used. In this example, the field is the recipient of the message. Double-click on the Sex field to open the properties dialog

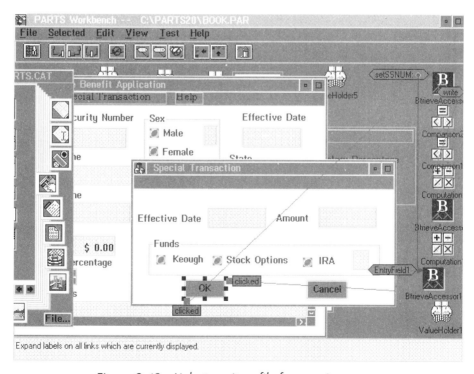

Figure 9.43   Links to write a file from various parts.

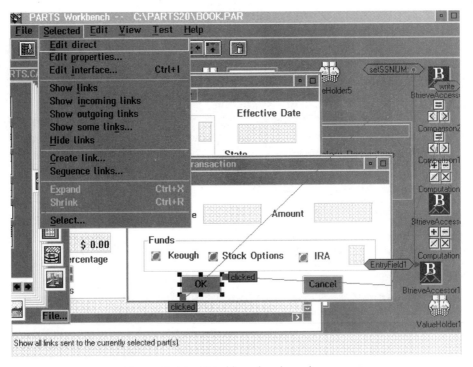

Figure 9.44   Workbench selected menu.

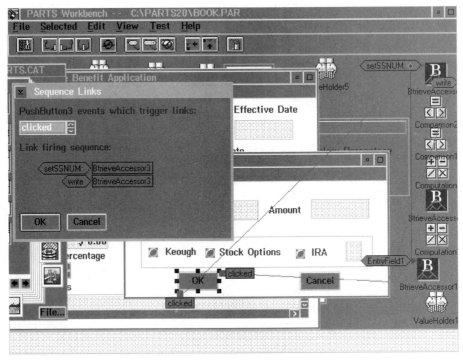

Figure 9.45   Link sequencing dialog.

for the field and select 'Interface'. Select the New option, write the required script, and save it. Figure 9.46 shows the custom script for our example. Two were actually written for the respective radio buttons: SetSexF and SetSexM.

Sample Application Links

It would be impossible to document all the links required in our sample application. While some examples follow this section, you should realize that setting up your linking tasks can be ordered in the same way in which we have thus far ordered our approach to building the application.

The following sequence should be followed to set up your links.

1. Set up the proper links on your windows. All windows that you drop onto the Workbench are automatically linked to fire when the application is started. If one window is to be a subordinate of another, delete the existing link and draw a new link from the parent to the child window. In our application, the only window that should be fired at startup is the logon window. When the user id and password are matched, the link to the Employee Benefit Window is fired.

2. Complete links for any unlinked fields. When you define a database using Pick fields with mouse, the update links are auto-

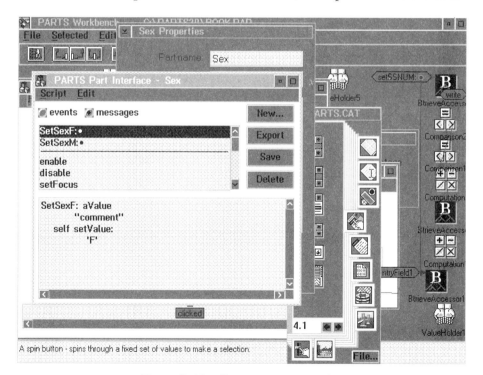

Figure 9.46   Custom message script.

matically set up for you. However, if you used the Create new field option as we did to store our salary percentage and fund data, you will have to manually create the links.

3. Create links to open and close files. When the Employee-Benefit window is fired, we want to open the file that stores the data. For example, a link will be required (opened . . . open) from the window to the accessor. Similarly, when we close the window we want to close the file. Another link (closed . . . close) would be drawn from the window to the accessor.

4. Set up links for selection items. Links will be required for all actions that result from clicking a radio button, checking a check-box, and so forth.

5. Link menu options. Set up links for all menu options. In our sample application, Logon will fire a link to the logon window (clicked . . . open) and Exit will will issue a close (clicked . . . close) to the workbench. Search issues a (clicked . . . getGreaterThanorEqualTo) to the Btrieve accessor for the employee social-security number displayed on screen and Select opens the Employee-Selection window (clicked . . . open).

6. Determine need for variables (value holders) and comparison parts, and set up the links. Our sample requires several value holders. For example, the salary percentage must always equal the total of the funds percentages on the Employee Benefit Window. All values are moved to value holders and an additional value holder is defined to hold the total of the funds percentages. Any time a file write is issued, the value holders are updated and a link to a comparison part, dropped from the computation page of the catalog, is fired.

7. Determine the need for dialog windows and code the links. *Dialog windows* are equivalent to the traditional programming functions of displaying error messages and collecting special information from the user. With PARTS, most of the tradition message functions are handled by default. For example, if you hit end of file while toggling through a set of records, the accessor will automatically display the end-of-file dialog. Some, however, we have to code ourselves. Look back at our example in number 6. When the value holders are in unequal state, a message dialog is required to warn the user. The message-dialog part is found on the window page of the catalog and the properties label can be updated with the literal message.

8. Determine the need for computational parts and link them. Remember the amount-to-invest field on the Employee-Benefit window? This field is used only for screen display and not stored in the database. However, whenever a record is retrieved, the

salary is changed, or the Salary Percentage spin-button value is changed, the amount to invest must be computed. The computation part is found on the computation page of the catalog.

9. Code any special message scripts required. In our sample application we have the Male/Female script discussed earlier and similar scripts on the Special Transaction screen where radio buttons are used to designate Fund Type.

Sample Links from the Employee Benefit Application

File Menu Save option. There is more than meets the eye in a file save. As a matter of fact, you will not find a direct file write being fired from this option. First, let's take a look at the links set up as shown in Figure 9.47. To clarify further, refer to Figure 9.48, which shows all links as currently sequenced. The first link fired places a total of the IRA, Stock, and Keogh spin-button values in a value holder. The next link fired is Comparison1. This compares the value-holder accumulators to verify that Salary Percentage is equal to the total of the funds percentages. A comparison part can trigger only one of two events: *true* or *false.* Comparison1 is set to *false.* The *false* condition fires the dialog window to display a message that the totals are invalid.

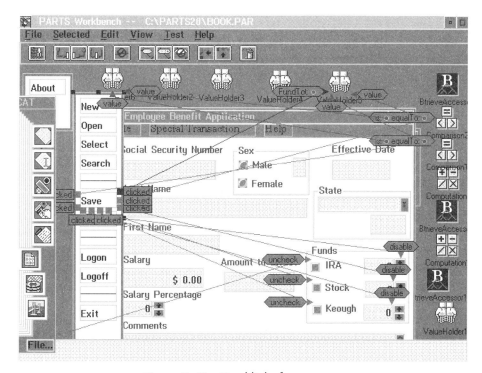

Figure 9.47   Fired links from a save.

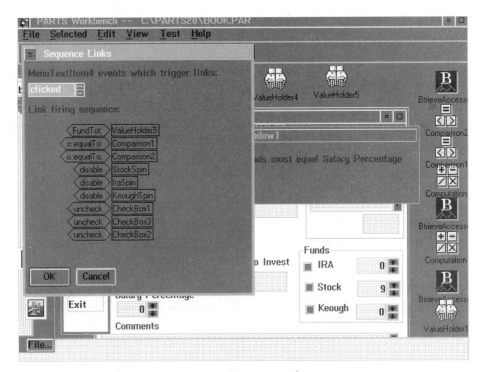

Figure 9.48   Link sequence for a save.

When the user closes the dialog window, Comparison2 is executed. The event is set to *true* in this comparison. Only when the value holders are equal does the comparison part sends the write message to the file accessor. The remaining messages uncheck the Fund's check boxes and disable the Fund's spin buttons.

Note that the only critical link in this sequence is the computation of the Fund's total percentage.

Amount-to-Invest Computation

The best way to understand this computation is to follow the firing path as detailed in Figure 9.49 and in the list following.

1. Spin button changed event sends a message to the computation part to calculate a product.

2. The computation part looks at its message, and gets the values from Salary Percentage and Salary, and performs the computation.

3. The result of the computation is passed via a result link to a value holder.

4. When the value holder changes (Figure 9.50), a message is sent to the Amount-to-Invest field to update its value through the script shown in Figure 9.51.

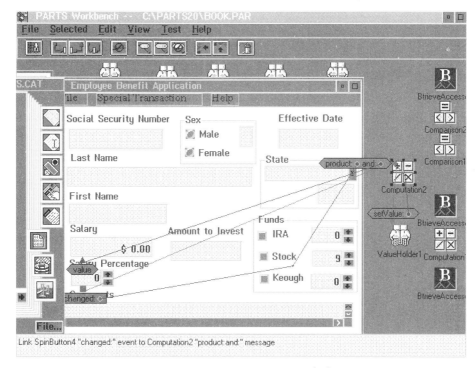

Figure 9.49   A computation link.

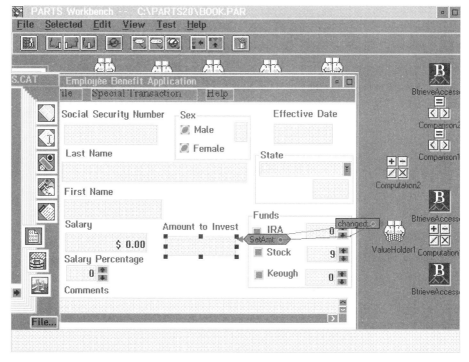

Figure 9.50   Changed value holder updates a field.

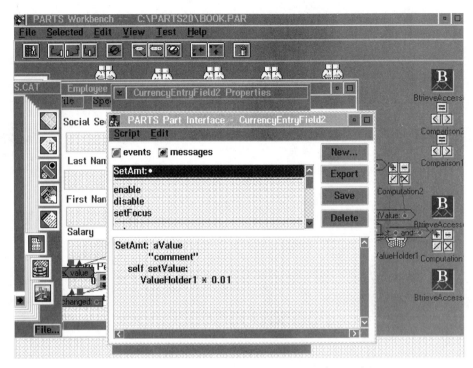

Figure 9.51   Computation script to move a decimal point.

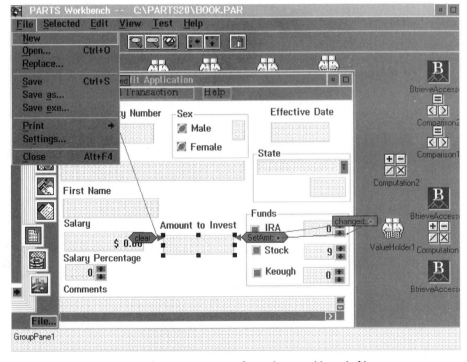

Figure 9.52   Select save as exe from the Workbench file menu.

Packaging the Application

To package your application to run from the OS/2 desktop, select Save as exe from the Workbench File menu (Figure 9.52). Your deliverables will include the .EXE file and your data files. The Btrieve accessor uses licensed programs. Before distributing an application containing a Btrieve accessor, read the file readme.txt in your PARTS directory for additional information.

Index